To Beth Moore,
my favorite Lece

Tom Ouflin
march 1995

Also by Thomas Griffith

The Waist-High Culture
How True: A Skeptic's Guide to Believing the News

HARRY AND TEDDY

HARRY AND TEDDY

The Turbulent Friendship of
Press Lord Henry R. Luce and His
Favorite Reporter, Theodore H. White

THOMAS GRIFFITH

Random House

New York

Grateful acknowledgment is made to the following for permission to reprint previously published material:

Tim Anderson on behalf of the Estate of T. S. Matthews: Excerpts from *Name and Address* by T. S. Matthews (Simon and Schuster, 1960). Reprinted by permission of Tim Anderson on behalf of the Estate of T. S. Matthews. • HarperCollins Publishers: Excerpts from *In Search of History: A Personal Adventure* by Theodore H. White. Copyright © 1978 by Theodore H. White. Reprinted by permission of HarperCollins Publishers, Inc. • Alfred A. Knopf, Inc.: Excerpt from "The Making of Theodore H. White" from *Scribble, Scribble* by Nora Ephron. Copyright © 1975, 1976, 1977, 1978 by Nora Ephron. Reprinted by permission of Alfred A. Knopf, Inc. • Random House, Inc.: Excerpts from *Witness* by Whittaker Chambers. Copyright © 1952 by Whittaker Chambers. Reprinted by permission of Random House, Inc. • William Morrow & Company, Inc.: Excerpts from *The Stilwell Papers* by General Joseph W. Stilwell, edited and arranged by Theodore H. White. Copyright © 1948 by Winifred A. Stilwell. Reprinted by permission of William Morrow & Company, Inc.

Library of Congress Cataloging-in-Publication Data
Griffith, Thomas.
Harry and Teddy : the turbulent friendship of press lord
Henry R. Luce and his
favorite reporter, Theodore H. White
/ by Thomas Griffith. — 1st ed.
p. cm.
Includes index.
ISBN 0-679-41179-8
1. Luce, Henry Robinson, 1898–1967—Friends and associates.
2. White, Theodore Harold, 1915– —Friends and associates.
3. Journalism—United States—History—20th century. I. Title.
PN4874.L76G75 1995
070.5′092—dc20   94-25763
[B]

Book Design by M. Kristen Bearse

Manufactured in the United States of America on acid-free paper

2   4   6   8   9   7   5   3

First Edition

To Robert Manning

and to the memory of T. S. Matthews, Roy
Alexander, Paul O'Neil, Alfred Thornton
Baker, Edward O. Cerf, Duncan
Norton-Taylor, and Louis Banks

Sturdy shipmates on a stormy crossing

Contents

HARRY AND TEDDY

Chapter 1

THE CHINA
CONNECTION

Teddy White came out of Harvard in 1938 with a degree
summa cum laude in China studies, an itch to see China,
and a traveling fellowship to get him there. With little money to
waste, he crossed Europe, took passage through the Suez Canal
on a Norwegian freighter, and landed in Shanghai. He loved the
English working people he met en route and thought Paris the
"swellest" of cities, but his enthusiasm for Europe quickly
changed in the months after Munich when, as he wrote home, he
grew nervous about "the Jewish situation in Germany and the
signs in Paris 'Mort aux Juifs.' . . . I hate Europe; God curse them
forever. . . . They're mean and barbarous. I hate them all . . . their
cafés and concerts and theatres and arches and parks. . . . God
bless America." He was happy to get to Shanghai.

That fabled city—the goal in Asia of adventuresome Americans during the depression, as Paris was the goal in Europe—
had lost some of its sybaritic seductiveness now that it was
ringed, but not occupied, by Japanese troops. But it still held
such appeal to footloose American newspapermen willing to
work for very little money that White could not find even an
office boy's job on any of the city's three ill-paying English-
language newspapers.

With his money running low, he bleakly considered his future as he sat in the Shanghai YMCA: "I had seen as much of life

in Japanese China as I wished; it had disgusted me." But before returning home in defeat to Boston, he wanted to see a China that was not ringed by Japanese troops. So he applied for a job with Chiang Kai-shek's government and, to his surprise, learned that a vacancy had just opened in the propaganda office: Could he fly immediately to Chungking?

Chiang's wartime capital in the remote interior was a craggy hilltop city sitting atop cliffs at the convergence of the Yangtze and Chialing rivers. There Chiang's government had retreated after two years of savage war during which the Japanese had not only surrounded Shanghai but conquered the great coastal and lowland cities of China—Canton, Peking, Tientsin, Nanking, and Hankow. Chungking was inconvenient and inaccessible but relatively impregnable. And strategically it protected China's richest province, Szechuan, a semitropical granary that was home to fifty million peasants.

On a sandbar in the center of the Yangtze where it passes the city of Chungking sat a tiny airstrip that could be used only until late spring, when raging waters from Tibet's melting snows flooded it. Teddy White flew to Chungking in May 1939, on the first airplane trip of his life. He had taken ship from Shanghai to Hong Kong, to fly from there over the Japanese lines at night to Chungking. When Teddy arrived at the Hong Kong airport with all his luggage, he was told that he would be allowed only eight pounds of baggage. So, as he gleefully wrote his family: "I put on my body the following clothes: six pairs of running pants, 6 athletic shirts, one pajamas, 2 sport shirts, 3 silk shirts, 2 vests, 2 coat jackets, a grey sweater, 9 prs socks, 2 prs of pants, 2 suspenders, one belt, 13 handkerchiefs, 3 ties." Over all of this he draped his overcoat. Unable to wear his second pair of shoes, he dangled them from the pockets of the coat. Then he talked the clerk into letting him take aboard a final bulky item, his secondhand typewriter.

As Teddy waddled off the plane at Chungking, hardly able to bend because of the layers of clothes he wore, he looked up at a chaotic collection of houses clinging to a steep gray cliff. Notched into the cliff were several hundred steps leading up to the city. He crossed a footbridge to the base of the cliff and placed himself in a hammock of bamboo slats slung between two bamboo poles. Two sedan-chair bearers, one fore and one aft, lifted the poles to their shoulders and, with their overdressed human cargo swaying precariously, set forth up the cliff, chanting in cadence as they climbed step by step.

Teddy, ever the careful notetaker, observed calluses "thicker than leather" on the shoulders of the leading bearer. Everything about the scene fascinated him and alerted his senses. His second exposure to Chinese culture was about to begin, an experience that would be more raucous, profound, and exciting than Harvard's academic preparation had led him to expect.

He had been in Chungking less than three weeks when the mists that usually protected the city parted, and on a clear cloudless day twenty-seven Japanese bombers, flying higher than the Chinese antiaircraft guns popping at them could reach, dropped loads of incendiary bombs on a city that had no military targets. Between three and four thousand men, women, and children were burned to death in what was at the time history's largest slaughter of defenseless human beings. (From that day on White never felt any compassion over destruction visited on Japan.)

That night the city was lit up by flames. Teddy and a companion, Robert "Pepper" Martin of the United Press, walked through crowds of panicky Chinese, who were fleeing to the countryside carrying screaming children, pots, pans, and bedrolls. Teddy had not been to his lodgings at Friends Mission all day, and when he returned at four A.M., he discovered that it had been bombed, and the force of the blast had deposited in his room the corpse of a woman. He moved out of the mission.

After that Teddy could usually be found at the new government press hostel, a thatch-roofed compound with barred openings for windows. At the hostel he joined the city's foreign press corps, a diverse little group of strays and loners trying to report, to a world not much interested, tales of distant battles based on scanty information. They lived in sparsely furnished rooms with mud floors and mud walls, sharing discomfort, danger, and undistinguished food. They were an odd lot. Most had found their way to Asia on their own, depression-era nomads searching for adventure. Till Durdin, the sage and taciturn *New York Times* correspondent, who later characterized his earlier self as a hippie in the days before there were hippies, had quit his newspaper job in Houston and worked his ship passage to the Orient by scrubbing decks and cleaning winches, then labored on English-language papers in China before latching on to the *Times*. Jack Belden, most poetic of the group, was roaming the world as a magazine writer when he jumped ship in Hong Kong with ten dollars in his pocket. Al Ravenholt of the United Press got to China by taking a job as chief cook aboard a ship without first admitting how little he knew about cooking.

Though perhaps the youngest of the lot, Teddy White dominated the conversation at the hostel table with his brash personality and endless flow of opinions and ideas. He was the only one among them who had prepared himself with college courses in China studies. As he held forth, his chopsticks stabbed at the bowls of food in the center of the table. With a fencer's dexterity, talking all the while, he could ward off the chopsticks of the others to make sure he got a particularly choice morsel.

Along with his Harvard degree, Teddy had a master's in street smarts from his upbringing in a Boston ghetto. Like the novelist Norman Mailer (ex-Harvard and ex-army), Teddy liked to couch his most serious thoughts in profane vernacular. Stocky and chubby-cheeked, White peered at life enthusiastically through thick-lensed glasses.

Not long after Teddy's arrival, a young John Hersey came to Chungking. One of his missions was to find a part-time correspondent for *Time* magazine. He was impressed by the twenty-two-year-old Teddy, "a small, slightly unkempt person who was living in squalor in Chungking, but . . . obviously the best-informed of all the Americans in town, including the seasoned correspondents (well, possibly excepting Tillman Durdin of *The New York Times*)." At the time Teddy White was earning sixty-five dollars a month translating and writing news stories in the office of Chiang Kai-shek's propaganda minister, Hollington Tong. Teddy's job, Hersey noted, gave him an insider's access to military and government leaders.

Hersey himself was only a year older than Teddy. He seemed, as White described him in his autobiography, *In Search of History*, enviably sophisticated and successful: "Blithe, handsome, tall, a Yale varsity football player, Hersey had every quality I then admired most in any contemporary, as well as self-possession and beauty." If this later assessment was laying it on a bit thick, Teddy was more candid in taking Hersey's measure in a letter home: He "has the right kind of parents and the right kind of luck; and you add to the fact that he went to the right kind of school, and is very good looking and tall and very attractive personally and is truly intelligent but nevertheless he has never held down a real job before and is green." By "the right kind of parents," Teddy meant that Hersey was a "mish-kid" (born in China to American missionaries), who had gone to work for *Time* magazine after Yale. He soon became the favorite of another China-born mishkid, the mighty Henry R. Luce, cofounder of *Time* and inventor of *Life* and *Fortune* magazines.

Hersey promised White a fifty-dollar-a-month retainer to work for *Time*, plus twenty-five dollars for each mailed report that found its way into a story in the magazine. This seemed skimpy pay to Teddy, but he reckoned that if he worked hard at it, he would be able to quit his government job. He began to churn out ideas, suggestions, and stories, and discovered that he had a flair for it. "*Time* was then," he would later acknowledge, "a far less responsible magazine than it is today, and delighted in quips, curiosities, anecdotes and quotes, whether true or not."

To impress the editors of *Time,* Teddy decided that he "needed a major story—a narrative, a scoop, not a feature." He reasoned that "all other newsmen in Chungking were bound by their jobs to the cablehead and daily deadlines" and could not spend the time he could to visit a hard-to-reach war front. So from the Ministry of Information he wangled a leave, a plane ticket to Sian, and a low-grade military pass. From Sian he headed for the Ch'in Valley in Shansi Province. Lying north of the Yellow River, it was then the only active front in the war against the Japanese. It took Teddy ten days by foot and horse-back to get there from Sian. Each night he filled his notebooks with the sights and sounds of the day. Because he had no inter-preter, and because others found his Harvard-taught Chinese unintelligible, he slowly picked up a "rough street Chinese." He joined up with a unit of Nationalist guerrillas who were march-ing to the front, sometimes crawling through mountain gaps while their officers (and Teddy) rode ahead on horses.

They encountered "villages where the war had come and passed, or the war had come and stayed." In his dispatch Teddy reported: "Houses were burned by [the retreating] Japanese sol-diery both out of boredom and deviltry and because they were cold and needed fire and warmth. The Japanese looted indis-criminately and efficiently. . . . In villages whose occupants had not fled quickly enough, the first action of the Japanese was to rout out the women and have at them. . . . Male villagers were stripped naked, lashed to carts and driven forward by the Impe-rial Army as beasts of burden."

White also noted, though he did not include the incident in the report he filed to *Time,* that when the unit he was with stopped to ask peasants for food and water for the horses, the leader identified his men as Communists. "I asked him why he said that; we were a Nationalist group. And he snapped at me,

'Shut up! If we tell them we're Nationalist guerrillas, they won't feed our horses or water them.' . . . The people were certainly not unfriendly to Nationalist troops, who, like them, hated Japanese, but their political leadership, in the most primitive way, had been won over to the Communists." Only much later would he appreciate the full significance of the lieutenant's lie.

White's vivid report of the Japanese fighting and pillaging in the Ch'in Valley created a stir in New York. *Time* magazine devoted a page and a half to it, awarding White the first byline ever given to one of its own "special correspondents." On his return to Chungking Teddy quit his government job. No longer was he regarded by the tiny foreign press corps simply as an eager supplier of government information and propaganda. He was now one of them, and as a journalist had already proven himself courageous, persistent, and perceptive.

He felt himself lucky to be working for a magazine whose publisher was entranced by China. To the American public, and to most newspaper editors at that time, what happened in Europe—the fall of France, the air blitz of London, the siege of Stalingrad—mattered more than events in Asia. Soon White was assigned to roving Southeast Asia as a full-time *Time* correspondent, gathering material about the background of the war in the Pacific that his editors thought near at hand.

Early in 1941 he was ordered back to Chungking and told to await a visit from the boss and his wife, the playwright Clare Boothe Luce, a prospect that "absolutely terrified" him. His fellow correspondents, knowing his cockiness, didn't for a moment believe him. They made bets on how soon after meeting Luce Teddy would be first-naming him. The winner thought it would take only seven words: "Welcome to China, Mr. Luce. Now, Harry, here's what we are going to do . . ."

Among those welcoming the Luces at the airport after their long flight from San Francisco were Teddy's old boss, Hollington

Tong, the propaganda minister, appropriately dressed, and Teddy himself, wearing shorts and a sun helmet.

"Harry was majestic," White recalled. "He carried himself like a king, and had more power than most kings." In his memoirs (written long after Luce's death) Teddy pictures Luce on his visit to Chungking: "At the height of his powers, burly, magnificently muscled, bursting with energy, his overset brows frowning from under a Panama hat."

White's family speaks tolerantly of "his tendency to mythologize." Those of us who worked many years for Henry Robinson Luce, as I did, can envision the airport scene: Luce would emerge from the plane, as he emerged from taxis, looking rumpled, no matter how expensive his tailoring; he would greet his welcoming committee in friendly fashion, but he was never one for small talk; he would size up his welcomers as persons delegated to watch over him and his luggage; he would be anxious to get on to wherever he was expected, and would so indicate with a brusqueness that could seem like rudeness. Not exactly a majestic presence, but neither was he a self-satisfied celebrity, expecting adulation. Luce was content to let his wife draw the cameras.

For a man so shrewd and sharp in judging people, and one whose magazines were so skilled in cutting well-known figures down, Luce had one odd trait. He was an ardent hero-worshiper of the few contemporaries he judged to be great. Just to be in General MacArthur's presence once brought Luce to tears he could not hide. He revered Eisenhower the general (but was disappointed in Ike the politician). He thought that Churchill, by his eloquent John Bullishness, had saved Western civilization. He saw Chiang Kai-shek not only as the man who alone could save China but as the one who might even convert it to Christianity, a prospect that would have delighted Luce's missionary father, who lived until the day of Pearl Harbor. As one sign of Luce's admiration, all of these men—MacArthur, Eisenhower, Churchill, and Chiang Kai-shek—had been honored on *Time*'s cover as Man of the Year; Churchill later would become *Time*'s Man of the Half Century.

To Chiang's beleaguered government, in the anxious period seven months before Pearl Harbor, Luce was China's single most powerful supporter in the United States. Until the "date which will live in infamy," when America was thrust into a Pacific war it did not want to fight, China stood alone in resisting Japan. Luce had joined with David O. Selznick, the movie producer, to raise millions of dollars for United China Relief. He once sent to every *Time* subscriber a plea to contribute; this was the only occasion he ever begged money from his readers.

Luce's magazines glamorously publicized Chiang and Mei-ling, the wife who had converted him to Christianity. They made celebrities of the famous Soong sisters. Mei-ling, Chiang's wife, had been educated at Wellesley College, spoke English easily, and understood the Western arts of publicity. Another Soong sister, Ch'ing-ling, was the venerated widow of Sun Yat-sen, the founder of the Chinese republic (she would become a heroine of the Communists); the eldest, Ai-ling, was married to the enormously wealthy H. H. (Daddy) K'ung, who at one time or another was Chiang's premier and finance minister, as well as Standard Oil's representative in China.

From the airport the Luces were lifted up the steep stairs to a waiting limousine. Luce wanted to know how many steps the coolies had climbed; Teddy didn't know—and after that made it his business to anticipate such questions. He perceived that Luce was insatiably curious, a condition that could be alleviated only by feeding him facts. This is not unusual among journalists, but where Luce differed from most journalists, and from most people, was in a trait discerned by John Knox Jessup, *Life*'s chief editorial writer: "He never pretended to knowledge he did not have, not even by the negative presence of silence." He was not ashamed to appear ignorant, and could ask simple questions, not easily answered, of economists, artists, or nuclear physicists, convinced that any of them should be expected, almost as a duty, to make the most recondite of subjects intelligible to a layman. That made him an ideal editor for mass magazines: an intermediary who did not talk down to audiences.

The limousine bore the Luces to the K'ung mansion, where they would be guests. The Luces did not stay with the Generalissimo; they lacked diplomatic status, and besides, things might have been awkward, since both Madame Chiang and Clare Boothe Luce were used to dominating any room they were in.

From their quarters at the K'ungs', the Luces began an endless round of banquets and toasts, interviews and ceremonial visits. But it was tea with Chiang and Madame Chiang that thrilled Harry Luce the most.

Madame greeted them first, graciously praising Clare's beauty; then into the room came the slim Generalissimo, dressed in khaki. "You got the feeling that there was no person in the room except the man who had entered it so quietly," Luce later wrote. Luce told Chiang that he was "the greatest ruler Asia has had since Emperor K'ang-hsi, 250 years ago." Then the Luces offered their presents. One was a portfolio of photographs of Chiang and his wife, many of them taken by *Life* photographer Carl Mydans; these the Generalissimo savored, grinning "from ear to ear." Then, knowing that Madame's cache of cigarettes had been destroyed when her pantry was bombed by the Japanese, the Luces generously replenished her supply. The Chiangs gave Clare a pair of silk pajamas and Harry a jade Tang horse. "An hour later we left," Luce wrote, "knowing that we had made the acquaintance of two people, a man and woman, who, of all the millions now living, will be remembered for centuries and centuries."

Once the formal Chinese hospitality had been sufficiently savored, the Luces wearied of it. But on the second day of their visit, Luce was exhilarated by his first air raid: he enjoyed the democracy of the shelter, where hundreds of Chinese—coolies and bureaucrats, merchants and children—gathered in shared peril in huge caverns that had been carved out of the cliffs by battalions of laborers after Japan's brutal air raid two years earlier.

One morning, White writes in his memoirs, Luce "commanded my presence and ordered me to get him away from the smothering government escort—and as we mounted rickshaws and sneaked off, it turned out he only wanted to practice his Chinese. He had not spoken Chinese since he was a boy growing up in a Shantung mission compound, but the tongue came back to him, and with glee at rediscovery, he commanded the rickshaw man this way and that, poked in and out of shops, examined prices and stocks, bargained in Chinese with ever-growing gusto."

That day's adventure was the beginning of the lasting friendship between Henry Robinson Luce and Theodore H. White. Superficially, they had little in common: Luce was tall, Teddy short; Luce was rich, Teddy poor. Their personalities differed sharply too: White, as his journalistic colleague David Halberstam described him, was "small, gnome-like, [with] a wonderful rich sweet-ugly grin and terribly weak eyes. He was Jewish-left instead of Presbyterian-right." White was gregarious and emotional, a warmhearted man, eagerly open to friendship; Luce was leery of it.

Luce was a loner, determined never to let emotional considerations stay him from what he must do or wanted to do. He shunned familiarity, fearing its obligations. The most memorable feature of his face was not his mouth or his eyes but his thick overarching eyebrows (did he instruct his barber not to trim them?). His wife, Clare, once taxed him for always looking so solemn. "I can't help it," he replied. "It's the face I was born with."

In conversation Harry listened earnestly and reacted quickly, sometimes registering bemusement, boredom, or impatience. Once he had heard enough, he would move to dismiss the subject or the person, not necessarily out of antagonism, but out of intellectual restlessness: he didn't like to waste time. His laughter was a quick snort. But if he thought he had scored some point in argument, he would lean back, inhale his cigarette with special pleasure, cock an amused eyebrow, and dare his opponent to rebut him.

His fellow mishkid John Hersey said of Luce that "emotions—feelings that had to do with a human touch—were enigmatic to him, but abstractions lit up his face. . . . His mind darted and jumped. He was astonished and delighted by whatever he had not previously known. He stammered because there were so many enthusiasms trying to make simultaneous escape across his Calvinistic tongue."

What united Harry Luce and Teddy White, a man young enough to be his son? First of all, their love of China. I think that day, as Teddy and Harry played hookey together from Luce's distinguished hosts, Teddy, with his gregariousness with the strangers they met, helped Luce to recapture the spirit of his adolescence in China.

But more than a fascination with China bonded them. As they talked, the two men, with their quick, impatient minds, discovered similar interests, shared passions, a love of the specific fact, and a delight in disputation. Volleying back and forth little balls of fact to contest each other's argument, they played a parlor game of finding patterns and meanings in events, a practice that would continue through their friendship. A journalist may feel constrained in what he can say in print, but he feels free in after-hours conversation to skip-jump freely over the news, constructing sweeping, and sometimes superficial, hypotheses when all the returns are not yet in. This intellectual foreplay is how he goes about the job: once these hunches are tested and confirmed, they harden into judgments. Such carefree theorizing is also fun. It added spice to the pleasure Harry and Teddy found in each other's company.

At this first meeting in Chungking they seemed to think

much alike. Both believed that it was in the American interest to oppose the Japanese invasion of China. Both spoke of their admiration for Chiang Kai-shek. This needs to be emphasized in view of White's later antipathy to Chiang ("He was a man I learned first to respect and admire, then to pity, then to despise"). The shift in Teddy's attitude helps to explain Luce's later feeling of betrayal. The evidence for White's earlier admiration for the Generalissimo and Madame Chiang is to be found in articles that White wrote for *Life* and *Fortune* in early 1941, the year of Luce's visit. In *Life:* "Probably no chief of state in the world, whether temporary like Churchill or with a pretense of permanence like Hitler, has such a hold on his country as does Generalissimo Chiang Kai-shek." On Madame Chiang Kai-shek, in *Fortune:* "It would be impossible to exaggerate her loveliness. No photograph does her justice because her beauty—aside from perfection of feature, a complexion that puts cosmetics to shame, and about the best figure in Free Asia—is electric, incandescent and internal." (In the disillusionment of his 1978 autobiography she becomes a "beautiful, tart and brilliant woman, more American than Chinese, and mistress of every level of the American language from the verses of the hymnal to the most sophisticated bitchery.")

If a love of China had first drawn Luce and Teddy together, a wrenching quarrel over China's future would later divide them. The issue was hardly trivial. In fact, when Senator Joseph McCarthy later exploited it to allege a pattern of treason in the U.S. State Department, what had been honest differences among many people over how to treat a postwar China became instead a vicious, acrimonious, and recriminatory policy debate that divided Americans for a decade. But that was in the far-off future.

At the moment, as John Hersey wrote, Luce was "dazzled, charmed, and challenged" by Teddy White. Clare was taken by Teddy's knowledge, his quick, cheeky wit, his capacity to ingratiate. He cheerfully toured her around, introduced her to important people, arranged interviews for her. Two days before the

Luces were to return home, Teddy writes, Luce "turned to me and, in that peremptory half-stammering speech of his, asked me if I could be packed and ready to leave in forty-eight hours. . . . He did not ask me whether it was convenient to leave China at that time or what my plans were. He had decided that I was to be Far Eastern editor of *Time*. Now."

In Hersey's view, Luce "took White with him, to make him an editor of the magazine—but more importantly, to adopt him, to take possession of him. As he had done, in a different but no less paternal way, over the years with me. Four years later, both White and I had, not without pain, torn ourselves away from him."

Luce's friendship with Teddy would prove more durable than his friendship with Hersey, despite Hersey's initial advantage. Luce and Hersey were too much alike, both Calvinistically sure of what they believed; Teddy was more pliant and less dogmatic. But, as the later painful interruptions in his friendship with Luce proved, Teddy could be pushed only so far.

The Luces, with their prize catch, Teddy, in hand, flew back to the States on the leisurely five-day Clipper route across the Pacific, stopping each night at the familiar Pan American stepping-stones of Guam, Wake, Midway, Honolulu. They were now Teddy, Harry, and Clare to one another, but the time had come for Luce to define the relationship more clearly. "As we were coming in to San Francisco, he harrumphed me over, stammered again and said, 'Teddy, you've read all this stuff in business magazines about how the boss's door is always open to everyone?' I said I had, and he continued, 'Well, that's not the way I run my magazines. Everybody's door is open to me. But my door is open to people only when I want to see them.' "

A MEATBALL AT HARVARD

When Teddy White set out to write his autobiography in his sixties he characteristically matched himself against the best literary model he knew, *The Education of Henry Adams*. Was it the memorable opening passage of Adams's great book that beckoned to him?

> Under the shadow of Boston State House, turning its back on the house of John Hancock, the little passage called Hancock Avenue runs, or ran, from Beacon Street, skirting the State House grounds, to Mount Vernon Street, on the summit of Beacon Hill; and there, in the third house below Mount Vernon Place, February 16, 1838, a child was born, and christened later by his uncle, the minister of the First Church after tenets of Boston Unitarianism, as Henry Brooks Adams.
>
> Had he been born in Jerusalem under the shadow of the Temple and circumcised in the Synagogue by his uncle the high priest, under the name of Israel Cohen, he would scarcely have been more distinctly branded, and not much more heavily handicapped in the races of the coming century, in running for such stakes as the century was to offer.

Theodore Harold White was born on May 6, 1915, within three miles of the Boston State House, in a house on Erie Street, Dorchester, in the Jewish ghetto. In his origins he was as distinctly branded as the patrician Henry Adams and could plausibly argue that he, rather than Adams, would be the more "heavily handicapped in the races of the coming century, in running for such stakes as the century was to offer."

Teddy White's first memory of that house on Erie Street was of listening, in a little bedroom off the kitchen, to a conversation between his parents, who thought him asleep. He heard his mother "crying to his father because there was no money to buy shoes for the children, who had to go back to school. Then his father came to bed; his father slept with him in the same bed, the two brothers on another narrow bed in the same room, his mother sleeping with his sister in the other bedroom. That night his father did not sleep at all."

Teddy seems not to have been drawn to his father; in his autobiography he calls him "as melancholy a man as I ever met." The youngest of seventeen children, David White ran away from Pinsk in Russia at the age of sixteen and somehow got to Boston. Unable to find a regular job, he spent summers selling from a pushcart and sleeping under it at night; winters he worked and slept wherever he could. Though descended from a long line of rabbis in Russia, he repudiated the old culture and scorned religion as superstition. (Teddy himself was always proud of his Jewishness, but he was never orthodox in his religion, probably owing to his father's influence.) David White quickly learned English and became a Socialist. After taking free law courses at night at the YMCA, he got through Northeastern University and was admitted to the bar. His clients were poor, and he charged them no more than they could pay (during the depression, this was often nothing). Short, stout, and gentle, he had (like Teddy) the brawny chest and forearms of a steelworker. Father fancied himself a scholar and a poet; money meant little to him except as a means to buy books.

At a Socialist clubhouse, Teddy's father met and fell in love with a nineteen-year-old volunteer waitress, Mary Winkeller. Because he was "learned," she eventually got her parents' consent to marry him, but soon she was mediating between two hopelessly antagonistic and irreconcilable forces—her Socialist husband and her Orthodox parents.

The newlyweds took over the first floor of her parents' house on Erie Street. "Upstairs was Yiddish-speaking. Downstairs we spoke English," Teddy wrote in his autobiography. His grandmother was a "hard, shrill, vigorous woman of violent piety" who, after fifty years in this country, spoke no English but raged eloquently in Yiddish. As the eldest son, Teddy became a bridge between the two households, invited upstairs on Friday for the prayers of the Kiddush, and often encouraged to stay for a dinner of chicken and chicken soup.

Young Teddy had a ravenous appetite for learning. At the age of eight, over his father's objections, he was sent to Hebrew school in the afternoons and though at first resentful at having to study an extra two hours a day, he was soon captured by the ancient Hebrew language, its images and cadences, and by the Bible's vivid stories. Mornings, like many of Boston's brightest students, he took the trolley downtown to that demanding magnet school Boston Public Latin, the oldest public school in America. One day he wrote in his diary, "I know now that I am brilliant."

He made a different kind of entry in his diary the day the stock market crashed in 1929: "No money all week, Pa brought home $2.00 today, Mama is crying again." His father was reduced to collecting rents in the Boston slums for landlords almost as poor as their tenants. His gentle spirit gave way; destitute and forlorn, saddened by the feeling that his oldest son was turning into a street tough, David White died in 1931. Teddy was then sixteen.

Forced to swallow its pride, the family went on relief, which was as much a humiliation as it was a help: for a family of five, the city of Boston offered a meager eleven dollars a week. Teddy's older sister quit college to work at the Boston Public Library for fifteen dollars a week—and was required to give back one day's pay a month to Mayor James Curley's political machine. Teddy's two younger brothers got up at six in the morning to sell papers on the street corner before going to school. His mother insisted that Teddy finish his last months at Boston Latin before becoming, as the oldest male child, the principal family breadwinner. For Teddy that meant getting up at five in the winter's cold to sell newspapers on the trolley ten hours a day, taking no time off for lunch. Mother looked after all the accounts ("From her, more than anyone else, I inherited my obsession with money"). For an additional fourteen dollars a week, Teddy taught Hebrew classes for two hours a night; listening to his students recite by rote from the standard books of the Bible so bored him that he had them read the Song of Songs, which he found more musical.

In Boston's ethnic scheme of things, streetcars were Irish territory, run by men from Galway. Most would let Teddy ride a few blocks, hawking his papers, then slow down so he could jump off to ride the next car back. But one among them, a hard-faced and profane motorman named Conley, warned Teddy to "stay the hell off" his trolley, even though Teddy wore the nickel-plated medallion that authorized him to sell Boston's four daily newspapers on the cars. One day Teddy hopped Conley's car; he writes, "I rode three stops trying to explain to him that I had to make a living, too, for my mother and the kids, and I had the right, and I didn't want to have to fight with him. Finally, he said, 'OK.' " Won over, Conley thereupon gave Teddy a key to the motormen's booth at the end of the line, where on cold winter mornings Teddy could stand beside an electric heater, thumbing through the papers for a catchy sales pitch in the day's news: "Read all about it! Twenty-seven babies' bodies found pickled in a barrel in East Boston!" A hustler by day, hearing Solomon's Song of Songs at night, Teddy, in his own telling, had no time for what passes as a normal adolescence. But among his papers is a letter to one Sarah Richman: "After all who am I, a mere ex-newsboy, that you should waste so much time and beauty on me? I'll be at Harvard next year. In my autobiography it will be Chapter III. (Chapter I. My life as a newsboy. Chapter II. I meet Sarah Richman. III. Harvard. IV.??? I and John Roosevelt and August Belmont II and John Penrose Saltonstall will study side by side in the cloistered halls of Fair Harvard! American democracy! Newsboy and President's son!"

Chapter II, the romance with Sarah Richman, must have been a brief episode in Teddy's life, like most adolescent crushes. But Chapter III, through a fortunate combination of circumstances, became reality. A $180 grant from the Burroughs Newsboys Foundation and a scholarship from Harvard College gave Teddy enough for a year's tuition. Living at home, Teddy took the subway to Cambridge for his classes, was back home by four in the afternoon, and then, every night from six to eight, through all four of his years at Harvard, he taught at the Hebrew school.

If this seems an unrelievedly grim existence, Teddy did not live it grimly. With his breezy confidence, he was not abashed to be among contemporaries from more affluent backgrounds. His days of hustling had made him an early master of the twin urban arts of ingratiating and needling.

The first Harvard faculty member he impressed was John Kenneth Galbraith, who spotted Teddy as the best student in his freshman class in basic economics. He recommended Teddy for membership in Winthrop House, a Georgian brick dormitory where Galbraith was a resident tutor. When Winthrop's admissions committee gathered to choose among the applicants, Galbraith was handed a list of names. Across the top of a ruled page were cryptic marks: the first stood for graduates of the four elite prep schools, who were to be admitted automatically; the next for Exeter and Andover graduates, heavily favored; O.P. meant

Other Private schools, whose graduates were tolerated; H.S. indicated students from public high schools, to be discouraged; and X indicated Jewish students, for whom a quota existed. These markings were the doing of the master, Ronald M. Ferry, whom Galbraith described as a biochemist "of warm heart and incoherent speech." Galbraith noted that Ferry's face turned dour when he spotted Teddy's name. "He told me that we were already up to our Jewish quota. I protested that White was not a Jewish name. He looked at me with a hopeless gesture," implying that anyone could change his name. "Teddy was disaccepted over my objection." Galbraith was so upset by the experience that for a long time he would cross to the other side of the street to avoid saying hello to Dr. Ferry.

Teddy may even not have known of his rejection, for he couldn't afford to live in a dormitory anyway. He was a "meatball," Harvard's derisive name for a day student or scholarship student who brown-bagged his lunch and studied not in his rooms but in the library. And it was as a meatball that Teddy was led to the choice of his career.

On the ground floor of one big lecture hall in Harvard Yard were two libraries, one always crowded with students, the other the almost-empty precincts of the Harvard-Yenching Institute. Teddy chose to study in the quieter one. Out of curiosity he pulled down some Chinese volumes from the shelf. They were made of "fine rice paper, blue-bound [and] bamboo-hooked"; he was entranced. He enrolled in a class in elementary Chinese, taught "by one of the most brutal men I have ever met," a teacher so prejudiced against undergraduates that Teddy, the only undergraduate among the four students in the class, feared that he would flunk the course and lose his scholarship. Teddy's sister remembers hearing Teddy in the adjoining bedroom, having spent the early hours of the evening teaching his Hebrew class, reading aloud from his Chinese language cards until long after midnight. Eventually he earned an A. By the time he finished Harvard he could recognize by sight three thousand individual Chinese ideograms.

He was also rewarded by finding a more sympathetic instructor. In his junior year Teddy met the man who would be as great an influence in his life as anyone but Henry Robinson Luce. These two men, Luce and John King Fairbank, with their sharply divergent views on China, would become continuing rivals for Teddy's loyalty and friendship. Fairbank, then twenty-nine, was a young Orientalist from the prairies of South Dakota, who had arrived at Harvard via Oxford and four years in Peking. Since Teddy was the only undergraduate majoring in Chinese history and studies, he found himself assigned to Fairbank. Unlike most tutors, who are "usually embittered graduate students," Teddy writes, "Fairbank approached me as if he were an apprentice Pygmalion, assigned a raw piece of ghetto stone to carve, sculpt, shape and polish."

How did Pygmalion set out to shape and polish this raw piece of ghetto stone? First of all, there was the matter of Teddy's lamentable manners. In Fairbank's memoirs, *Chinabound,* he wrote charitably: "All he lacked was social experience—balancing a teacup, presenting letters of introduction, being au courant with the theater and books of the moment, having made the grand tour of major European capitals, and the other superficial frills. These he picked up overnight when the time came."

Fairbank and his wife, Wilma (whom he met when both were Harvard undergraduates and married later in Peking), were young faculty, not much older than their students. They lived in a charming yellow clapboard nineteenth-century cottage rented from Harvard, only fifteen feet wide but equipped with six fireplaces. There, every Thursday at five, they held an open-house tea, where, as Fairbank wrote, "foreign students practiced their English, girls met boys, visiting dignitaries were entertained." There too Teddy learned "to balance a teacup properly" and also, since he often took meals with the Fair-banks, "by observation," he learned "proper table manners at a properly set breakfast table."

Fairbank was "soft-spoken, with an unsettling conversa-tional gift of delayed-action humor," Teddy writes. He was also "a painstaking drillmaster." In his "absolute devotion to forc-ing [Teddy's] mind to think," he made him spend "six weeks plowing through St. Thomas Aquinas." Teddy became Fair-bank's first, "most exciting," and favorite pupil. "A session with Teddy was like Fourth of July fireworks," Fairbank later recalled:

> Ignite an idea and he would take off like a rocket. How come Confucius and Plato, Mencius and Aristotle were roughly contemporaries? Are civilizations really individual organisms—born, grown, productive, and senescent like you and me?
>
> Gibbon said Rome fell from "barbarism and religion." China was equally conquered by Buddhism and barbarian invaders from the north. How was China able to put it all together in the great T'ang empire while Rome perished?

Such intellectual jousting was good preparation for Teddy's later matches with Luce. Fairbank found Teddy "very good at grasping the whole, a genius at looking at a thousand bits and pieces and finding a pattern," though this could also lead Teddy to overheating his metaphors and pushing his hypotheses too far. Teddy's fascination with Big Questions animated his best work but sometimes flawed it. This tendency surfaced early. When the time came for Teddy to choose his senior thesis, he wanted to write about the role of force as the engine of history, as exemplified by China's modern warlords; Fairbank thought it too broad a theme for a college senior to take on and proposed instead a narrowed, more scholarly subject, the Twenty-one De-mands of Japan on China in 1915. They had "an affectionate quarrel," which Fairbank finally won by overcoming White's belief in the supremacy of force in history. Many are the causes of human action in man, Fairbank wrote to him: "force forces them at times, fear of force more often—and ideals still more often."

Master and pupil by then had became so close that Teddy, perhaps for the first and only time, broke the rigid compartmentalizing he insisted upon between those who knew him in his Erie Street life and those he knew at Harvard. He invited Fairbank to his home. The family worried over how Fairbank might respond to "that hard, shrill, vigorous woman," Teddy's grandmother. But the occasion went well because, in the words of Teddy's sister, Gladys, Fairbank had "acquired a Chinese attitude toward the elderly," and treated her with grave respect.

Fairbank had an even more subtle influence in guiding Teddy's choice of his future career. In Fairbank's view Teddy lacked the right background for diplomacy or the right temperament for teaching. Therefore he should put his China studies to best use by becoming a journalist—a remarkably discerning piece of advice.

With his summa cum laude degree and his traveling scholarship, Teddy wrote Fairbank in October 1938: "Dear Chief: Off to seek my fortune. Whee!" Ten months later Teddy was being lifted in a sedan chair up the steep steps to Chungking. The secondhand typewriter he carried in his hand had been a parting gift from his old tutor, John Fairbank.

Before leaving Boston, Teddy, as the family breadwinner, had to reach a family agreement about money. There wasn't much to go around. Teddy and his mother decided that his mother, sister, and two brothers could all get by, if skimpily, on a budget of $20 a week. Teddy would provide what he could. Out of his $1,500 traveling scholarship, his round-the-world ticket cost him $600; he reckoned on another $300 for living expenses en route to China. The remaining $600 he put in the family budget. Once his scholarship money ran out and he began to earn money from *Time* and other publications, he had all his paychecks sent to his sister, Gladys, in Boston. She would then send him an allowance of $50 a month, which he insisted was all he needed. He was indifferent about how he dressed, and he could live cheaply in the press hostel in Chungking. Sometimes, if there was a little money to spare in the family budget, Teddy would write home: "Buy momma some clothes."

Then as Teddy's income gradually rose, he planned a grander surprise for his family. His brother Robert, seven years his junior, was about to enter Harvard. Teddy was determined that Robert must not become a subway-commuting "meatball" as Teddy had been. Teddy suggested to Gladys that he and his sister should set aside enough money so that Robert could live in a college dormitory, participate in bull sessions, make friends, go for afternoon walks with a girl on the grassy banks of the Charles, and see football games. (In four years at Harvard Teddy had seen not one game: Saturday afternoons were for studying.)

Along with this proposal came a touching letter of guidance to Robert from Teddy:

> Now listen to me, brother, for what I'm going to say is damned important. . . . I dived down the subway every night. I butchered my whole career at school. I got good marks but little else. . . . The important thing isn't the courses, it's the guys you meet. They're all brilliant young men there, and they'll be running America some day; you're as smart as any of them so learn to live with them. Keep out of the path of the stinking, long-nosed aristocrats from Back Bay and New York. Meet the boys who have the brains. DON'T BE AN INTELLECTUAL. This is the age for men who can do something. . . . If you major in literature, government, economics or history, I'll disown you, so help me. You must study such things as mathematics,

chemistry, engineering (a field that intrigues me more and more is meteorology). . . . Harvard has one of the finest weather departments in the world—but no pupils; magnificent equipment but none to use it. . . . The field for weather experts is just opening up. . . . You must be useful first, then civilized.

When I graduated from Harvard I knew all about the world but nothing about people. I was a rude, untutored, uncivilized, unpleasant Erie St. barbarian. I did not know how to eat at table. I was coarse in manners and expression; I was without poise. I was "cheap." I know we have good stuff in us, us Whites, but Erie Street has built a shell around us. . . . It's the coarse laugh, the rough manner, the gracelessness of our bodily movements that betray us—you and I both. Start now on the little things: the clear voice; the deference to women; the clean table manners; the well-turned phrase; the constant reserve.

In fact, Robert did choose meteorology as his career, for as he later explained: "Yes, he was very influential. He was more than a brother, a sort of father of the house. OK?" In the Army Air Force during World War II, Robert served in the Pacific, forecasting the weather over Japan for B-29 bombing raids. A short, outgoing man with a close physical resemblance to Teddy, Robert M. White pursued his distinguished career with an ebullient energy like Teddy's. In time he became chief of the U.S. Weather Bureau in Washington.

Financial necessity had held the family together during the hard years, but eventually each went his or her way. When, after three years in China, Teddy returned to the United States with Harry and Clare Luce, he hurried back to Boston, eager to show off his correspondent's uniform, arriving in white tropical sharkskins and a pith helmet. His sister, Gladys, greeted him: "You still look Jewish to me, Teddy."

Teddy, usually so loquacious in his autobiographical writing, describes this homecoming tersely: "My family laughed at my costume; and I was annoyed. But I loved them and told them of my promotion and they rejoiced. But Boston was no longer home, the old ghetto no longer my place."

As the years went by the family kept in touch mainly by letters and by telephone; they were a walled-off part of Teddy's life, separate from his career, his travels, his friendships. Or as his brother Robert put it, "The Whites don't gather to celebrate being Whites."

Teddy was living more glamorously now: editing in Manhattan at *Time* magazine, and weekending at the Connecticut country home of the Luces, who invited him often, fearing he might be lonely. There, he writes, "I might meet the head of British Intelligence, famous writers like John Gunther and Walter Duranty, Broadway personalities, various Rockefellers. Luce would drily instruct me as to who was who and who did what, enjoying both my goggle-eyed wonder and his wife's pleasure in her great parties."

It is doubtful that grander living impressed him much; because he had experienced the depression, financial security meant a lot, but luxury was never a necessity to Teddy. And much as he was grateful for the hospitality of the Luces, this ambitious young journalist knew he had made a mark but not yet a reputation. He wasn't where he most wanted to be. Less than six months after his return to the States, the Japanese bombed Pearl Harbor. He was free now to resume the career he cared most about, reporting. He got himself assigned to Asia and set forth on uncharted seas.

THE UTTERMOST PLACE

The odd but enduring friendship that had sprung up between Harry Luce and Teddy White seems at first a bizarre amalgam of incongruities and dissimilarities. One was shy, the other forward; one was Jewish, the other a Christian who, in the prejudice of the day, thought of Jews as somehow set apart from everyone else.

Perhaps the older man saw something of his earlier self in the younger man. At school both had been loners, outsiders (almost outcasts), who had to earn their way, and who reached the top of their class by dogged, dedicated study. By the time that Luce met Teddy White in China, Luce was the rich boss, the powerful press lord, the influential opinion molder fawned over by China's rulers. But in fact Harry Luce's beginnings were in many ways as humble as Teddy's.

They came to their mutual interest in China by totally different routes. Teddy's curiosity about the country was an intellectual one; the spark was not ignited until he was in college. For Luce the fascination was basic, instinctive and emotional: he was born in China and there he spent his childhood.

That accident of birth marked Luce's personality, acting as both a strength and a weakness. It made him feel an outsider not only in the country where he was born but also, when he got there, in his own country, the United States.

Once, at a dinner with his colleagues in New York, he confessed to those of us present: "You could never guess what I have missed most in my life. It is that I have never had—and cannot have—a hometown, an American hometown. . . . You see, an American always explains himself satisfactorily by citing where he comes from—be it the sidewalks of New York or the farmlands of Illinois, or Houston, Texas. 'Where do you come from?' I would give anything if I could say simply and casually, 'Oskaloosa, Iowa.' "*

For Luce, the correct answer to the great American where-are-you-from question was "Tengchow, China."

He was born there on April 3, 1898, in a mud-walled mission compound without gas, electricity, or plumbing. His parents had arrived at this desolate and isolated Presbyterian mission with little baggage except their courage, commitment, and faith. His father, the Reverend Henry Winters Luce, was a wholesale grocer's son from Scranton, Pennsylvania. At Yale, where Luce's father was called Lucifer for his red hair and hot temper, he had intended to become a lawyer, but during a burst of religious fervor in America at the turn of the century, he wrote this resolve in his diary: "God willing . . . I propose to go to the foreign field and witness for Him as best I may in the uttermost parts of the earth."

The uttermost place he chose was China. The bride who accompanied him was Elizabeth Root, a tactful and dedicated young woman whom he had met in Scranton, where she was doing social work for the YWCA among factory girls.

Together they had arrived in Tengchow, an ancient walled port city with steep and narrow streets on a promontory jutting into the Yellow Sea in the northern province of Shantung. The

---

*Hearing of this, for Luce was by then famous, Oskaloosa in 1965 made him an honorary citizen.

Presbyterian mission was sheltered from the surrounding poverty, unrest, disease, and banditry by a fortresslike brick wall with an enormous gate that was locked at night. The walls however were not high enough to ward off the Boxer Rebellion, the cresting wave of xenophobic fury that swept over China shortly after the Luces got there.

The Boxers were fanatics whose war cry was "Kill the foreign devils" and who believed that the purity of their cause would exempt them from death. Fearing that Boxers were about to invade the mission, the Luces fled the compound in the middle of the night, father leading young Harry, just two years old, by the hand. Mother followed, carrying Harry's month-old sister in her arms. Hidden from sight by fields of fifteen-foot-high sorghum, they made their way to the nearby shore.

A Chinese gunboat was riding at anchor in the sampan-filled harbor. Its captain, a friend of the missionaries, took the Luces aboard. After several days in an overcrowded refugee camp at nearby Chefoo the Luces sailed across the bay to Seoul, Korea, where they stayed for nearly a year, until an international army of eighteen thousand soldiers (mostly European) savagely quelled a rebellion that in itself had been unforgettably savage. Before the rebellion was put down, the Boxers had killed two hundred missionaries, along with wives and children. They also murdered an estimated thirty thousand Chinese converts, scorning them as "rice Christians" who professed this alien religion only in order to be fed.

Harry was too young to remember the experience, but he absorbed it as part of the family lore. Later, when it was possible to examine the clash of cultures that led to the rebellion, some of the blame fell on missionaries who, in their revulsion at Chinese customs such as opium smoking and foot binding, and in their ignorance of the riches and strengths of Chinese culture, arrogantly antagonized many Chinese in their single-minded zeal to save heathen souls. Such a criticism did not apply to Harry's father, the Reverend Luce, who was not interested in

setting records for the number of souls he could claim as converts but aspired to educate a class of Christian-trained leaders.
Convinced that he could learn from as well as teach the Chinese,
he surrounded himself with long-gowned Chinese scholars to
help in his teaching and translating. Strong-willed and pious,
the Reverend Luce was intelligent and fair-minded, an admirable man—but lacking in personal warmth.

For his family he laid down a strict and spartan regime: rise
at six, cold bath and a half hour of Bible study before breakfast
at seven, three hours of Chinese lessons in the morning and
again in the afternoon, a fifty-minute walk before supper. In the
evenings the Reverend Luce would play the violin, accompanied
by his wife at the upright piano; at weekend gatherings in the
compound, everyone would join in the singing. Mother was the
one who provided the affection and the discipline, both of
which her husband seemed to regard as woman's work.

In the wholesome, hermetic atmosphere of the mission
Harry developed some of the traits that would mark his later
career as editor and publisher. Some, such as steady work habits
and religious devotion, were inculcated; others, like the self-
reliance of an essentially lonely man, were natural by-products
of the way he was brought up. Eager to prove to his father his
religious dedication, Harry at the age of four was dictating to
his mother earnest little sermons he had written himself; when
he was six, he lined up all the children of the house, including
the children of the Chinese servants, and preached a sermon to
them.

The Reverend Luce encouraged all the children to speak up
at mealtimes, but it was Harry that he was most attentive to,
treating him as an adult. They would solemnly discuss religion
and politics. Harry was instructed in the noble history of the
United States, from its origins in the Declaration of Independence to its present embodiment in a president the Reverend
Luce greatly admired, Theodore Roosevelt.

Harry got his first look at the United States at the age of

seven. The Reverend Luce and his family were sent home to the States on a fifteen-month furlough, during which time the father was to raise funds for a new mission college in China. Leaving his wife and children in San Francisco, he journeyed to Chicago, with a letter of introduction in hand, to call on the immensely wealthy widow of Cyrus H. McCormick, the man who invented the reaping machine and founded International Harvester. After listening sympathetically to the Reverend Luce's proposal for a few moments, and noting his evident fatigue, the pious and regal Mrs. McCormick broke in: "You are very tired. Come with me."

She led him across the hall to a suite of rooms. "These are my son's rooms, but he is not here now. I want you to go right to bed. I will send to your hotel for your bags. Later in the evening I want you, if you will, to tell me about your work in China." As the Reverend Luce remembered it, "Never again did we talk of finance," but one day a check arrived for $20,000, which laid the foundation for the endowment of Shantung Christian University, a rather grand name for the gloomy gray brick school that would shortly rise at Wehsein.

Eager for his wife and children to meet his new benefactress, the Reverend Luce sent for them in California but did not prepare them for the opulence of the McCormick mansion. Mrs. Luce was conscious of her own shabby dress and the ill-fitting clothes her children wore. The two girls sat stiffly on a sofa, their legs unable to touch the floor. But it was grave young Harry, looking out the window in awe of the passing carriages, that Mrs. McCormick was captured by. She offered to contribute money to the college and mission, then expressed a fear that in China young Harry would not be able to get the right schooling, and offered to adopt him and educate him in America. After praying together for guidance, the parents declined her generous offer, preferring to raise the boy themselves in China. Mrs. McCormick would continue to help support the family and often sent Harry money when he was going to college in America, but Harry never forgot his horrified, but incorrect, impression that Mrs. McCormick was bargaining to buy him from his parents. He considered it the most terrifying memory of his childhood.

The new university in Shantung, to which the Luces now moved, had no gas or electricity or adequate plumbing but was more comfortable than the Tengchow compound had been. There were about fifty Westerners and two hundred Chinese students at the mission, but in winter, because the college could not afford coal, classes had to be shut down. For the Luces this meant more time for home instruction; by the light of kerosene lamps Mrs. Luce read to the children from Dickens, Gibbon, and Shakespeare. An amah taught them Mandarin, and Harry improved his kitchen Chinese playing with the children of the servants.

From the mission, evangelists spread out into districts where contagious diseases (bubonic plague, typhus, and cholera) flourished, and on their return they were often quarantined for weeks in rough shelters outside the gates of the walled compound. The college itself was outside the town, and young Harry, on his walks, was fascinated by the endless, crowded procession of life on roads whose ruts were deepened by centuries of passage. As he would put it later, "I came to know the Chinese with their strange tenderness, sentimentality and paradoxical cruelty." On hikes he shuddered at the sight of the white towers where desperate parents abandoned the children they could not afford to feed.

As the older son, Harry was constantly favored in the family. He took a dislike—a "pig-headed dislike," his sister Beth said—to a Prussian-like governess who had been hired to teach the children German. The girls had to put up with her, but Harry was excused. Instead he was sent off alone to an English boarding school in Chefoo. There he discovered how American he was.

"I hated it and I loved it," Luce said of Chefoo, but his hatred of the English school is easier to document than his love for it. The school was run by a martinet who prescribed canings on the knuckles or buttocks for hundreds of offenses, of which the most serious was speaking to any Chinese person—a strange injunction for the fourteen Americans among the one hundred twenty students, since most were mishkids, used to the company of Chinese. "The British code, flogging and toadying, violated every American instinct," Luce later said. "No wonder that hardly an hour passed that an American . . . did not have to run up the flag. A master insists that Ohio is pronounced O-*hee*-o. What are you going to do? Will you agree? The American can't agree; it would betray every other American. So, first your knuckles are rapped, then you get your face slapped by the Master, then you are publicly caned. By this time you are crying, but you still can't say O-*hee*-o."

Solemn and religious, Harry liked best the fiery Sunday sermons but also credited God's help in the classroom; he prayed to get through a tough algebra exam, and when he did, he wrote to his family that "it was all God." He studied French, Latin, and Greek under teaching so rigorous that he later found it easy to make A's in college courses in America.

Much of Harry's memory of Chefoo was of homesickness, of chilblains, of bloody noses and skinned knees and "a shameful, futile, endless two hours on Saturday afternoon when I rolled around the unspeakably dirty floor in the main school with a little British bastard who had insulted my country."

At a staff dinner in New York he once tried to describe his early stirrings of patriotism. He had been derided by sophisticates for his naïveté in proclaiming the twentieth century the American century. Derision might cause him to reexamine his ideas but never to reject what he believed. "I probably gained a too romantic, too idealistic view of America," he told his colleagues. "This was not simply because America looked better at a distance. And it had nothing to do with America being an El Dorado. Indeed I was brought up to think that if anything was wrong in America, it was that too many people were too rich, and rich people were apt to be more sinful than other people. . . . The idealistic view of America came from the fact that the Americans I grew up with—all of them—were good people. . . . I was never disillusioned with or by America, but I was, from my earliest manhood, dissatisfied with America. America was not being as great and as good as I knew she could be, as I believed with every nerve and fiber God Himself had intended her to be."

Young Harry had noticed the difference between the behavior of Americans and that of other Westerners when, on summer holidays from Chefoo, he rejoined his family at the seaside in Tsingtao, a pretty colonial town that had been seized by the Germans as indemnity for their losses in the Boxer Rebellion. Luce rather liked the clean town, the German bands, and the beer, but he "learned about Germans in relation to Chinese rickshaw coolies. Germans beat rickshaw coolies; they beat them over their bare backs with their sticks. Britishers on the other hand never beat coolies; Britishers were simply high-handed; after a long pull they would give the coolies only a minimum fare or less and walk haughtily away. The Americans didn't beat coolies; they always overpaid."

Harry's romanticized view of America and Americans would soon be tested against reality. Having won a scholarship to the Hotchkiss School in Lakeville, Connecticut, Harry was about to leave China, but its sights and sounds and distinctive smells would always remain with him—"the mountains descending to the sea, the tilled fields." Later he wrote, "I loved China but I was immunized against any illusions about her."

The Americanization of an American born abroad was about to begin. But first something had to be done about the stammer that had afflicted Harry Luce since he was eight. His mother blamed it on the trauma he had suffered during a tonsillectomy when the anesthesia wore off before the operation was over. It added to his self-consciousness. "Use your native Lucepower," his father would enjoin him. At Chefoo Harry had helped to organize a debating society, hoping to get practice in public speaking. By using his native Lucepower he managed to get through an entire debate without stammering; but the stammer returned.

Luce's father had heard of a school outside London whose headmaster claimed success in treating stammerers. The Reverend Luce thereupon took a daring chance on young Harry's character: he sent the fourteen-year-old boy off to Europe on his own. From Shanghai, Harry took a German ship to Europe via the Indian Ocean and the Suez Canal. In Rome and Florence he faithfully followed the cultural routes that he and his father had worked out together from guidebooks. But when Harry at last reached the English school, he found that the remedy for his stammer, using breathing exercises, promised help but not a cure. After four and a half months, Harry got his parents' permission to drop out. He spent the rest of the year cycling around England, then touring classical sites in France, Switzerland, and Italy.

When Harry entered Hotchkiss the following year he was better prepared academically, more mature, and certainly more widely traveled than his classmates, but he was regarded by them as something of a dour oddball. They called him Chink. In his tacky Chinese-made suit he was ill at ease among the well-dressed sons of the well-off. He had trouble following their conversation or understanding their slang. He didn't know how to talk baseball; he regarded athletics as a waste of time. Among his classmates he was not popular, but he was respected and could count among his friends Thornton Wilder, the future playwright of *Our Town*, who had been a classmate at Chefoo, and would be again at Yale.

Young Harry was one of only six scholarship students in a class of sixty-four. Assigned to wait table and clean up, he didn't know how to use a broom (at the mission, Chinese servants had done that). "I detested it, but I wasn't humiliated," Luce said. He was just glad to be at Hotchkiss.

It was at Hotchkiss that Harry met the classmate who would be the most important influence in his life. It was a case of meeting someone with whom he had little but talent in common. Briton Hadden was the cocky, gregarious son of a prosperous banker from Brooklyn. In contrast to the sober and earnest young Harry, Hadden loved baseball, disdained seriousness, and affected a tough-guy manner, chewing gum and talking gangster-style out of the corner of his mouth. But he was every bit as smart, ambitious, and competitive as Harry. They were rivals through prep school and college, and then, with full respect for each other's talent, would become partners (though never close friends) in inventing *Time, the Weekly Newsmagazine.*

Of the two, Luce was always the better scholar. At Hotchkiss, he was on the Honor Roll, Leader of Class. On his College Boards in Greek Harry scored the highest in the country (in celebration the headmaster declared a school holiday). In other match-ups, where personal popularity mattered, Hadden usually won. He became the editor of the school paper, with Luce as his assistant; Luce edited the literary monthly. Hadden was the class orator, Luce the class poet.

At Yale their rivalry continued. Both "heeled" for coveted staff positions on the *Yale Daily News;* Hadden finished first, Luce second. Of course, Hadden enjoyed the advantage of not having to earn his way through Yale, while Luce waited tables, solicited orders for a tailor, and managed several student eating houses. Luce made Phi Beta Kappa, Hadden didn't. A Greek major, Luce achieved the highest marks in that subject in Yale's history.

But it was Hadden, competing for what mattered most to both, who became board chairman of the *Daily News;* Luce, having lost by one vote, became managing editor. To his family,

Harry gamely wrote: "Happily I have the greatest admiration and affection for Brit which, in some measure at least, is reciprocated." Hadden in turn wrote to his own family: "Luce is the best competition I ever had. No matter how hard I run, Luce is always there. I have to get better acquainted with Chink Luce, with whom I will have to work in the next few years."

Both would be tapped for Skull and Bones, Yale's solemnly sacrosanct secret society. Luce graduated summa cum laude in 1920 and was voted most brilliant; Hadden was voted most likely to succeed and "the man who had done most for Yale." Looking on at the rivalry with fascination, and already sharpening the skills that would make him celebrated as a waspish culture critic, Dwight Macdonald wrote of his classmates that they were "polar opposites" in every way but one:

> Luce/Hadden: moral/amoral, pious/worldly, respectable/raffish, bourgeois/bohemian, introvert/extrovert, somber/convivial, reliable/unpredictable, slow/quick, dog/cat, tame/wild, efficient/brilliant, decent/charming, Puritanical/hedonistic, naïve/cynical, Victorian/18th Century.
>
> The one important quality they had in common was an enormous respect for American-style success and a 24-hour determination to achieve it.

How did Harry Luce, pious and introverted, decide to become a journalist? As a boy he had aspired to be an orator, and though he was never good at it, he retained the itch to instruct and persuade. Mrs. McCormick, his patroness, hoped he would become a minister, like his father, but the idea never seems to have appealed to him. At Hotchkiss, when asked to name his career, Harry wrote "undecided." He sometimes talked of going back to China to make his fortune in some business enterprise. But he enjoyed a summer job on the Springfield (Mass.) *Republican* so much that he decided that journalism might be the best way to reach his real ambition, which was to enter politics and public life. First he had to earn enough money to be independent; journalism would give him that.

But when he confided his ambition to a man he greatly admired—Dr. Amos Wilder, a prominent member of the Yale faculty and father of Harry's friend Thornton—he got a shocked response. Wilder, who had once been a newspaper editor, pleaded with tears in his eyes: "Harry, don't. Don't go into journalism. It will turn you into a cynic. It will corrupt and corrode you. It will turn your wine into vinegar. You will lose your soul."

(Years later Luce told his biographer John Kobler: "To the extent that I have become corrupted and corroded I can't blame it on journalism.")

Luce didn't leap into journalism, he sidled into it, in company with Brit Hadden. On the college paper both had written fiery editorials about the war in Europe, and when the United States declared war on Germany in 1917, Luce and Hadden, full of patriotic fervor, spent the summer of their junior year in officers training camp, as student instructors of draftees at Camp Jackson, South Carolina. At the end of one very hot day Harry and Brit took a long evening walk together; they bemoaned how ignorant of the world the draftees were—as Luce put it, "Their knowledge didn't equal their interest"—and talked about how a lively, interesting newsmagazine might find a large audience in an ignorant world. "I think it was in that walk that *Time* began," Luce said later.

But the idea was still vague, and after finishing Yale, Luce set off for Europe with two classmates on what he called "my last opportunity to have a good time" before embarking on a career. With money he had saved from his editor's salary on the college paper, and with a one-thousand-dollar graduation check from the ever-helpful Mrs. McCormick, he enrolled at Oxford. He read history, bicycled, played tennis and chess, and took long vacation trips to the Continent. Then, his holiday year over and his money gone, he returned to the United States with two Savile Row suits, a mustache, and a cane.

He was in love with a girl he had met in Rome, Lila Ross Hotz, who came from a wealthy Chicago Presbyterian family. He followed her to Chicago but told her he couldn't afford to marry her yet. Finally he got a job on the Chicago *Daily News,* gathering material for Ben Hecht, a crusty romantic who wrote a tough-sentimental column extolling, with more fiction than fact, the lives of the city's "little people." It was Hecht who, with Charles MacArthur, would later immortalize Chicago's rough, street-smart journalism in *The Front Page.* Luce was hopelessly out of place in that shabby, cynical world and after six weeks was fired.

He was, therefore, without a job when Yale's mutual-protection network came to his rescue. He received two letters from Yale classmates. One was from Walter Millis, who had done so well as an editorial writer on the Baltimore *News* that his editor had asked him, "Do you know any more Yale boys who write as well as you?" Millis offered Luce a reporter's job at forty dollars a week. The other letter was from Brit Hadden, who had received a similar offer from Millis. "If we're ever going to start that paper, this looks like our chance," he wrote Luce.

Hadden and Luce rented an apartment together in Baltimore, spent their days as rival reporters on the *News* and their evenings cutting up copies of *The New York Times* and cannibalizing articles from weekly reviews. Their simple idea was to give readers in one hour's reading time all the important news of a whole week, much as all-news radio stations would later promise, "Give us twenty-two minutes and we'll give you the world." They practiced collapsing seven days of a running news story into one pithy narrative; they compartmentalized the news by subjects (adding a few that most papers slighted, such as news of art, medicine, and religion). Their biggest concern was whether they were legally entitled to steal the news from newspapers, and they were relieved to learn of court decisions that news could not be copyrighted. The manner of describing events might be protected, but the *facts* about any event, such as a murder, once reported, quickly lost their exclusivity and entered the public domain. The courts' decision that news could not be monopolized was sound public policy, but it had the effect of reinforcing a condescending attitude toward newspapers in Yale's two young men, who thought newspapers long-winded, mealymouthed, and boring. They had little idea of how much effort, how many hours of sitting through monotonous trials and legislative hearings, how much skilled questioning of evasive bureaucrats, it took to produce the raw material that they simply appropriated, pared, and commented on brightly. For many years, experience as a newspaperman was a handicap to getting a job at *Time*. The magazine preferred Ivy Leaguers with a quirky smattering of culture and the knack of being wittily concise. Newspapermen were regarded as hacks without imagination; many newspapermen in turn regarded the people at *Time* as arrogant, overpaid amateurs, not serious professionals.

Once Luce and Hadden had produced a dummy of their newsmagazine, they issued a manifesto to describe its aims. Why, they asked, is the American public "for the most part" so poorly informed? "This is not the fault of the daily newspapers: they print all the news," nor was it the fault of the weekly reviews, which *Time* intended to crib from. And only a "facile cynic" would think that ignorance was the public's own fault. No, the trouble was that "no publication has adapted itself to the time which busy men are able to spend on simply keeping informed." *Time* would gather information from "virtually every magazine and newspaper of note in the world," chop and dice it into one hundred bite-sized pieces, none longer than four hundred words. That was the formula: take somebody else's reporting, compress it, and retell it with panache.

The final ingredient in the formula would be a brash, inventive, irreverent style. Verbs carried the action: people didn't speak, they snapped or gushed; they didn't eat, they wolfed down; they didn't walk, they strode. Quips flourished and puns went unpunished. From Homer *Time* stole the double-barreled adjective ("fleet-footed Achilles") and used it to describe, deflate, and diminish people ("moose-tall," "beetle-browed," "pint-sized"). If a phrase pleased the editors ("fireplug-shaped Fiorello La Guardia"), it would be repeated endlessly, until it seemed attached to the person's name. Even when *Time* praised, it did so with a smirk (*The New York Times,* from whom it appropriated so much, was always "the good, grey *Times*"). Pictures were often chosen to ridicule, their captions to titillate. Though Edmund Wilson complained of *Time*'s "jeering rancor," its malice was tempered by sophomoric high spirits. *Time* was catchy and became addictive: at dinners readers would quote the latest example of its impudence. The style was Hadden's more than Luce's (though when the mood was upon him, Luce could be just as feline in crafting a mouse-taunting insult).

Would the new magazine be as stodgily neutral as its well-established competitor, the *Literary Digest,* or would it be opinionated? On this point Luce and Hadden elected to be forthrightly ambiguous: "*Time* gives both sides, but clearly indicates which side it believes to have the stronger position. . . . But this magazine is not founded to promulgate prejudices, liberal or conservative. 'To keep men well-informed'—that, first and last, is the only ax this magazine has to grind."

Already the ambiguities of the prospectus—the readiness to acknowledge certain prejudices while swearing *Time* had no ax to grind—was an indication of the split personality that the magazine would have as long as both Hadden and Luce were involved in editing it. Hadden, the amused observer of the passing scene, was the one with no ax to grind. Luce, his Presbyterianism always astir just below the surface, saw a journalistic duty "to foment and formulate" and would later disingenuously scorn the promise to give both sides: "Are there not apt to be three sides or thirty sides?" He would also say: "Show me a man who claims he's completely objective and I'll show you a man with illusions."

With their typewritten dummy and prospectus in hand, Hadden and Luce set out to solicit criticism and to seek support. H. L. Mencken, the Sage of Baltimore, said, "Nobody will read it"; William Randolph Hearst declined to invest. Hadden and Luce had originally believed in the Yale solution: simply persuade each of ten rich Yale classmates to put up $10,000 each. The trouble with this notion was that it was the *parents* of these classmates who had the money. Two Morgan partners, urged by their sons, finally came in; then, after futile months of knocking on doors, Luce and Hadden ran into luck with another Yale classmate, son of a Rockefeller partner, whose mother put up $20,000. That gave them $86,000; they decided to launch.

In a succession of cheap, drab offices in lower Manhattan, a tiny staff got out the magazine. The print order for the first issue, dated March 3, 1923, was 25,000; it sold 8,600 copies. According to the original agreement, Hadden and Luce were to trade places every year, one running the business side, the other editing. Brit won the toss to edit, but when they traded jobs at the end of the first year, Brit proved so inept with finances (and Luce was so good at them) that Brit, much to Luce's disappointment, continued to edit the magazine for its first three years and set its breezy tone.

In an atmosphere decidedly collegiate, the staff worked long hours without letup. Hadden presided boisterously from a roll-top desk, sending clippings to his three writers, usually with terse instructions: "Let's blurb this"; "Let's blat this"; "Flay!" Thus did opinion get made and airily expressed in *Time*'s first years.

From these amateurish and bizarre beginnings came habits and practices that would continue to dominate the magazine when it became successful, sedate, prosperous, and influential. Over time, responsibility moderated the impulse to be clever; *Time* gradually shed some of its more grating mannerisms. But in ways that would affect Teddy White in China and other top-flight journalists when *Time* at last decided to hire its own correspondents, it would still be a magazine where writers and editors prevailed, where people sitting in their little cubicles in a New York skyscraper read newspapers and magazines, stared at the wall or out the window, sent queries for information to correspondents the world over, did no reporting themselves but sat in judgment on those who did, and decided for themselves—in consultation with their editors—what the news was and how it should be interpreted. Correspondents had few rights, not even the right to know before an issue went to press what had been used from their files, or what else had been put in. It was a formula for friction, and friction was inevitable.

"CERTAIN DARK POSSIBILITIES"

After Pearl Harbor it took Teddy White more than six chaotic months to get back to Chiang Kai-shek's mountain
lair in Chungking, cadging transportation as best he could.

Time had first assigned him to Singapore as a war correspondent, but before he could get there, Singapore had fallen,
and the Japanese were advancing south through the Dutch East
Indies. Teddy's ship was diverted to Australia. From there
White made his way to India, where he first met the doomed
war hero Lieutenant General Joseph W. Stilwell.

Teddy, like Luce, had his personal heroes. Luce's were warriors—MacArthur, Churchill, Eisenhower, Chiang—the kind
whose emotions would be stirred on hearing "Onward, Christian Soldiers" played by a regimental band. Teddy's were a
working journalist's heroes, valuable as sources, unlike one another in their beliefs, but each magnetic, articulate, and activist.
First there was Stilwell, then Chou En-lai, and finally John F.
Kennedy. Stilwell, the crusty commander of Allied forces in the
China-Burma-India theater, had also been appointed chief of
staff of Chiang Kai-shek's armies. As the first foreigner allowed
to command Chinese troops, he had an impossible mission.
White found Stilwell angry and bitter. The Chinese army in
Burma had been unable to defend the Burma Road, China's
only land bridge to the outside world. They, and the British

troops beside them, were decisively defeated by the Japanese invading Burma. Though in the first months of the war the Japanese were crushing all resistance everywhere, Stilwell blamed his own defeat on the man who had sent him there and then sabotaged him: Chiang Kai-shek.

While thousands of refugees and soldiers in chaotic flight clogged the major roads, Stilwell gathered a small nucleus of twenty-six Americans, thirteen British, sixteen Chinese, and a motley collection of Burmese nurses and Indian cooks and mechanics, and together they made their way out of Burma through the jungles on foot. At fifty-eight Stilwell was almost totally blind in one eye from an explosion in an ammunition dump during World War I and, with poor sight in the other, was unable to distinguish the fingers of a hand at three feet. But he was a man of indomitable spirit. After traveling over dirt roads and jungle trails, fording streams, beset by snakes and insects, exhausted by heat and soaked by showers, he and his party came to a range of forested razorback mountains, which they spent eight days climbing to reach the Indian border and safety. They had journeyed one hundred forty grueling miles without the loss of a single life.

In these first dark months of World War II, when American forces from Pearl Harbor to the Philippines were concealing their losses to deceive the enemy and to bolster morale at home, Stilwell had been characteristically blunt and refreshingly honest when reporters questioned him: "I claim we got a hell of a beating. We got run out of Burma."

Shortly after that defeat Teddy White got his first look at Stilwell. The general had flown to India, concerned by reports that Indian troops were rioting for independence from the British, and wanting to make sure that his own base would be secure. White found this wiry, gnarled plainspoken soldier occupying an oversized suite in the Imperial Hotel in New Delhi. Scowling over a cigarette, Stilwell appraised White and decided to be candid: "The trouble in China is simple: We are allied to an ignorant, illiterate, superstitious, peasant son of a bitch."

"I gulped," Teddy White recalled in his autobiography: "I had never heard Chiang Kai-shek described that way before, not even by Chou En-lai."

Within two years the quarrel between Chiang and Stilwell led to a disastrous open break. The reporting of this dramatic event would sunder for many years the friendship between Teddy White, who favored Stilwell, and Harry Luce, who favored Chiang. The falling-out itself became news, in a fashion that enhanced White's reputation and diminished Luce's.

Perhaps such a split was inevitable, despite the genuine affection that had sprung up between Teddy and the Luces in Chungking in the spring of 1941. Shortly before their first meeting Teddy had written to his family in Boston: "It's always fine to work in close proximity to the big boss. But I know Mr. Luce will disagree with me politically and it will be hard to keep my mouth shut. Mr. Luce will probably also want to use me as an office boy, and I don't know whether I can do that or not."

But before long Teddy had forgotten an original intention to go back to Harvard to teach; he enjoyed experiencing history in the making, and hobnobbing with the famous: "The Hemingways were here and I breakfasted with them twice; turned down a third invitation because I don't like Hemingway. His wife is a nice girl. At present, the Caldwells are here; Erskine Caldwell ('You Have Seen Their Faces,' 'Tobacco Road') and his wife Margaret Bourke-White. They too are queer people. Less glib than the Hemingways but I think they will wear better. I have by now decided that all famous authors are six-footers, big-bellied, married to attractive wives and are only ordinary people."

The following week, just before the arrival of the Luces, Teddy had again written home: "I'll probably quit *Time* in a few months. I don't think I'm going to get along with them, and I'd like to look for work in the early fall. I don't like *Time*'s news policies or general politics. At present I'm staying till Luce comes and then I'm off."

Yet get along the Luces and Teddy memorably did. A mutual love of China, and a fascination with its struggles, united them. But Luce got the distinct impression, which proved not to be true, that Teddy shared his own enthusiasm for Chiang. Teddy's autobiography makes clear that his disenchantment with Chiang began earlier. After his visit to the battlefront in Shansi for the story that in 1939 brought him his first byline in *Time*, White had concluded that Chiang and the men around him were no longer "a real government. They had no control of events, and I had an immense desire to separate from them."

Luce certainly had good reason to believe in Teddy's admiration for Chiang, whom Teddy had described in *Life* as the man who might one day win "greater influence than any other single being of our age." Did Teddy really believe what he wrote then? The likely explanation is that Teddy was still the "bespectacled hustler" he called himself on emerging from Harvard. If so, he wouldn't have been the first careerist to establish a foothold before displaying his fearlessness. Later, when he had become a successful and established journalist, had as it were secured his base, Teddy White would fight courageously and tenaciously for what he believed.

As for Harry Luce, the quarrel with White would fix him in journalistic legend as an editor blinded by his loyalty to Chiang, gullible in his trust in the Generalissimo, consumed by a hatred of Communism, and unwilling to hear or to print anything contrary to his prejudices. There will be much to criticize in Luce's later behavior, but in the first two years of the friendship, until the quarrel over Stilwell, Luce was, contrary to the legend, ever solicitous of Teddy's views, receptive to Teddy's tough reporting about Chiang, and concerned to get the balance and the facts right about China. Teddy White himself would acknowledge that.

■ ■ ■

The story of Joe Stilwell, as Teddy reported it, was that of an inspired soldier too honest to function as a diplomat as well. Stilwell was a special favorite of the army chief of staff, George Catlett Marshall. He was Marshall's first choice, after Pearl Harbor, to plan and then command the Allied invasion of North Africa. Instead, Stilwell's peacetime past caught up with him. In the somnolent between-wars period of the 1920s and 1930s, Stilwell had been sent to language school to learn to read and write Chinese and had served several tours of duty in Asia. Now, as Japanese armies swept swiftly across the South Pacific and west to Burma and India, Chiang complained petulantly that the Allies had given Asia too low a priority. To placate him the U.S. Army sent its top Asian specialist to Chungking as Chiang's chief of staff. That meant Stilwell.

He arrived in Burma just ten days before Rangoon fell. He was put in command of two Chinese armies and was empowered to shoot any soldier up to the rank of major (one of Chiang's favorite methods of changing commands). He quickly discovered that his commanders were receiving private messages from Chiang, often giving instructions contrary to Stilwell's, because of Chiang's fear of heavy battle losses. At first Stilwell was understanding: "It is expecting a great deal," he wrote in his diary, "to have them turn over a couple of armies in a vital area to a goddam foreigner that they don't know and in whom they can't have confidence."

But his patience ran out when the "pusillanimous bastards" would delay movements of troops until it was too late to employ them, thus to "create a condition by failing to act, and then plead it as an excuse for not acting." If Stilwell had been empowered to shoot a general, his choice would have been the man in charge of supplies, who filled his trucks with goods to take back to China instead of using his trucks to transport troops.

This fellow turned out to be a cousin of Chiang's and untouchable.

Stilwell, after his initial "hell of a beating," was convinced that the Burma Road had to be retaken. The only alternative—flying in supplies over a spur of the Himalayas called the Hump—was a dangerous undertaking that helped but could never supply all that China needed.

On his return to Chungking, Teddy White found the atmosphere of the besieged capital had visibly darkened in the fifteen months since he had gone back to the States with the Luces. Chungking's population had swollen by a quarter of a million Chinese refugees. Sealed off by Japan's blockade, with most of the great coastal cities in enemy hands, the Chinese economy was a shambles, presided over by officials who were frequently incompetent and often corrupt. Inflation had doubled while White was away and would double again in months. People suffered and in desperation stole and cheated. Correspondents found that once-faithful employees could no longer be trusted. The black-market money changer who had previously sneaked into the press hostel now marched in trailed by a bearer carrying a basket crammed with bundles of wadded banknotes to trade for American dollars.

Of this the American public knew little. People in the States were preoccupied with the rearrangements of their own lives—enlisting, getting called up in the draft, going to work in war factories, learning to shop with ration coupons. The foreign news they listened to on the radio or read about in the papers concentrated on the war in Europe of Churchill, Hitler, and Stalin. In the Pacific, Japanese and American carrier groups sought each other out in heroic battle. But in China itself the Japanese, so busy elsewhere, were content to stabilize their front without massive battles. What little news did come out of China now had to get past American censors, who could be almost as zealous in excising information that might embarrass the Chinese as were the Chinese themselves.

In times of war Americans tend to romanticize their allies, celebrating dictatorships as strong and reliable partners. Though ignorant of China's deteriorating condition, the American public felt a newfound affection for its ally, particularly as personified in China's leadership—Chiang the simple soldier who had been converted to Christianity, and his wife the Wellesley graduate who was one of the three sisters of the much-publicized Soong family.

The Luce magazines, whose traditional formula was to describe events through the personalities of the people involved, had made the Soongs household names to their readers. Chiang, with or without his wife, had been on *Time*'s cover nine times. *Life*, with big picture spreads, portrayed the Soong sisters glamorously. T. V. Soong, their brother, had served as president of the Central Bank of China, minister of finance, foreign minister, and acting president of the Executive Yuan. The Soongs were in fact a tight little inbred clique that wielded great power and enriched itself doing so. When they were seen close up, as Stilwell saw them, their glamour soon wore thin.

One of Stilwell's responsibilities was to ration the thin trickle of supplies flown in over the Hump. It peeved Chiang that other theaters of war had stronger claims for money, men, and matériel, but even when the Allies could send China more supplies, everything at the final stage had to pour through a narrow bottleneck. At first only fifteen tons a month could be airlifted over the Hump by pilots flying clunky transports at twenty thousand feet across mountains and jungles while dodging Japanese airplanes. Within a year, they were able to deliver three thousand tons a month, but this was hopelessly inadequate; it fell to Stilwell to decide who got what, an exercise Stilwell likened to "trying to manure a ten-acre field with sparrow shit."

He couldn't satisfy everybody, least of all Chiang. Now that

Chiang was an ally, he felt entitled to all the supplies he could get for his five hundred million people, his four million soldiers, and his own feeble war industry. And as China's inflation got out of hand, space also had to be found on the overcrowded transports to ferry in great bales of new Chinese currency printed in the United States.

Even more insistent was the need to bring in enough gasoline to keep Brigadier General Claire Chennault's "Flying Tigers" in the air. Chennault, another authentic American hero, was a lanky Texas aerial genius who, because of his strident advocacy of airpower, had been forced to retire from the U.S. Army in 1936. He signed on as a mercenary to fight for China and assembled a ragtag collection of brave, cocky Americans who had flown in the army or the navy. His American Volunteers Group, flying P-40s painted with menacing snouts, had proven highly effective in combat against Japanese planes. After Pearl Harbor they were incorporated into the U.S. Fourteenth Air Force, and Chennault was welcomed back as a brigadier general.

Chennault and Stilwell were both proud, colorful, and determined mavericks, brilliant tacticians and natural leaders. They became bitter enemies, a "soul-trying" situation for Teddy White, who liked and admired both. Chennault and Stilwell (who outranked him) quarreled initially over how to divide the meager supplies arriving over the Hump. Chennault thought the war could be won quickly by airpower alone, with his planes creating havoc over Japan's interior sea-lanes. Stilwell argued that this would inevitably invite retaliation against Chennault's air bases in East China, which could be defended only by the battleworthy Chinese ground forces that Stilwell would train.

Stilwell also needed supplies and equipment to carry out his own assignment from General Marshall, to modernize, retrain, and remold the badly led and ill-equipped Chinese army. Marshall, looking ahead to eventual invasion of the Japanese mainland, saw the Chinese as the largest manpower pool the Allies could tap. It was Marshall's plan to land American troops on the Chinese mainland and join with Chinese troops for the final grand assault on Japan once the European war was won, once the navy and MacArthur's troops had closed in on Japan and the navy had cleared the seas.

One day Stilwell was summoned to a meeting in Chungking which he suspected had been rigged in advance. Chennault (a great favorite of General and Madame Chiang, in part because his air successes cost a minimum of Chinese lives) said he wanted two hundred planes. Chiang wanted another three hundred for his own air force. Madame Chiang then turned to Stilwell and said, "That's your job to get it in." When the others left, Madame indicated to Stilwell what his reward would be: "And we're going to see that you are made *a full general*." In his journal Stilwell wrote: "The hell they are."

Tired of being treated as an errand boy, Stilwell found an occasion to remind "Madame Empress" that in addition to being Chiang's chief of staff, he wore other hats, including that of commanding general of the U.S. Army Forces of the China-Burma-India theater, with responsibilities outside China. As a U.S. Army officer, he was sworn to uphold the interests of the United States. "If she doesn't get the point, she's dumber than I think she is." Two days later, Madame Chiang called to ask what Stilwell had recommended to Washington. "She got hot on the phone and started to bawl me out so I said I would like to see her."

After being kept waiting two hours, Stilwell patiently explained what it would take to fly 5,000 tons a month over the Hump: 304 planes, 275 crews, 3,400 officers and enlisted men on ground, five fields at each end, each to take 50 transports. "She began to get some light." He added that he thought her husband "wanted a soldier and not a rubber stamp or transmitting agency. And I told her that at the first sign of lack of confidence, I wanted to go home." After writing this in his diary, he added a final line: "Developed gut ache and had it all night. Puked five times."

Yet Stilwell had a qualified admiration for the woman he sometimes called Madamissima in his diary: "a clever, brainy woman. Sees the Western viewpoint." Stilwell had no respect at all for her husband and constantly referred to the Generalissimo as Peanut, even in the presence of Chinese subordinates (with the result that the insult inevitably got back to Chiang). In a letter to his wife in California, Stilwell called Chiang a "stubborn, ignorant, prejudiced, conceited despot who never hears the truth except from me and finds it hard to believe."

The novelist Pearl Buck had done more than anyone else to stir in American hearts a friendly feeling for the Chinese people. In *The Good Earth,* which sold two million copies worldwide and was made into a fine film, Pearl Buck had portrayed China's long-suffering peasantry so vividly that more than a decade later her novel still defined America's impression of the Chinese. She was now concerned by the wide gap between the actual situation in China and what the American public understood about it. This led her to write a letter to Harry Luce. Though their politics differed, Pearl Buck was a mishkid like Luce.

She proposed to write an article for *Life* because she was "so fearful that certain dark possibilities now looming in China will materialize and cause disillusionment and pessimism about China over here." Luce commissioned the article, "What's Wrong with China," which ran in *Life* on May 10, 1943. She argued for more military aid to China and said that the Chinese still regarded Chiang as a great man, but she reported that the liberal voices of China were being silenced, the Kuomintang bureaucracy was becoming more oppressive, and corruption was increasing. How Chiang's greatness would be measured in the future, she wrote, depended on how effective he was in "dealing with these evils on the negative side, and in providing the people with a technique of democracy on the positive side." Unless America brought more pressure on Chiang for reform, "we are in the process of throwing away a nation of people."

Such statements were a startling departure for the Luce magazines, which had sometimes acknowledged defects in Chiang's regime but usually cushioned such criticism with references to the magnitude of his problems. But Pearl Buck had obviously found a direct route to Luce's conscience. He sent a "Private Memorandum" to his editors:

> I am interested in publicizing Pearl's article on China for two reasons:
> 1) As one who is given credit or blame for helping to increase American interest in China for the past two years, I do not want to be found guilty of having misled the American people—bringing their friendship for China to the "verge of sentimentality" which "will inevitably end in disillusionment."
> 2) Being considerably, if not fully, aware of the faults or evils in Chinese administration, I would naturally welcome anything that can be done to remedy the actual situation.

But he wondered whether Pearl Buck's article might do more harm than good, in "returning the whole matter of China to a state of confusion worse than the previous state of indifference." Then he began to roll the question around in his head:

> What exactly is the serious fault in the American view of China? Do Americans actually love the Chinese too much, "adore" them, etc.? I think that's ridiculous. Most Americans are just getting out of the "laundryman" stage of opinion.

Furthermore, Luce wrote, consider Pearl Buck's worry about democracy:

Actually not ten percent of the American people have any opinion of the Chinese government—except the Generalissimo and Madame Chiang. So the actual semantic question turns on Chiang and the Soongs. If we want to talk straight, isn't that the real point?

The plain fact is that China has been struggling into modernity—her own modernity, but modernity nevertheless, and that for 16 years the Generalissimo and the Madame have led that struggle. Could there have been better leaders—or worse? Could they, being the leaders, have done substantially better or substantially worse? Surely, these are not easy questions.

At least Luce himself was not finding the answers easy. As a man whose life had been shaped by two cultures, he felt himself uniquely equipped to serve as a kind of bridge between them. As Pearl Buck had sensed, though he supported Chiang, Luce, both as an editor and as a friend of China, wanted to be right with history. Teddy White, too, sensed this, and aware of Luce's deeper doubts, he would skillfully exploit the crevice in Luce's loyalty to Chiang.

A One-Man Free Press

For Teddy White the experience that would, more than any other, sharpen his disagreements with Harry Luce began with an item that appeared one day in February 1943 in *Ta Kung Pao*, Chungking's most independent newspaper. It told of a famine in the northern province of Honan. For daring to mention one of the most terrible famines in Chinese history, *Ta Kung Pao* was shut down by the government for three days. Teddy decided to go to Honan to see for himself.

With a colleague, Harrison Forman of *The Times* of London, he flew to Sian, where the stump of a railway line led to Honan. The route was under Japanese gunfire for much of the way. After dark, three trains a night—their flatcars, boxcars, and old coaches crowded with refugees perched on the roofs and clinging to the sides—sneaked by the guns. In the daytime the Japanese gunners did not bother to intercept targets they thought too small, so it was possible to make the thirty-mile journey on a handcar, manned by two soldiers at each handle. In such fashion, huddled in the cold winter wind in soldiers' padded robes, White and Forman rode in the open pumpcar, front-seat witnesses to a passing parade of horror.

They saw people—some dead, some dying—who had fallen from the rooftops of the refugee trains the night before because their fingers, numbed by the cold, had lost their grip. One man, still alive and crying, must have fallen under the wheels of the train; his leg was severed at the shin. Along each side of the track an endless procession walked in the cold, or dropped from hunger and exhaustion, and lay there. "A dozen times an hour some father pushed a wheelbarrow past, the mother hauling at it in front with a rope . . . or the woman of the family sat sidesaddle on her mule with her baby in her arms, like an unhappy madonna, while the father belabored the rear of the mule with a staff. Old women hobbled along on bound feet, stumbled and fell; no one picked them up. Other old women rode pickaback on the strong shoulders of their sons, staring through cold black eyes at the hostile sky."

When they arrived at the provincial capital of Loyang, the two correspondents met the bishop of the Loyang Catholic mission, "a great-hearted American," Thomas Megan of Eldora, Iowa, who gave them warm food and then offered to be their guide to the land of the dying. They set out on horseback for Chengchow, epicenter of the famine, once a city of one hundred twenty thousand but now shrunk to thirty thousand. Along the way they saw a young girl, "her face shriveled about her skull," dead a day or more, snow covering her eyes. "She would lie unburied until the birds or the dogs cleaned her bones. . . . We stopped to take a picture of dogs digging bodies from sand piles; some were half-eaten, but the dogs had already picked clean one visible skull. Half the villages were deserted; some simply abandoned, others already looted."

What Teddy White had seen was horrifying enough; what he and Forman heard from the missionaries—European and American, Catholic and Protestant, unselfishly working together—was worse.

> In one village a mother was discovered boiling her two-year-old to eat its meat. In another case a father was charged with strangling his two boys to eat them; his defense was that they were already dead. . . .

What appalls me most, as I read back into the notes of my trip, written each evening, is my increasing callousness. At first I was frightened; and of course the matter was too large for grief. But then I became increasingly hard. Riding a horse through a cluster of beggars lying in wait for you in a village street was a serious matter, dangerous. If you stopped, they might tear the horse down and eat it, and then you yourself would be left on foot with the starving. So I learned to flog my horse to a gallop through any cluster of people, sometimes whipping hands off, sometimes throwing out handfuls of peanuts or dried persimmons to make a safe getaway, and sometimes casting Chinese dollars into the wind to decoy them with paper.

Through the years, somewhere in its vast territorial reach, China has always known famine, but this was Teddy White's first experience of it. The rich flat plain of Honan, usually fertile with wheat, corn, millet, and soybeans, had seen no rain for two years. In the province's ten hardest-hit districts, where eight million of its thirty-two million peasants once lived, perhaps two million had died and five million had fled as refugees. At first, shaken by what he had seen and heard, Teddy accepted this vast tragedy as an act of nature, its havoc unpreventable, its suffering fatalistically to be borne. But then, as he listened to the accounts of the missionaries, and interviewed officials and the army officers who ruled the province, Teddy's attitude changed to anger at

> what purported to be the government of China; or at the anarchy that masqueraded as government. For though the famine had come from the heavens, in the worst drought since the reign of Emperor Kuang-hsu in 1893, death might have been avoided had government acted. But this death was man-made. . . .
>
> The government was fighting a war against Japan; it was relentless in collecting taxes for the war. But since it did not trust its own paper money, its armies in the field

were instructed to collect taxes in grain and kind for their
own support. . . . The army's tax, I found, was usually
equivalent to the full crop, but in some cases it was
higher—and where the grain tax was higher than the yield,
peasants were sometimes forced to sell animals, tools, furniture, for cash to make up the difference. . . . Army store-
houses bulged with surplus grain—which officers sold for
their own profit, and which missionaries and good officials
bought from the black market to feed the starving.

Teddy filed his dispatch to *Time* from Loyang, but instead of its
being forwarded to Chungking, to be censored (and probably
killed), the bulk of it was sent directly to New York. Teddy
never knew how this happened: Had some unknown telegraph-
key-tapper, moved by conscience, deliberatedly bypassed
Chungking in defiance of regulations? (The final section of his
file was sent to Chungking, where censors saw to it that it never
did reach New York.)

Teddy's report, which created such a stir when published in
the States, was widely disbelieved when word of it got back to
Chungking. In the capital there had been some awareness of a
food shortage in Honan, but not of a famine; layer upon layer of
officials reporting to their superiors had minimized the severity
of the situation to cover their own failures. Teddy was reproached for sensationalism, denounced for bypassing censorship, even accused of plotting with Communists in the telegraph
administration to have his dispatch sent directly to America.

As he wrote to his New York boss, the chief of correspondents, "I went and am sorry that I went. I have been mentally
sick ever since I came back—nervous, depressed, unhappy."
Having become the center of controversy, he found that many
of his news sources refused even to speak to him. Determined
that attention be paid, Teddy set out "to raise hell." He wrote
his boss, "I know it is not my place in China to create free public
opinion or to constitute myself a one-man free press, but I had

to do something. I saw everybody I knew and yelled to high heaven. I tried to reach Chiang Kai-shek with the story; I ran about screaming 'People are dying, people are dying.' "

Finally, with the help of the most politically liberal of the Soong sisters, Madame Sun, he was able to get an appointment with the Generalissimo. Madame Sun wrote Teddy: "May I suggest that you report conditions as frankly and as fearlessly as you did to me. If heads must come off don't be squeamish about it . . . otherwise there would be no change in the situation."

Chiang, impassive as ever, greeted Teddy with evident distaste, standing stiffly to meet him. When Teddy described the famine testimony of peasants, Chiang turned to an aide and said, "They see a foreigner and tell him anything." Teddy spoke of cannibalism (impossible in China, Chiang said), of dogs eating corpses (impossible, Chiang repeated). Teddy sent for his colleague Harrison Forman, waiting in the anteroom, to show his pictures of dogs standing over corpses. "The Generalissimo's knee began to jiggle slightly in a nervous tic." Then he wanted to know places and dates and the names of officials, which he carefully wrote down with a brush pen on a little pad. Chiang thanked Teddy, saying that Teddy had been a better investigator than any he had sent on his own.

Soon heads began to roll. And so did food: trainloads of grain arrived in Loyang, as Father Megan happily wrote Teddy. The provincial government opened soup kitchens all over the country; even the army distributed some of its grain stocks, all of this confirming to Father Megan that "the famine was entirely man-made." The arrival of food ameliorated conditions somewhat, but Teddy was now convinced that Chiang could no longer govern China: "Of all marks in my thinking, the Honan famine remains most indelible."

Emotionally spent by the infighting in Chungking, and "in a state of nervous collapse," Teddy flew off to the U.S. Air Force base in Kunming, "to live under the American flag for a few weeks, and get myself mobilized and fit again. . . . I swear I'll never again try to clean up Chinese politics by myself. Let them do it on their own."

For months Madame Chiang had angled for a trip to the United States to capitalize on her popularity. To many Americans this eloquent and poised Wellesley graduate was the embodiment of America's brave and besieged Chinese ally, a view that Pearl Buck thought dangerously unrealistic and sentimental. So did the Roosevelt administration, which delayed her visit as long as it could. As General Stilwell wrote to his wife, the Madame had apparently planned a royal tour of the United States, "turning on the charm all over the place, and keeping the suckers in line."

She was cheered in wartime Washington when she addressed both houses of Congress. One enthusiastic journalist wrote that Madame Chiang was worth ten army divisions to her husband, but considering how corrupt and inefficient Chiang's troops were, this may have been a smaller compliment than he intended. After initially glorifying the Madame, the American press began to print stories about her haughtiness. Eleanor Roosevelt was irritated at the way Madame Chiang, while a guest at the White House, clapped her hands imperiously to summon servants. Madame Chiang was also criticized when, staying at hotels, she refused to sleep on anything but the silk sheets she had brought along. In New York seventeen thousand people crowded Madison Square Garden to see her at a benefit to raise funds for Harry Luce's favorite charity, United China Relief. But at the last minute she refused to read her speech, saying that it would not be proper for her to beg for money. (Luce's sister Beth read it to the audience instead.)

Madame was still in the United States when Teddy White's critical account of the Honan famine appeared in *Time*. She was furious, and demanded that Luce fire Teddy. But as Teddy noted in his autobiography: "He refused, for which I honor him."

■ ■ ■

Several months after Madame Chiang's visit to the United States, Harry Luce wrote to Teddy that he wanted to communicate "something pretty vague" about the "vast question about how to tell the truth about China." Luce had grown troubled by the accusations that his magazines were presenting too favorable a picture of Chiang Kai-shek's China.

> So we published Pearl Buck's article in *Life,* which you no doubt have seen—and we published this on top of a number of things from you which were distinctly bearish.
>
> I believe that by now we have pretty thoroughly discharged our obligations to print the bad with the good. As a matter of fact, we are, if anything, now over on the bear side. The plain fact, the great fact, the glorious fact is that China still stands. Considering all the odds against her, within and without, that is the fact that needs explaining. In Chungking, you are, of course, daily confronted with all the things that are not being done as well as they should be. But just think, Teddy—the great fact is that Chungking is still there!

Was this letter meant to cheer up a depressed Teddy, in the hope of making his coverage more optimistic? Or was it the letter of an editor deceiving himself, unwilling to recognize how bad the situation was, or how deep was Teddy's disenchantment with Chiang? Luce continued:

> You have always had immense faith in China and the Generalissimo. This faith in China was communicated to the American people in the past two years. Perhaps you felt that you have communicated too much faith—or a too easy faith. I simply write to say you need have no such fears. It is still the faith—and not the defects of the faith—which it is most important to communicate.

If ever a journalist did a real job, you have done it. And here's looking forward to many a Peking duck in Peking with you.

Luce was an indefatigable writer of off-the-top-of-his-head memos. It was his way of keeping in touch with his troops, or with the many in public life to whom he sent crisp comments on current events. He wrote several dozen such memos a day, in pencil, in longhand, on long yellow legal pads. These memos were, like his conversation, terse, devoid of small talk, to the point. They kept him in communication with his reporters and the editors of his three magazines. Before technology perfected the sending of messages electronically, these handwritten memos, dispatched around the building by a small army of college-student office boys, gave a personal touch to the editing process.

Harry's memos to Teddy were more considered than the spontaneous, elliptical give-and-take ones he wrote to colleagues in New York. Teddy White, too, spent great care on his memos to Luce, supplementing the dispatches he filed to the magazines. He wanted to keep Luce personally informed of a deteriorating situation that Luce was unable to see for himself because of President Roosevelt's personal edict barring Luce from visiting China.* Luce countered Teddy's gloomy facts

---

*Just how petty Roosevelt could be when Luce was involved is exemplified by the president's shabby treatment of John Hersey as described in Robert E. Herzstein's *Henry R. Luce*. As a *Time* correspondent with the Marines in Guadalcanal Hersey spotted several wounded men coming under heavy Japanese machine-gun and mortar fire; he rushed to their side and got them to a first-aid station some distance away. The following day he rescued another group of wounded Marines. The commanding officer of the Seventh Marines called Hersey's behavior "outstandingly conspicuous by reason of his being an observer and therefore not required to undergo the dangers he subjected himself to." The commanding general of the First Marine Division recommended a Silver Star for Hersey; Admiral William F. Halsey, commander of the South Pacific Force, endorsed the recommendation; so did the navy's Board of Awards; so did Secretary of the Navy Frank Knox. But Roosevelt turned them all down on the grounds that anyone "who had red blood in his veins . . . would do the same thing."

with professions of faith. In his autobiography White brags of the "remarkable intellectual volleying between us. The quality of Luce's mind and learning" was the reason "so many of us served him loyally for so long."

When one reads these exchanges today—divorced from the passions of the time and the tensions between a correspondent jeopardizing his job by criticizing editorial policy and a boss hoping to win arguments by persuading rather than ordering— they seem less profound than Teddy thought them to be. Rather than great intellectual exchanges, they often read as if the two men were dragging up half-remembered history and philosophy from their college courses, each trying to overwhelm the other.

In one such memo, Luce invoked Christianity, Confucius, and the schizophrenia of Western thought to argue that China had to discover a morality of its own, not simply lift it from the philosophically confused West. Teddy rebutted with a memo "invoking Alfred North Whitehead and Science and Reason against Christ and Confucius. It was exhilarating."

Exhilarating perhaps, but ultimately, from Teddy's point of view, not effective. In the spring of 1944, Teddy decided to fly back to New York to persuade Luce that "we must now, finally, tell the truth about China, for Chiang Kai-shek was doomed unless he could be shocked into reform by America."

After hearing Teddy out, Luce promised him space to make his case in a major article in *Life*. Luce was sufficiently concerned that in a "strictly confidential" note to his top editors he wrote that "as a result of what [Teddy] writes and our further deliberations with him, our attitude in certain Chinese questions may undergo a change." Luce mentioned one particularly sensi-

---

Shortly thereafter, one of Roosevelt's favorite congressmen, Lyndon Baines Johnson of Texas, eager to have a touch of war service on his record, was sent to the Pacific by Roosevelt for a tour as an observer. He flew one combat mission, coming under attack by Japanese Zeroes over New Guinea. For this he was awarded the Silver Star by General Douglas MacArthur. As Robert A. Caro notes in his biography of Lyndon Johnson, none of the plane's crew, the men who fought off the Zeroes, got a medal.

tive point: "The most difficult problem in Sino-American publicity concerns the Soong family. They are or have been the head and front of a pro-American policy. It ill befits us, therefore, to go sour on them. On the other hand, they are probably increasingly less popular in China. During the next year we may try to work our way through this problem."

Teddy's article, when it finally ran, was called "*Life* Looks at China." Its very title indicated that this was not Teddy's view alone, but the magazine's, which gave Harry a justification for toning down Teddy's angriest passages. As Teddy saw it, he and Luce had bickered over "whether to do a skin-flaying exposé of Chiang's government, or a sorrowful, hopeful story." He writes, "I pushed Harry as far as he would go (publishing that Chiang's Kuomintang combined 'the worst features of Tammany Hall and the Spanish Inquisition'), and he restrained my angers, still heated by the Honan famine, as far as I could let myself be restrained."

Afterward, Teddy fulsomely wrote Luce: "I know that to permit publication of such a piece in *Life* must have been a great wrench to you. I was scared as Hell, Harry, at what I thought would be an inevitable clash between my convictions and your policy. And therefore I feel now I want to tell you how profoundly happy it made me to be allowed to publish in *Life* the things I wanted to say. Our friendship, I hope, will be long-lasting and grow firmer in years; but right now I'm all aglow. . . . Speaking as newspaperman to his editor, it was a god-dam inspiring experience."

If for the moment the compromise satisfied Teddy, later it did not. "The gist of that article," as he explained to a friend, "was that Chiang was OK, but the guys around him were bad, that if only he would reform his government we would love him." That formulation did not long appease Teddy.

In his autobiography he writes: "Only when I returned to

China, after the colloquy, was I persuaded by facts, murder, execution and incompetence that Chiang was no longer a useful vessel either of American or of Christian purpose. I was more pragmatic than Luce. I could not ignore what I saw; and he would not print it, for it destroyed his philosophy of the world."

"The Man
I Then Adored"

There was one man in Chungking whose dislike of Chiang was even deeper than Teddy's. In General Stilwell's case the dislike was both professional and personal. Teddy and Stilwell had both come to believe that Chiang was incapable of reform and was a hindrance to the prosecution of the war.

Out of friendship and admiration, Teddy did much to establish Stilwell's reputation, and later in sorrow and anger to chronicle his downfall. In his diaries (which were edited by Teddy after the general's death and published as *The Stilwell Papers*), the general described how much he loathed the claustrophobic court atmosphere in Chungking: "The 'intellectuals' and the rich send their precious brats to the States, and the farmer boys go out and get killed—without care, training or leadership. And we are maneuvered into the position of having to support this rotten regime and glorify its figurehead, the all-wise great patriot and soldier—Peanut. My God."

He found it "impossible to compete with the swarms of parasites and sycophants" around the Generalissimo. Stilwell wasn't winning any battles in the field and he wasn't winning many arguments at the court. The dispute over who should get the biggest share of the meager supplies being flown in over the Hump grew so acrimonious that President Roosevelt summoned Chennault and Stilwell home to resolve it. At the time

Winston Churchill was also in Washington, and he took part in many of the discussions. The British, having been driven out of Hong Kong and Singapore, wanted the major war effort concentrated in Europe and never considered Chiang an equal partner in the Alliance.*

Churchill was willing to endorse Chennault's six-month bombing campaign launched from China, but he completely dismissed Stilwell's proposal to reopen the Burma Road using Chinese troops (the British counted on winning Burma back at the peace conference and didn't want someone else liberating it first). "Roosevelt wouldn't let me speak my piece," Stilwell complained. He was convinced that Churchill had the president in his pocket. At a farewell lunch Churchill said, "Mr. President, I cannot but believe that an all-wise Providence has draped these great events, at this critical period of the world's history, about your personality and your high office." "And Frank," Stilwell noted, "lapped it up."

To anyone who would listen, Stilwell argued that China "was on the verge of collapse economically. . . . That any increased air offensive that stung the Japs enough would bring a strong reaction that would wreck everything and put China out of the war." This was a sound prophecy, but it was Chennault who won the argument and was assigned four fifths of all cargo flown over the Hump.

An embittered Stilwell returned to Chungking, "to find Chiang same as ever—a grasping, bigoted, ungrateful little rattlesnake." The reader of *The Stilwell Papers* soon wearies of all the invective: "This insect, this stink in the nostrils, superciliously inquires what we will do, who are breaking our backs to

---

*Roosevelt himself was fascinated by China, where (as he told Stilwell) his grandfather had made a million dollars in the China trade. In a letter to General George Marshall, the president wrote that Chiang "came up the hard way to accomplish in a few years what it took us 200 years to attain. . . . One cannot speak sternly or exact commitments from a man like that, as if he were a tribal chieftain." This was a caution to Stilwell against too many condescending references to the Peanut.

help him, supplying everything—troops, equipment, planes, medical, signal, motor services . . . bucking up his bastardly chief of staff, and general staff, and he the Jovian Dictator, who starves his troops and who is the world's greatest ignoramus, picks flaws in our preparations and hems and haws about the navy. God save us."

Though contemptuous of Chiang, Stilwell never patronized the Chinese foot soldier, whom he had come to respect in his earlier days in Asia. Stilwell believed, far more than did Chiang's top generals, in the superior qualities of the Chinese infantryman, if properly trained, fed, and led.

It was an army of conscripts, many of whom had been shanghaied into service. They lived in cramped quarters and were undernourished and prey to dysentery, malaria, scabies. For every soldier killed in battle, ten died of disease, or deserted. Discipline was brutal: at a commander's whim a man could have his ears cropped, be flogged, or be forced to kneel in the broiling sun, hands tied behind his back, until he collapsed.

Stilwell vowed to change all that. He undertook to train and re-equip thirty of the hundred Chinese divisions to American military standards. Once he had set up camp at a British base in Ramgarh, India, sixty-six thousand troops were flown over the Hump to be trained. Chiang had promised the pick of troops, but 68 percent of the men in one shipment couldn't pass a physical. At Ramgarh they got full meals and put on an average of twenty pounds apiece. Hospitals treated their diseases. And the pay that they earned, however meager, was given to them, instead of being stolen by their officers. They were taught to use modern weapons and learned about sanitation, care of the wounded, and how to load a mule with artillery. They were drilled rigorously.

Within two years four Chinese divisions had been trained, and Stilwell was eager to prove not just their courage (which he knew about) but their professionalism when pitted against a first-class modern army like the Japanese. He wanted to battle-test his troops personally in Burma: "I prefer associating with soldiers and sleeping on the ground to this bickering and dickering that I've gotten into."

He was sixty years old, and his wiry frame had been weakened by dysentery and jaundice. A man of his rank should have stayed at his headquarters. Instead, in a dirty khaki uniform, a cigarette dangling from his lips, he set out to lead his inexperienced troops on a long march, to surprise a dug-in and battle-hardened enemy at Myitkyina, the Japanese base in northern Burma. To do so, his troops had to cross two hundred miles of jungle, swamp, and mountain before the heavy rains began in late April. As Teddy White described it in *The Stilwell Papers*: "It was snakes in camp at night; K rations and dried rice; snipers and ambush; darkness during the day and the rustling jungle at night. It was hike, kill, and die, or, as Stilwell noted in his diary after one of his everyday marches through the muck: 'Up the river, over the hog-back—slip, struggle, curse, and tumble.'"

After one climb on a hot day, Stilwell wrote: "Damned near killed me. All out of shape. No wind, no legs. Swore off smoking then and there. Felt like an old man when I struggled in."

Stilwell advanced with two Chinese divisions trained at Ramgarh, and another he would keep in reserve; all had Chinese officers. They were about fifty thousand men, about the same number as the enemy they would face. To guard against the possibility that his green army might retreat, Stilwell abandoned regular supply lines and made his men dependent on airdrops alone.

While the Chinese troops advanced frontally, on their flanks Stilwell sent a tough and skilled American commando unit, Merrill's Marauders, to move behind the Japanese to cut off their escape. The Marauders marched almost one hundred miles over a six-thousand-foot mountain range, then broke radio silence to announce that they had reached and captured the airstrip at Myitkyina. This enabled Stilwell to fly in several regiments of Chinese troops to reinforce his own; transports and gliders shuttled in day and night, carrying supplies and equipment.

But all was not yet over. The monsoons began, and the Japanese, rather than surrender, decided to make a suicide stand. Several weeks passed before Stilwell could write his wife in Carmel, California, proudly claiming victory: "THE FIRST SUSTAINED OFFENSIVE IN CHINESE HISTORY AGAINST A FIRST-CLASS ENEMY." The Japanese lost an estimated twenty thousand lives.

The real victory for Stilwell was in the faith the Chinese soldiers now had in themselves ("Their tails are up"). Once scorned, they had in Burma earned the respect of the enemy and of their allies. Stilwell himself was promoted to four-star general, a rank he shared only with Generals Marshall, MacArthur, Eisenhower, and Hap Arnold of the U.S. Air Force. There was one absentee from the general acclaim: when President Roosevelt asked Chiang to name Stilwell commander in chief of the Chinese armies, Chiang was in no hurry to oblige.

In Stilwell's judgment, he was now in position to begin the slow and difficult reopening of the Burma Road, which would give China a chance to break the Japanese blockade and bring in all the goods and supplies China desperately needed.

But perhaps it was already too late. Teddy dates the spring of 1944 as the time when Chiang lost "the Mandate of Heaven," the traditional symbol of a regime's legitimacy. Like most dynasties in the past, the Nationalist government lost its control in a paroxysm of runaway inflation.

In the large provincial capital of Chengtu, White reported, the local price index had risen 174 percent since the start of the war; workmen's wages went up 104 percent—while at the distinguished university, salaries of professors had risen only 19 percent. The academics, like bureaucrats in the civil government, had to beg, steal, or bribe to survive. For this reason Chiang lost the crucial support of the intellectual and professional class. Inflation also made life hard for the quarter of a million Americans in wartime China—including the military and thousands of advisers and civilians. Often they and their government had to buy at the official rate of exchange, set at twenty Chinese dollars to one U.S. dollar, when the actual rate was two hundred to one. Living under a regime they considered corrupt and inefficient, Americans were frustrated and outraged.

At this low point in Chiang's fortunes the Japanese, who had previously been content to stabilize their front in China, decided to attack. By 1944 the Japanese were retreating elsewhere, aware that they were losing the war, but China offered a tempting opportunity to open their last major offensive.

They began in the north, moving into Honan, which had never recovered from the famine once so vividly reported by White. The Japanese found the peasants still angry at the Chinese army overlords who had extorted grain and ignored the starving of the people. With knives and pitchforks and bird guns, the peasants turned on their own soldiers; within weeks fifty thousand Chinese troops had been disarmed by their countrymen. The Chinese army, ill-trained, low in morale, and short of ammunition, collapsed, giving the Japanese possession of the northern end of the north-south railway. They were in position to split China in two.

Their major target, five hundred miles south, was the vast American complex of air bases and supply depots of the U.S. Fourteenth Air Force at Kweilin, from whose runways Chennault's fighters and bombers had destroyed more than a million tons of Japanese shipping. The Japanese knew, as Stilwell knew, that the bases were poorly defended by Chiang's demoralized armies.

As Chinese armies collapsed before the advancing Japanese, panic swept Chungking. Chiang summoned Stilwell back to the capital and urged him to abandon his effort to open the Burma Road, and to fly his troops to bolster the East China front. Stilwell instead wanted Chiang to release the twenty divisions of crack Chinese troops that Chiang kept idle in the north as a barrier against the Chinese Communists. A showdown over the long-standing ideological issue that divided the United States and Chiang could no longer be postponed.

The Americans wanted Chiang and the Communists to patch up their differences to defeat the common enemy, Japan. At the beginning of the war such an alliance did exist, but the Communists, growing stronger as Chiang weakened, were now unwilling to play a subservient role in a coalition with Chiang; nor was Chiang himself willing to compromise. In view of the later history of China, Chiang's answer to American demands seems prescient: "The Japanese are a disease of the skin; the Communists are a disease of the heart."

The Chinese government looked upon the United States as the richest and most powerful nation in the world, able to defeat the Japanese and by 1944 already in the process of doing so. Why, then, Chiang reasoned, should he squander the armies and resources that he would later need to defeat his own domestic enemy, the Communists? He would not budge.

Stilwell flew to Kweilin, saw how desperate the situation was as the Japanese closed in, and with a heavy heart ordered Chennault to destroy the base and its vast surrounding arsenal—bombs, gasoline, spare parts, and repair shops—every ton of which had been brought in over the Hump with great effort and the expenditure of millions of dollars. The Fourteenth Air Force, as it evacuated its great base, destroyed as many of its supplies as it could not take out. Stilwell wired Marshall that the situation had become hopeless because of Chiang's unwillingness to commit his 250,000 soldiers in the north, who were keeping the Communists at bay. The Generalissimo would "not listen to reason, merely repeating a lot of cock-eyed conceptions of his own invention."

Stilwell's cable was forwarded to Marshall in Quebec, where Roosevelt and Churchill were again conferring. Now it was the turn of an angry Roosevelt to treat Chiang like a "tribal chieftain." Roosevelt was in the last year of his life, in the midst of a political campaign for an unprecedented fourth term, and worn down by the burdens of the war. In Roosevelt's fatigue and anger, he was uncharacteristically blunt in the cable he sent to the Generalissimo on September 18, 1944:

> . . . my Chiefs of Staff and I are convinced that you are faced in the near future with the disaster I have feared. . . . For this you must be prepared to accept the consequences and assume the personal responsibility. I have urged time and again in recent months that you take drastic action. . . . Now, when you have not yet placed General Stilwell in command of all forces in China, we are faced with the loss of a critical area in east China with possible catastrophic consequences. . . . It appears plainly evident to all of us here that all your and our efforts to save China are to be lost by further delays.

Among those most offended by this message was Joseph Alsop, a socially well-connected journalist (he was a cousin of Roosevelt's) who was in China as an adviser to General Chennault. To Alsop this was "one of the most mystifying and nearly lunatic messages ever used to a high wartime purpose. . . . It was a message such as Roosevelt in health and vigor would never have sent to any Allied chief of state."

To add to the sting, Roosevelt directed that his message be delivered personally by a messenger guaranteed to give further offense to Chiang. Stilwell was delighted with the assignment. He drove out to the Generalissimo's country residence, to find Chiang and his chief military counselors meeting with American emissaries who were trying, as they had been trying for three months, to pin down Stilwell's appointment to head China's armies. For a few minutes all drank tea together. Then, Stilwell writes in his diary, after the other Americans had left but with Chiang's staff still present, "I handed this bundle of paprika to the Peanut and then sank back with a sigh." Chiang read the Chinese translation quickly, said, "I understand," and ended the meeting.

Three days later an elated Stilwell sent this doggerel to his wife:

> *I've waited long for vengeance—*
> *At last I've had my chance.*
> *I've looked the Peanut in the eye*
> *And kicked him in the pants.*
>
> *The old harpoon was ready*
> *With aim and timing true,*
> *I sank it to the handle*
> *And stung him through and through.*
>
> *The little bastard shivered,*
> *And lost the power of speech.*
> *His face turned green and quivered*
> *As he struggled not to screech.*
>
> *For all my weary battles,*
> *For all my hours of woe,*
> *At last I've had my innings*
> *And laid the Peanut low.*

Stilwell miscalculated by celebrating too soon. Chiang had been furious at the insulting letter and humiliated that it had been entrusted to Stilwell to deliver. After Stilwell had left, Chiang broke into convulsive sobbing, as Alsop learned from his friend T. V. Soong.

Chiang was further disturbed by the knowledge that Stilwell had received two emissaries from the Chinese Communists the previous day. They had indicated a willingness to rejoin the coalition under Stilwell's command, but would not serve under Chiang; if their conditions were accepted, Chiang would become a mere figurehead.

As the days passed, the triumphant Stilwell began to sense

that he, not Chiang, might be the one in whom the harpoon was being sunk. Chiang began his belated response to Roosevelt, in calligraphy brushed in by pen, by saluting him: "Oh hope for the world! Oh light of the West!" However, his advisers persuaded him that this was the wrong tone to take. They consulted with Joe Alsop, who said that Chiang should declare Stilwell *persona non grata* and blame him in large measure for China's difficulties.* And thus Chiang replied to Roosevelt that as he was head of state, there could be no question of his right to dismiss any officer. Secondly, he wrote, "It was made manifest to me that General Stilwell had no intention of cooperating with me, but believed that he was in fact being appointed to command me. . . . If, ignoring reason and experience, I were to appoint General Stilwell as Field Commander, I would knowingly court inevitable disaster." Stilwell must go.

Sensing at last that events were moving against him, Stilwell summoned White and the *New York Times* correspondent, Brooks Atkinson, to his austere Chungking villa. (Atkinson, the best theater critic on Broadway, had taken a wartime leave from the theater to cover the greater melodrama in China.)

Stilwell got right to the point: Within a few days, he began, he would be relieved of his command. "And suddenly," White wrote later, "I could see him as an old soldier stripped of authority, shriveled overnight. . . . I remember him scratching at his arms, infected with the jungle itch he had contracted in Burma." Stilwell was brooding, bitter. Someone must know the truth, he said, but for the time being they were not to print the story. For the next few days White and Atkinson could come

---

*Since this was at such odds with Teddy White's attitude, it is of interest to note the relationship between these two distinguished journalists. In a memoir published posthumously in 1992, Alsop wrote: "I always thought of Teddy White as a great reporter and we were not unfriendly during those months in China. We came out of our particular wartime experiences with radically different views and prejudices, however. In later years Teddy and I had to agree not to discuss the China days for fear one or the other of us would grow apoplectic and seek to do personal harm."

and go at his headquarters, reading the "eyes only" cables arriving from Washington. It shocked Teddy that the man he "then adored" was ready to "violate his military oath of secrecy, his personal loyalty to George Marshall, to carry his story to the court of future opinion."

Two days later the radio message from General Marshall arrived, ordering Stilwell home, removed without any public announcement. On the day after their thirty-fourth wedding anniversary Stilwell wrote to his wife:

> The axe has fallen and I'll be on my way to see you within a few days. The politicians are in command so this kind of monkey business is to be expected. Some of the boys here were confident that F.D.R. would stand up to the Peanut. I felt from the start that he would sell out. "The war is more important than the individual," etc.
>
> So now I am hanging up my shovel and bidding farewell to as merry a nest of gangsters as you'll meet in a long day's march.

Having won his victory, Chiang sent a minor functionary to Stilwell to offer him China's highest military decoration given to a foreigner, the Special Grand Cordon of the Blue Sky and White Sun. (Stilwell wrote in his diary: "Told him to stick it up his ——.") Chiang next invited Stilwell to tea and thanked him for all he had done, and said that "*it was only because of the differences in our make-ups that he was asking for my relief.* Hoped I would correspond with him and continue to be China's friend. I told him whatever he thought of me, to remember my motive was only China's good. . . . The G-mo even came to the door."

Only a few members of Stilwell's inner staff who helped him pack his bags and briefcase knew of his recall. In his diary, Stilwell noted: "Told White and Atkinson. They also were horrified and disgusted. Atkinson going home to blow the works."

Teddy's job was to remain at his post, but he was just as determined to be heard.

An agitated Teddy White sat down at his portable typewriter to tap out, with his usual quick staccato, a file for *Time*. It was a lengthy, emotional dispatch full of special pleading. He was reporting the downfall of the soldier he admired most; he was recording the tactical triumph of a ruler he thought was the biggest barrier in China to prosecuting the war to victory. He was not only horrified and disgusted; he was angry as well.

Unlike Brooks Atkinson, who on his return to New York would be given all the space in the paper he needed, subjected to a minimum of editing, and given a byline, Teddy was an anonymous correspondent for *Time* who knew, in submitting his raw material, that "if there was a history that framed it all, then the editors back in New York decided what the history meant."

As a special favorite of Harry Luce's, he had long since become more than a mere supplier of raw material. His command of that material—his knowledge of conditions in China as a whole, in the capital, and in the army; his meticulous amassing of detail; and his intimate acquaintance with people in high places and shrewd perceptions of them—gave weight to his judgments, even when they ran contrary to Luce's. His files had become increasingly impatient and dogmatic. He knew he was antagonizing Luce, but he felt he had to.

Of late Teddy had also become aware that whatever he now wrote had to pass before the skeptical eyes of a new Luce favorite, Whittaker Chambers, a man he barely knew, who had been made the foreign editor of *Time*. It was Whit who would edit *Time*'s coverage of Stilwell's recall, deciding what to use and what to reject and setting the tone of the finished article. Chambers would later become notorious in the ugly history of the 1950s, with his accusation that a high State Department official, Alger Hiss, had been a Communist. Until that accusation, Chambers was known in the corridors of *Time* not as a Soviet spy but as a taciturn, mysterious figure, a gifted writer and autocratic editor who, as a reformed Communist, saw Communists—in the popular expression of the day—under every bed.

On a drizzling, overcast day T. V. Soong and the minister of war (whom Stilwell had tried to get fired) appeared at the airport to pay their brief farewell respects to Stilwell, then drove away. Stilwell turned to an aide, said, "What the hell are we waiting for?," and climbed aboard the plane, followed by Brooks Atkinson. Teddy had given his dispatch to Atkinson to take with him to New York so it would escape censorship. As the plane took off, only Teddy stood on the airstrip to wave Stilwell a melancholy good-bye.

In New York, Whittaker Chambers edited the Stilwell cover story into what Teddy, still fuming more than thirty years later, would call in his autobiography, "a lie, an entirely dishonorable story."

Teddy got his first inkling of what Chambers had done when he heard a broadcast quoting from the Japanese news agency, Domei. Of course Japanese propaganda could not be trusted, but enough of the account seemed factual to enrage Teddy. He cabled Luce: "If what Domei said is true, I shall probably have to resign as have no other way of preserving my integrity." In his cabled reply, Luce sought to placate Teddy, but with a touch of sarcasm Luce made it clear that he was now listening to a different drummer: "Keep your shirt on until you have full text of Stilwell cover story. . . . Your views have always been respected here but I do not think it becomes you to get angry if for once your editor does not instantly follow your instructions."

THE PERILS OF
WORKING FOR LUCE

Six years after Teddy White was hired in Chungking as a correspondent for *Time,* I went to work for *Time* as a writer in New York. We both knew what we were getting into by joining an opinionated newsmagazine whose opinions were not always the same as our own. We both faced one question from our friends. Sometimes it was bluntly put, sometimes tactfully. Sometimes it was only implicit in an embarrassed silence. How *could* you go to work for Luce?

Friends were of course glad that we had good jobs that presumably paid well, but would we have to sell our souls? The experience reminded me of my puzzlement as a child at the attitude of the Roman Catholic side of my family, my mother's side, toward a friend in Tacoma, Washington, who was also of Irish extraction and whom they loved dearly but treated as if she were somehow different. She was an admirable woman, but during the potato famine back in the old country her family had joined the other church in order to be fed. In the devastatingly dismissive phrase used by my relatives, "They took the soup."

In going to work for Harry Luce, had Teddy and I "taken the soup"? We were young (born the same year) and somewhat priggish about how incorruptible we were as journalists, but we did not deny the dangers and professed ourselves ready to quit at any moment. That readiness to quit was often on Teddy's mind, as it was on mine: it was the only way either of us could feel independent enough to stand up to Harry Luce. I remember one sign of that concern, a resolve my wife and I made: although I was making more money than I ever had before, we would never live up to the limit of that New York salary so that I would always be free to quit. Long afterward I read a remark in the autobiography of Luce's eventual successor, Hedley Donovan: "I went through a kind of drill with myself every time I got a promotion: Okay, what would it be like to give this up—the money, the recognition—where would I start job hunting, where would we cut the family budget, etc." Donovan recalled the advice of an old boss of his on *The Washington Post*: "Always edit with your hat on."

The annals of *Time* are full of the accounts of gifted men and women, proud of the magazine they worked for, who at some crucial moment, or after an accumulation of discontents, decided to leave. Some quit in anger; some with regret. The record is also full of people who loved their work and treasured the companionship of talented colleagues; the pleasure they took in their demanding and frustrating jobs exceeded their misgivings. It was that kind of place.

Henry Robinson Luce was one of the last of a vanishing species, the press lord, and of his kind something of a mutant. His predecessors, like William Randolph Hearst and Colonel Robert R. McCormick, were autocrats whose whims were commands. Every night from Hearst's California castle at San Simeon instructions ("The Chief says") were wired to his editors in twenty-eight American cities, telling them which stories to splash on page one, which of Hearst's enemies to ignore or condemn, and which favorites to glorify. In a petty pique against Stanford University, Hearst for a time forbade the mention of its name (driving sportswriters on his San Francisco paper to desperate circumlocutions to describe the athletic feats of "the boys from Palo Alto"). Because Hearst loathed Franklin D. Roosevelt, the New Deal was always referred to, even in the news columns, as the Raw Deal. The eccentricities of Colonel McCormick, the bristling autocrat of the *Chicago Tribune,* ranged from phonetic spelling to a militant isolationism and a hatred of Roosevelt similar to Hearst's.

In an era when such blatant bias was commonplace in American newspapers, I emerged from college in the depression year of 1936, full of idealism about the craft of journalism, righteously critical of its practice, and in need of a job. My choices were to seek a job either on the local Hearst paper (which I haughtily refused to do) or at its more respectable rival, the *Seattle Times,* a conservative paper run by a paternalistic owner, one Colonel Blethen. His biases and peccadilloes were less flagrant than Colonel McCormick's, but his animus against Roosevelt and labor unions was just as strong. I had no alternative—jobs were hard to find—so I chose the *Times.* We brown-bagged our lunches to eat in our parked cars and, having no union, were paid less than the typesetters and printers. We were plantation slaves, but we were a friendly, competent crew and enjoyed our work. To us in Seattle the arrival of each issue of *Time* was a breath of freshness: we envied its interest in subjects our paper barely touched—art, music, theater, books; we liked *Time*'s outspokenness, enjoyed its audacity and cleverness, and admired its professional flair. I longed to work there: it promised more freedom.

Having disdained the safe, ponderous mediocrity of most American newspapers, Luce and Briton Hadden had from the beginning recognized that the livelier, opinionated journalism they favored meant hiring people of independent mind, unwilling to write to the boss's order. That realization was what most separated Luce and Hadden from press lords like Hearst and McCormick (or Colonel Blethen). Yet Luce and Hadden were just as eager as any press lord to be successful, influential, and profitable. Hadden's ambition was to be a millionaire by the time he was thirty, and he almost made it. Neither Luce nor Hadden wanted to publish a mere journal of opinion, which would confine them to a small circulation and to the margin of events.

After five years of losses, *Time* became profitable; the partners were on the way to becoming rich. Then in 1929 Hadden died at the age of thirty, from an infection that modern antibiotics could quickly have cured. From then on Luce was on his own; the ambiguity of what kind of a magazine *Time* should be was now resolved. The phrase in the original prospectus about having no axes to grind had clearly reflected Hadden, who was content to put out a newsmagazine that was a clever bauble. Harry believed in self-improvement for himself and his readers; to be an editor was to be an educator, even at times a preacher.

He was an ardent capitalist but a maverick among businessmen; for him profit wasn't everything. Though he worshiped success, success for him meant making money by doing something socially worthwhile. All those cold baths in boyhood and the half hour of Bible study every morning before breakfast had had their effect on his beliefs and his character.

As *Time* itself became big business, Luce came to believe that business "is essentially our civilization." Fascinated by those successful businessmen that *Time,* giving an old word a new meaning, called "tycoons," Luce concluded that they were in need of both celebration and redemption. To give "business a literature," he would start a glossily designed magazine called *Fortune,* selling for a dollar at a time when most magazines sold for ten or fifteen cents.

Before *Fortune*'s first issue could appear the stock market crashed. Luce consulted the best economic experts he could find and, after being assured by them that the depression would not last more than a year, went ahead with publication. The bad advice from the economists confirmed Luce in his distrust of experts and strengthened his faith in his own instinctive judgment.

Again, as with the launching of *Time,* he went looking for the best minds he could find to be writers and editors. For his purposes they didn't have to be experts; Luce believed it easier "to turn poets into business journalists than to turn bookkeepers into writers." He began, as he and Hadden had before, by snobbishly narrowing his search to the Ivy League, and particularly to "the best Yale brains . . . on the current market." He chose well. As the depression worsened Luce found himself editing not a paean to capitalism but a magazine whose trenchant reporting of economic conditions was informed by the social consciences of writers like Archibald MacLeish, who was not only a gifted poet but an idealistic reformer; the wittily sardonic economist John Kenneth Galbraith; and the cantankerous gadfly Dwight Macdonald, who sported a goatee in tribute to his hero Trotsky. The masthead listed a board of editors in which the name Luce did not come first but was in its alphabetical place.

MacLeish was a find. He, like Luce, had attended Hotchkiss and Yale; he would become a man of many careers—lawyer, professor, playwright—and would win three Pulitzer prizes, but he spent many years as *Fortune*'s best editor-writer.

Luce's talent hunt also led him to invite to lunch Eric Hodgins (later the author of *Mr. Blandings Builds His Dream House*), who left a memorable account of his first brush with the thirty-nine-year-old Luce: "a young man with thinning red-brown hair, a stammer, a plodding-through-snowdrifts gait, and an intensity of gaze and manner. 'Know anything about *Fortune?* Ever read it?' Luce asked. . . . Luce had a grunt that simply cannot be rendered into the Roman alphabet; you came to learn that it indicated impatience, displeasure or both." At their second lunch Hodgins said, " 'I think it's only proper I should tell you that politically I incline toward the Left.' Luce did not even grunt."

Another poet recruited for *Fortune* was James Agee, later *Time*'s distinguished cinema reviewer, whose feeling about working for *Fortune* varied from "a sort of hard, masochistic liking to direct nausea," but who needed the money. His sleeper classic, *Let Us Now Praise Famous Men,* with haunting photographs by his friend and collaborator Walker Evans, would be commissioned by *Fortune* but then rejected as too sprawling and idiosyncratic. Agee, a hillbilly with a Harvard education, told friends that he sometimes felt like murdering Luce and fantasized the occasion: He would walk into Luce's office, and while Luce sat at his desk unsuspecting, Agee would steady his gun barrel on the desk and fire at chest level. The shot would echo up and down the halls as Luce slumped over, whereupon other writers would emerge from their offices cheering.

Luce thus created his own problems by hiring independent minds, hoping to elicit their best, yet reserving to himself the final say over what ran in his magazines. To be original, his writers needed—and Luce would allow them—looser reins than more autocratic press lords tolerated. But reins existed nonetheless, and this was the source of the tensions and the stimulus and the frustrations of working for Luce.

The first writer ever hired by *Time,* Manfred Gottfried—he later became the only man to share with Luce the title of editor of *Time*—once said to him, "Harry, I wish you wouldn't give us as much argument. Why don't you just give us a few orders?" But Luce regarded his writers and editors as peers and hoped to get his way by persuading them he was right. Frequently, however, it was not so much a matter of convincing them as of doggedly wearing them down. He wanted a collegial operation, but it was never a pure democracy in which all votes counted equally. Authority was necessary, Luce argued, because "we cannot evade the demand for a general coherence and a general sense of direction."

But there was a simpler reason why his vote counted for more: these were his magazines. Time Incorporated was something like a poker table in Las Vegas: the odds favored the house, but there had to be enough chance to win for the players to stay in the game.

Luce compounded his problems by choosing, for the most part, writers and editors who were politically liberal. If they quarreled and left, Luce could expect to be savaged in print by writers who, if nothing else, were distressingly articulate.

One of the stout liberals on *Fortune* was John Kenneth Galbraith, the Harvard economist whose later best-selling books were brilliant attacks on just about everything Luce stood for. "Political differences notwithstanding," Galbraith insists, "Harry Luce and I maintained a friendship and a certain reciprocal respect." Galbraith sometimes shocked his liberal friends, to whom Luce was anathema, by telling them, "Harry taught me how to write." At a small lunch with *Time* editors for President-elect John F. Kennedy, I remember, Luce wryly bragged to Kennedy, "I taught Ken Galbraith how to write and have been regretting it ever since."

What exactly did Luce "teach"? Though a great editor, Luce was not a particularly good writer—he wrote what I call proprietor's prose: plain, didactic, and without nuance. But we all learned from his editing: he had an instinct for grasping the essence of any subject and an unerring eye for whatever was flaccid, redundant, or superfluous in the writing. Long after leaving Luce and *Fortune,* Ken Galbraith, a master of ornate irony that sometimes ran to excess, would read over prose that he had just written, inwardly hearing Luce say of one paragraph after another: "This could go."

Louis Kronenberger, who as *Time*'s theater critic wrote with the Johnsonian balanced sentences of the eighteenth-century authors he most admired, was once summoned by Luce, who complained that a *Fortune* article Kronenberger had turned in was "too well written." Luce cut out the first sentence of each paragraph, making the story more jagged and abrupt but livelier. "I had to admit," Kronenberger told me, "that it read better." Wilder Hobson, another fine writer, once made the mistake of writing "and so, to repeat . . ." Luce angrily penned in the margin: "Make your emphasis come from STRUCTURE, not STATEMENT."

According to Galbraith, Luce hired liberals because they were better writers, and he never liked conservatives as writers because he already knew their arguments and got little stimulus from people who agreed with him. Hedley Donovan, Luce's successor and a man of dry humor, wrote that Luce welcomed "argument so ardently that it takes a certain amount of intellectual courage to agree with him when he is right, as is bound to happen from time to time."

If a conservative, Luce was an unpredictable one. This made life difficult for those I used to call the Anticipators, those poor fellows who survived by trying to guess what the boss wanted to hear and then giving it to him. That was like customer's tennis: I thought Luce deserved a better game, for his own good. The Anticipators sometimes prospered at Time Inc., but only for a while, because Luce's prejudices never followed the undeviating path of assembly-line conservatives. In arguing with liberals, Luce was unyielding in his belief in free enterprise, but his support for capitalism was qualified by his insistence that it have a responsible moral base. In a memo to the managing editor of *Fortune* about an article describing a battle between two wealthy men for control of a railroad, Luce complained:

> . . . and about your statement about making money being the No. 1 motive. In this case I resent the fact that Kirby and the Murchisons are fighting for a huge chunk of the "national estate" . . . without there seeming to be any point in the fight. Neither Kirby nor Murchison seem to stand for a damn thing. Kirby seems to be an utterly pointless man and I resent his having $300 million. Old Father Murchi-

son had something—in the old Texas robber baron sense. But what about those two boys: if they stand for anything *Fortune* didn't tell me. Yes, what we always want, in some sort of sense, are heroes and villains. There doesn't seem to be any sense of villainy in this thing and certainly no heroism. The more I think about it the more resentful I get. This is the sort of thing that turns one against capitalism. I resent having these great railroads owned by pointless men like these. . . . And as for these vast investment trusts, I am inclined to think they should be abolished. Vast money-power without any sense of creative responsibility. So there!

Luce died in 1967, but this casual memo to one of his editors suggests how offended he would have been by the speculative Wall Street atmosphere of the 1980s, by the amoral indifference to social consequences of "pointless men" (and women!), and by the obscene incomes they made.

Luce had many ways to exert editorial control. Ignoring the conventional levels of command in between, he might walk into any writer's or editor's office to make a point, particularly with staff members he knew. Or the staff member could be summoned by telephone. In the days before robot electronics took over, switchboard operators rang once for ordinary calls but twice if Luce was calling—this infrequent double ring was enough to make any of us jump out of our chairs. Luce, brusquely: "Can you come up?" or "Meet you at the drugstore in ten minutes, huh?" Sitting on a counter stool, drinking a cup of coffee in a Rockefeller Center drugstore (unrecognized by anyone in the place), Luce would say what was on his mind, often reaching into his suit pocket to bring out rumpled newspaper clippings, from Brussels or Butte or wherever he had been the day before, to suggest a story to pursue or to make an observation.

As his empire grew, as first *Life* and then *Sports Illustrated* came along, and as he began to publish Time-Life books, an early-warning system sprang up to give Luce a preliminary say on subjects he was most interested in, among all the millions of words, on an endless variety of subjects, that were ground out each week in that word factory, the Time and Life Building. Editors were expected to write "Show Luce" on copy that might create controversy on any subject on which Luce had strong views, or on any references to public figures who were his friends. Mostly he just wanted to be informed, but on some occasions he would weigh in heavily. If a story was highly critical of a friend but Luce thought it deserved to be printed, he would sometimes say, "Can you hold it until next week, when I'll be away?" This would give him a chance to plead ignorance when the friend called to complain. The story, not the friend, usually won out.

But the most crucial exercise of Luce's influence was the Friday "managing editors" lunch in a private dining room atop the Time and Life Building, with Luce, surrounded by his editors, sitting at the center of a rectangular table in what I always thought of as the Jesus position, so that the scene looked like a pagan parody of the Last Supper. There was indeed a mystical or superstitious aspect to the occasion. With each editor bringing along a colleague or two from his magazine, the assemblage ranged from ten to fifteen people; but if the number at the table totaled thirteen there would be a flurry of last-minute phone calls, and the most junior of the guests would be disinvited.

Often the lunch conversation was random, casual, and gossipy. Luce's private comments on politics were more down-to-earth, candid, shrewd, and impartial than what appeared in his magazines. The occasions most dreaded were those when he wanted to ruminate on a deadly topic like World Peace Through Law, a subject about which Luce was uncharacteristically woozy in his thinking. In his idealistic fervor, he simply ignored the frequency with which sovereign nations, including his beloved United States, disregarded legal mechanisms that were already in place, such as the United Nations and the World Court. Luce's monologue would go on until he exhausted the subject, having earlier exhausted the rest of us.

One of the purposes of these lunches was to make sure that all the editors were singing from the same page, so that *The New Yorker* would not be able to set one quote from *Fortune* against a contradictory one from *Time* under the mischievous heading "Which Luce Paper D'ya Read?" On the major issues of the day editors wanted to reach a consensus, but a loose one, leaving them free to vary their responses while staying within the boundaries agreed upon at lunch. Hedley Donovan admired Luce's talent for "sharing authority without diluting it." Editorial policy existed in Luce's mind but was rarely written down, which gave editors some leeway in interpreting it.

Harry Reasoner once asked Luce in a television interview: "I've heard it said that you think one of your major problems is to get good editors who will think for themselves and have independent opinions without just trying to determine psychically what you would like. Is that true?"

Luce: "Absolutely. I like to see independent thinking. If it's going the wrong way, I'll straighten them out soon enough."

Those of your friends who asked the question "How could you work for Luce?" thought, of course, that they knew the answer. You had a cushy job, but you had to park your conscience. The perks were indeed good, but the job was never cushy. You were matched against the best; the hours were long; the standards— tightening up stories, satisfying the editor's questions, stuffing in new information, rewriting, cutting—were demanding. By deadline time each week most writers and editors were so exhausted that they often spent the first day of their two-day weekend just resting up. Contention was always in the air, for Luce was never satisfied and didn't want his editors to be. That tension gave a spark to the magazine, and ulcers to a number of writers and editors.

Yes, Luce paid well; he did so out of the conviction of a Christian capitalist that he should. He provided good health benefits before most employers did; he set up a savings and profit-sharing plan that would match or exceed employee contributions; expense accounts were tolerantly monitored (in those days); and the staff was compensated for the long work-weeks by generous vacations. If a demanding boss, Luce was a good employer.

To get the best people while insisting (in those days) that their work be anonymous, Luce had to pay better than *The New York Times,* where the visibility of bylines was not only satisfying to the ego but helped to establish your name. Being the correspondent from *Time* or *Life* got you into most places but did little to establish your reputation with others in the field and nothing at all to make you known to the general public. The philosophy of *Time* was like that of *The Times* of London or *The Economist:* the authority to be believed was the institution, not its individual contributors.

The perk on Luce's magazines most valued by the staff was the company of bright, quick-witted people working together, traveling the world, spending whatever it took to do the job right (economizing was never an acceptable excuse for not getting a story you should have done).

Another magnet that drew writers to the Luce magazines was the large and well-informed audiences they catered to. We on the staff, with our own set of beliefs and prejudices, valued the audience he had assembled as fully as Harry Luce did, and we were just as eager to influence it. Would I, would Teddy White, have been happier to work on a small journal of opinion whose prejudices coincided with ours? That would be like playing tennis with the net down. I came to believe that it was healthier for me to be forced constantly to defend my views against Luce's before they could reach print. So long, that is, as Luce didn't too often win the argument simply by pulling rank. When Luce years later turned over the editorship of his magazines to Hedley Donovan, he asked Donovan how often he expected to prevail in lunchtime arguments with his editors. "At least two out of three," Hedley said. Luce replied that he would settle for fifty-fifty.

In his later years, Luce still deferred on occasion to his senior colleagues, and sometimes to his writers, though not as often as he had earlier. He still believed in the process of "group journalism," a phrase spoken derisively by writers at *Time,* who considered themselves too heavily edited. Luce knew that his own prose could only benefit from someone else's pencil. T. S. Matthews, my own favorite among managing editors of *Time,* told me of one such occasion. In the tense prewar days of 1941, when the nation was sharply divided between isolationists and interventionists, Luce was so offended by a strongly isolationist radio broadcast by the flying hero Charles A. Lindbergh (*Time's* first Man of the Year back in 1927) that he volunteered to write *Time's* account of it. Matthews, then editing the National Affairs section, thought Luce's first paragraph fervently patriotic in tone but good. He put his initials on the story and sent it along to Gottfried, the managing editor. Gott announced that he wanted to fiddle with it, which usually meant that he would turn a story upside down. Later that day Luce dropped into Tom Matthews's office to see how matters stood. Tom handed him Luce's original version, with Matthews's initials on it, then Gott's edit. Luce studied the Gottfried version a while, recognized a few phrases as his own, and said with relief, "Quite a lot got by." "But your lead paragraph is gone," Matthews remarked. "Oh, you liked that?" Luce asked and, thus emboldened, went off to Gottfried's office to appeal. He came back a few minutes later to report his triumph to Tom: "He says we can restore the first paragraph, and the first sentence of the second paragraph, but all the rest of it has to make sense."

Alas, Luce was not always so amenable to challenge. The years of the mid-1930s and the 1940s, when so much else changed in the world, brought changes in Luce, too. As he became more powerful he became more imperious. In 1935 he divorced his wife and married the handsome, brilliant, and brittle playwright Clare Boothe Luce, becoming, despite all his social awkwardness, something of a celebrity by association. In that same year Luce launched the big picture magazine *Life,* whose runaway success in its first year almost bankrupted the company because advertisers got a free ride on its unexpected explosion in readership. Luce lost five million dollars on that "wild steer ride" but commented, "Believe me, that was an awful lot more excitement than I ever got out of *making* money."

By now, *Time,* as Luce said with pride and some misgivings, had become "the most powerful publication in America," and its editors felt the need to make it more responsible, while keeping it lively. World and national problems had become too complex to be left to clever dilettantes from Yale, Harvard, and Princeton. Just as the rival *New Yorker* down the street had decided in the mid-thirties that its flippant lorgnette sophistication, and its preoccupation with the fripperies of a shallow society, was not the right tone for a depressed nation and a world at war, *Time* decided (reversal of reversals!) to hire experienced journalists to add a touch of professionalism to its reporting. As one of the newspapermen so hired, I remember, I was subjected to the condescension of "back of the book" characters, whom we in turn referred to, in friendly disparagement, as "the poets." The loss in felicity in writing in *Time* was offset by a gain in knowledgeability as smart-aleckiness gave way to seriousness, and sometimes to sententiousness.

Luce himself was taking his own role, and himself, more seriously too. To Roy Larsen, Luce's closest business colleague, who had been with him since the earliest years, Luce wrote, "I think you and I share a kind of reluctance to use power. . . . To see *Time* in perspective is to realize its tremendous potential power. . . . I don't particularly like it. I don't think you do much—but there it is."

The atmosphere around the building had become more impersonal, and Luce himself more remote and often testy. With all his other interests, and with the growth of the editorial staffs of all his magazines, Luce no longer was known to everybody. He may have been reluctant to use power, but he certainly felt more confident in venting his opinions. He found it easier to override a new generation of editors. His attitude was now more like Winston Churchill's, as Churchill had once lightheartedly described it: "All I asked was compliance with my wishes after reasonable discussion."

Some of the old hands were getting old, or departing. One of the biggest losses was Archibald MacLeish, the poet and playwright, who had known Luce since leaving Yale; he was *Fortune*'s most dependable writer. In a farewell letter to Luce when he quit, MacLeish wrote with the frankness of an old friend: "I will admit (with resentment) that *Fortune* is not the association of mutually assisting journalists it was for five or six very exciting years. I will admit (without enthusiasm) that it is now a part of a publishing enterprise in which not more than a dozen or so people know each other's names and not more than half that many wish each other well enough to stand by each other." He advised Luce to make more of an effort to tell people "when their work is good, because if you don't, the last element of personal humanity will drain out of that organization and you will be left with nothing on your hands but a business which earns money."

■ ■ ■

Many of the newer hands at the Luce magazines, having no memory of the days when the editorial family was smaller, more informal, and freer, accepted the working atmosphere as they found it. A photographer climbing a scaffold to photograph the ceiling of the Sistine Chapel for *Life* or a music writer interviewing Duke Ellington for a *Time* cover story could ignore—even be oblivious to—internal quarrels about *Time* policy and feel sufficiently rewarded by performing his own work well. Yet all of us, working at a place we liked, could be embarrassed or angered by outright dishonesty in *Time* magazine's coverage (*Life,* as a mass magazine, was less tendentious) and made to feel guilty by friends in academia or in our own craft of journalism. Most of the criticism centered on two subjects about which Luce was most headstrong—the Republican Party and the Republic of China. In these two areas he was willing to jeopardize the integrity of his magazines. *Time* magazine could no longer be counted on to treat each side fairly; it distorted or concealed facts favorable to the other side; by its selective use of pictures and acerbic adjectives it maligned its opposition. Readers in America, with other sources of information, could spot the biased reporting of American politics. But many of them had no alternative source of news about China.

Out in Chungking Teddy White was trying to report what he regarded as the dismal truth about Chiang Kai-shek's China and found his own magazine unwilling to publish it.

Chapter 8

"Those Lyric Fall Days in Yenan"

Having brazenly sacked General Stilwell, Chiang Kai-shek became jittery at his own temerity and worried how President Roosevelt might respond. During this moment of uncertainty in Chungking in October 1944, Teddy White saw an opportunity that might not come his way again.

Before long Chiang would try to shut down the American contact with the Communists—officially known as the Dixie Mission—in their remote caves in Yenan. Teddy had never been to Yenan and wanted to go there. In the interim before a new American commander arrived in Chungking, Stilwell's staff was still in place. Outraged by Chiang's dismissal of Stilwell, his people were happy to cut orders to fly Teddy to Yenan on the next day's courier plane.

Teddy's companion on the flight was an old friend, John Paton Davies, Jr., a mishkid, now thirty-six, and a rising star in the State Department. Later Teddy wrote that Davies was "to suffer humiliation and degradation far greater than mine for those lyric fall days in Yenan."

On his first night in Yenan, Davies met with Mao Tse-tung, Chou En-lai, and Chu Teh, commander of the Communist Chinese armies. He pressed them on how much help the Communists could give—mobilizing peasants, cutting railway lines, providing support—if, before invading Japan, American troops were to land on the China coast, much of it occupied by the Communists. Davies, scrupulously professional, confided none of this to Teddy. But Teddy, as the only American journalist on the scene, gained what he called a "spurious importance" by arriving on Davies's plane and, shielded by his own old friendship with Chou En-lai, found himself treated by the Communists as a "semi-official and friendly reportorial arm of the American government."

"A reporter could not have found himself in a happier situation," Teddy remembered. "Those weeks in Yenan were a time of laughter and gaiety," in an atmosphere of "joviality that, even now, I cannot conceive as feigned.

"Those of us who have been so criticized for romanticizing the Chinese Communists can claim forgiveness for those weeks in Yenan in October and November; Chinese Communists were different then; we were not duped. . . . Chu Teh and Chou En-lai would wander around on foot unannounced to visit the outpost of Americans as friends, chatting and whiling away the hours." Seizing the occasion, Teddy interviewed eleven of the thirteen members of the Chinese Politburo, in separate talks that often went on for three or four hours. All of them, eager for American support, made the same argument: We can help you; Chiang cannot.

One morning Teddy was awakened at seven and told that if he wanted to see Chairman Mao he should prepare to breakfast with him at once. In Mao's personal cave—not at his office, which was in another cave—Teddy White met the leader. A husky, commanding presence, Mao sat slouched, smoking heavily. He spoke softly, calmly, and surely, permitting no interruption or contradiction. Their formal interview lasted an hour.

Mao saw no hope of resuming the coalition with Chiang but said he would not attack the Generalissimo as long as Chiang maintained his part of the front against the Japanese. Mao did not object to America's sending limited supplies to Chiang, but he warned that if America equipped twenty or thirty divisions, Chiang would use them against the Communists, not the Japanese. It would be better, Mao suggested, for the United States not to supply either side, but if the Americans decided otherwise, Mao demanded that they distribute supplies proportionate to each side's effectiveness in fighting the Japanese. (White had promised to submit his report of this interview to Mao for clearance; it came back so censored, cut, and mangled as to be unpublishable.)

As they continued to talk informally, Mao asked Teddy to stay for lunch. It was served by Mao's third wife, Chiang Ch'ing, later to become, after Mao's death, the feared leader of the Gang of Four, but at this meeting "she seemed quite harmless there in the cave serving the great thinker—smiling, pleasant, compliant." Teddy asked Mao what Communist rule would be like once it came to power; Mao assured Teddy that there would be freedom of speech and freedom of the press, except for "enemies of the people." ("I did not think then to ask him who would define what an enemy of the people was," but the idea "kind of scared me.")

By good fortune Teddy had arrived in Yenan at a historic moment: an ingathering for a party congress of men and women who ten years earlier had suffered together along the heroic Long March to exile in Yenan. Since then their ragamuffin remnant had swollen to an army of six hundred thousand men, with a supporting militia of a million. This growth in recruits was in sharp contrast to Chiang's loss of a quarter of a million troops in the previous six months.

Coming together now in Yenan the Communist leaders were cocky and confident and greeted one another warmly as brothers. In his autobiography, White wrote: "Later, twenty years later, they would purge each other, kill each other. . . . Perhaps power changed them before they knew they were changing, when they learned that power meant they could afford the harsh luxury of purging and killing each other. . . . Lin Piao would go on to conquer Manchuria and North China; P'eng Te-huai would go on to command Chinese forces against MacArthur in Korea. Then both would be purged and Lin Piao would be killed."

Indeed, when the Communists did come to power they acted with a systematic ruthlessness that made Chiang's authoritarian rule seemed random and amateurish. Not only did the Communists treat the Chinese people harshly but they sustained savage feuds among themselves.

At the time of Teddy's Yenan visit, however, when the revolution was in embryo, their comradeship was most evident at a Saturday night dance in the army headquarters auditorium, where tunes like "Marching Through Georgia" could be detected even when rendered on a mouth organ, drums, a few Chinese fiddles, and paper-covered combs. Men and women danced on the beaten mud floor, dressed alike in shapeless thick-padded jackets and pants and wearing visored caps. "Sex was undeterminable except by the cut of the hair," John Davies recalled in his book *Dragon by the Tail*. He was flattered to be asked to dance so many times by young ladies until he realized they really wanted to practice their English. "The whole thing was like a church sociable with everybody seeming to know everybody else." Teddy White on the other hand was reminded of Jewish weddings he had known as a boy.

A reader looking back today at this innocent idyll and trying to see the era as those involved saw it must make two leaps of the imagination. The first leap is to put aside the notion of inevitability, that what happened was the only thing that could have happened. The players of the time saw their circumstances differently. They believed themselves actors still able to shape and control events.

The reader then has a second, more difficult hurdle to surmount. This is to escape the subsequent poisoning of the history of those times by Senator Joseph McCarthy. In his desire to discredit the Truman administration, McCarthy—a demagogue both cynical and sinister—almost casually chose the question "Who lost China to the Communists?" as the best weapon with which to attack his opponents. With malevolent ignorance Joe McCarthy saw the history of wartime China with cartoon-book simplicity as a tale of heroes, dupes, and betrayers whose exposure would bring him a political payoff. The actual history of that period in China is far richer in nuances and contradictions. Had Joe McCarthy really been serious in studying the period he would have found much to surprise and confound him. The Chinese he chose as heroes and villains had at one time been colleagues. This was particularly true in the interwoven careers of Luce's hero Chiang Kai-shek, and Teddy's hero Chou En-lai.

Much of this entwining can be blamed on that noble figure Dr. Sun Yat-sen, the father of modern China, an early believer in what came to be known as popular fronts. Sun was a Cantonese with socialist leanings who had been educated in Hawaii and had lived in exile abroad for many years. He was determined to break the power of the warlords who kept his country impoverished and fragmented, and equally determined to drive out the foreigners from their special enclaves. After several failures to win popular support by persuasion, Sun in 1922 decided to create a revolutionary army, and for help he turned to the Communist leaders who had just been successful in Russia. The Communists suavely told Sun just what he wanted to hear: China was not ready for Communism; national unity and independence must come first, and in this Stalin could be of help. Stalin, then in the process of grabbing power from the dying Lenin, sent Sun a political strategist, Mikhail Borodin, a sad-eyed cosmopolitan revolutionary who, until the Russian revolution of 1917, had taught school for years in Chicago under his real name, Michael Grusenberg.*

Besides Borodin, Stalin sent Sun a number of Soviet officers to help him set up a revolutionary military academy at Whampoa to train the officers who would lead Sun's army. The Soviet advisers were much impressed by a slender young peasant soldier of ascetic habits, Chiang Kai-shek. They packed him off to Moscow for six months' indoctrination.

Chiang liked neither Moscow nor the Russians, but he admired the way the Communists ran their one-party dictatorship, using centralized authority, propaganda skills, and police terror. He would later send his son, Chiang Ching-kuo, to be educated in Russia. On Chiang Kai-shek's return to China, he modeled his own Kuomintang party on the Communist party, and did so with the help of Borodin, who even framed the new party's constitution—writing it in English. To ensure that the Communist party and the Kuomintang worked together, Sun chose Chiang to run the Whampoa academy, and the Communist Chou En-lai to be the political director. One result of this bizarre partnership was that Mao Tse-tung, one of the founders of the Chinese Communist party and then just turning thirty, became not only a member of the Communists' Central Committee but also an alternate member of the Kuomintang's Central Executive Committee.

After Sun's death, Chiang resolved to rend asunder what Sun had brought together. His chance came in 1927 when Chiang's troops captured Shanghai, where the Communists inside the city, led by General Chou En-lai, had already risen in insurrection against the local warlord. With the help of Shang-

---

*When he went to China Borodin enrolled his two Chicago-born sons, Fred and Norman Grusenberg, in the Shanghai American school. There Fred became a classmate of the mishkid John Paton Davies. (The boy explained to Davies that his father was a lumber merchant in Canton.) After Borodin's period in China as Stalin's agent, he returned to Russia to edit the English-language *Moscow News;* he ran afoul of Stalin's displeasure and died in a Siberian prison camp.

hai's criminal street gangs, Chiang turned suddenly on his Communist allies, disarmed them, executed most of them, and forced the party underground. (Chou En-lai was among those captured but talked his way free and escaped.) This destruction of the Communist leadership in Shanghai led an angry Trotsky, Stalin's chief rival in the Kremlin, to denounce Stalin for having "lost China," a foretaste of Joe McCarthy's later accusation that the U.S. State Department had similarly "lost China." Both accusations were absurd: vast, chaotic China was never in the power of either country to win or lose.

Chiang by now was the dominant political leader in China. He had secured the backing of businessmen and landlords, who saw him as a man who would bring stability to China, and skillfully bought off or crushed once-powerful warlords, some of whom were allowed to keep their private armies.

Not long after their defeat in Shanghai, the Communists evacuated all of southern China. Weighted down with bags, baggage, and archives, thirty thousand Communist men and women set forth on a grueling six-thousand-mile exodus, which they would later glorify as the Long March. It was a journey of suffering and savagery; they were harassed constantly by Chiang's troops, and they themselves wreaked destruction on villages they marched through. At last, in Northwest China, they reached the bleak safety of Yenan and set up their base.

Chiang continued to pursue the Communists until he himself was kidnapped in 1936 at Sian by a young Manchurian warlord, Chang Hsueh-liang, who accused Chiang of not giving sufficient priority to resisting the Japanese invasion of Manchuria. One of the paradoxes of this freak episode was that the man who negotiated Chiang's release was the man Chiang had earlier tried to capture, Chou En-lai. As part of the settlement, Chiang promised to forgive Chang Hsueh-liang, but he then had thrown him into prison and even, as Teddy White wrote, "carried him, besotted with opium and weakened by concubines, in captivity to ultimate exile in Formosa."

Isolated in Yenan, the Chinese Communists nursed their wounds, regained their strength, and—under Mao's tutelage—set out to give Communism a distinctly Chinese face. They felt abandoned by everybody, including their presumed comrades in Russia. The Russian formula for revolution, gaining power through an urban proletariat, had failed in China; the way to power in China, Mao concluded, lay in winning over the peasants. Mao promised them land, gained their loyalty, and armed them, as Chiang—allied to the landlords—never dared do. Some Western visitors to Yenan admiringly characterized the Communists as mere agrarian land reformers, but Teddy White never did. He had heard the leaders proudly proclaim themselves Communists, and he saw that what bound them together was the discipline of their dogmatic beliefs.

In revising Communist thought, Mao invoked the sacred texts of Marxism, but in a decidedly Chinese form. Mao made all the ritual gestures to international Communism, but he was far too independent and nationalist for Stalin's taste. While the rest of the world, and many Communists themselves, were misled by the propaganda of harmony and friendship between Stalin's Russia and Mao's China, the reality was different. In time Stalin would have tried to purge Mao just as he purged so many Communist party leaders in Eastern Europe after the war. Fearing Stalin's infiltration of his movement, Mao got rid of the Twenty-eight Bolsheviks, a pro-Russian faction of Chinese who had been trained in Moscow.

If Mao was a nationalist, so also was Stalin. To defend Russia's eastern front, Stalin wanted a strong China to hold off a militant Japan. With money and matériel, Stalin supported Chiang as China's head of state, and he didn't want Mao to jeopardize Chiang's power. In the 1930s, when the Japanese invaded China, Soviet Russia had sent gasoline and planes to Chiang's government at a time when the United States was selling scrap iron and oil to Japan. Even after World War II broke out, and Russia was fighting for its life against the Nazi armies menacing Leningrad and Stalingrad, Moscow continued scru-pulously to funnel all its aid to China to Chiang.

This strategy of Stalin's would have been incomprehensible to Senator McCarthy, whose understanding of events was prim-itive, or to all those editorial writers in the United States who enlisted their typewriters in a war against "monolithic Commu-nism." Throughout World War II, Teddy White reported, the Chinese Communists "received not so much as an airplane, a ton of gasoline or a crate of munitions directly from the Soviet Union. From 1937 to 1945 no more than five Russian planes made trips to Yenan"; each of these flights had Chiang's prior approval, and an inspector was aboard to check what was sent.

This behavior by the Russians helps to explain the welcome Chinese Communists gave to visiting Americans like John Paton Davies and Teddy White, those representatives of the imperial-istic capitalist enemy. The war against Japan had generated an overriding nationalism among Chinese Communists. Russia's war in Europe meant little to them; they knew that the United States, not Russia, was doing most to defeat their Japanese enemy.

The view from Yenan, isolated as it was, was highly paro-chial. Ingrown in their outlook, beset by their own problems, toughened by their hard existence, the Communists were in fact, with one important exception, remarkably ignorant of the rest of the world.

The exception was the Chinese Communists' ambassador to the rest of the world, Teddy White's urbane friend Chou En-lai. The two had known each other for years, ever since Teddy, fresh out of Harvard and eager to learn everything about China, had found his way down one of Chungking's muddy back alleys to No. 50, Tseng Chia Ai, the ramshackle compound that housed Chou's mission to the court of Chiang Kai-shek, at a time when the Communists were presumably working in tan-dem with Chiang against the Japanese. Over the years Chiang and Chou, colleagues at Whampoa, had alternated between warring with each other and sparring diplomatically in uneasy coalition.

Chou's mission occupied the first and third floors of the compound, living in awkward intimacy with Chiang's secret police quartered on the second floor. It was part of Chou's job to wangle arms and supplies from Chiang, to whom not only all Russian aid but also American Lend-Lease was sent. Chou's headquarters in Chungking was a Communist listening post, alert to the outside world, and to what was going on inside China. Chou distributed to the foreign press corps in Chungking the news his radio tower picked up from Yenan, and these reports of skirmishes against the Japanese by either Chiang's troops or Communist guerrillas often proved more accurate than the clumsily exaggerated propaganda of the Kuomintang.

Correspondents found Chou a worldly intellectual. Unlike Mao or Chiang—who were peasants risen to power—Chou was the son of a well-to-do mandarin family. He had studied in an American missionary school in Tientsin (where he learned his choppy English) before being sent to Japan and then to Europe for more schooling. In France he joined the Communist party and organized a strike at the Renault plant; then, at the age of twenty-seven, he returned to China to join the revolution. An adroit diplomat, he was also a tough commander of troops. After escaping capture by Chiang in Shanghai in 1927, he had fought in many battles before and during the Long March, and had arrived in Yenan so wounded and exhausted from skirmishes along the way that he had to be lifted off his horse, close to death.

Once he regained his health, he was assigned to Chungking and spent five wartime years there. On rainy afternoons Teddy was often to be found in Chou's tiny reception room, which contained several dilapidated armchairs and a lumpy sofa covered in coarse blue peasant cloth. Teddy was fascinated by Chou's inside knowledge of what was going on in Chiang's sycophantic and corrupt court. "It is very rare that a young reporter meets a great man who has nothing at all to do except to play watchman at a political outpost, and who has the human need to gossip about what he learns," Teddy wrote in his autobiography.

Oddly enough, Chou is barely mentioned in *Thunder Out of China,* the wartime best-seller that first made Teddy's reputation; was Teddy already concerned about being considered too sympathetic to the Communists? Chou is briefly described in the book as "the brilliant and tempestuous revolutionary." Only an "older and wiser" Teddy would acknowledge in his autobiography how influential Chou had been in his life. If Chou, Joseph Stilwell, and John F. Kennedy were the three men "in whose presence I had near total suspension of disbelief or questioning judgment," it was Chou who proved the most disillusioning to Teddy. He writes: "I can see [him] now for what he was: a man as brilliant and ruthless as any the Communist movement has thrown up in this century . . . and yet he was capable of warm kindness, irrepressible humanity and silken courtesy." And "I retain an irrepressible affection for Chou Enlai still, even though I know he, as any Chinese Communist, would have sacrificed me for his cause."

Their friendship became strained on Teddy's visit to Yenan in 1944. Teddy had found Chou just as warm, chatty, and relaxed as in the old days. But only at first.

To Americans it made pragmatic sense that the Chinese Nationalists and the Communists, equally interested in expelling the Japanese invader, should work together. But whatever chance there was to bring the two sides together was diminished by Franklin Roosevelt's disastrous choice of Patrick J. Hurley to do the job. Hurley was one of a number of Republicans (among them Frank Knox, James Forrestal, and Robert Lovett) brought in by Roosevelt to give a bipartisan cast to the war effort. The best of these Republican acquisitions was Henry Stimson, elderly but respected, to be secretary of war. One of the worst was the egregious Hurley, who was sent, with the assigned rank of major general, as Roosevelt's personal emissary to mediate between the two Chinese leaders. A flamboyant and wealthy lawyer from Oklahoma with flowing white mane and outsized ego, Hurley had been one of Herbert Hoover's floor managers at the 1928 Republican convention and for that service had been made Hoover's secretary of war. Hurley knew so little about the Chinese that he had to be told that Shek was not Chiang Kai-shek's last name. (Hurley's habit of pronouncing Mao Tse-tung's name "Moose Dung" was not so innocent an error.)

One morning, unannounced and unexpected, Hurley flew into Yenan. Teddy happened to be at the airstrip awaiting a mail plane when he saw Hurley's plane buzz the field, circle it, then land. Out stepped Hurley, six foot three and grandly dressed in a general's uniform. Considering the surprise landing, Teddy marveled at how soon Mao, Chou, and Chu Teh, who had been hurriedly notified, arrived at the runway in Mao's "limousine," a war-scarred ambulance that was one of only four automobiles in Yenan. Hurley greeted the leaders with an eardrum-rattling Choctaw war whoop.

As the ambulance drove off, carrying Teddy, too, Hurley glanced out the window and saw dry riverbeds, which reminded him (he said) of rivers in Oklahoma so dry in summer that you could tell when a school of fish passed by the cloud of dust it raised. Hurley's easy, earthy humor put everyone in good spirits at first, and the cheery mood continued at tea at the Dixie Mission. Between tea and that evening's grand banquet (where Hurley let forth another piercing "yahoo") Hurley and Teddy White had a private chat. Teddy confided to him the details of his interview with Mao, it being fairly common practice during World War II for American correspondents to brief high-ranking visitors (a courtesy that ended abruptly in the Vietnam War in the mutual distrust that sprang up between army, government, and the press). Teddy confided to Hurley Mao's dismissal of any reunion of Communists and Nationalists. Later, when the diplomat Davies also warned Hurley of Mao's attitude, Hurley ordered him to return immediately to Chungking.

Hurley had brought with him a proposal from Chiang: that in return for one seat in Chiang's Supreme National Defense Council, the Communists would dissolve their armies, which would then be reorganized under Chiang's command. Just as White and Davies had predicted he would, Mao angrily rejected Chiang's offer. After this rebuff, Hurley asked Mao for his ideas, then worked much of the night writing his own proposal, without consulting a single American adviser. His plan was breathtakingly impractical.

He proposed a genuine coalition of Communists and Nationalists, reinforced by a full line of American-style guarantees, including freedom of speech, of assembly, and of the press, and the right to habeas corpus, along with two freedoms thrown in from Roosevelt's wartime Four Freedoms, freedom from fear and freedom from want. There was something touchingly naïve in Hurley's belief that two harsh dictatorships could so easily dissolve their enmity and jointly promise sweeping liberty to their people.

Nevertheless Mao leapt at the proposal. He might not have understood all that American talk about liberty and freedom, but Mao saw instantly that both sides would be considered equal partners in fighting Japan and that "supplies acquired from foreign powers will be equitably distributed" between them. Best of all, Chiang's dictatorship would be replaced by a United National military council. On such terms, Mao would be happy to fold his troops into a coalition government. In an outdoor ceremony on a sunny November afternoon, Mao signed Hurley's draft with his personal signature instead of stamping it with his chop, to show how much importance he gave to it. A blank space was left for Chiang to sign.

Would Chiang sign? Chou, who apparently feared his life would be in danger in Chiang's capital, had to be persuaded by

Mao to fly with Hurley to Chungking to negotiate with Chiang.

On the turbulent flight to Chungking, Chou treated Teddy coldly. Teddy thought he knew why. In one of Hurley's sessions with Mao, the blundering Hurley had repeated everything Teddy had told him in confidence. Mao's interpreter angrily confronted Teddy: "Mao trusted you; we thought you were a friend." From then on, neither Mao nor Chou would confide in Teddy.

Nonetheless Teddy was euphoric about the agreement Mao and Hurley had signed. In Chungking he dashed off a "rhapsodic dispatch, an emotional dispatch" to his editors in New York "about how peace had come to China at last." He would later write: "*Time* magazine did not publish my dispatch, the filter of distance removing the editors from my emotional writing, which was in truth winged with a hope and passion that were entirely unreal." Though this was written thirty years after the event, it was a rare acknowledgment from Teddy that his New York editors might on occasion be right.

For of course Hurley's foolish proposal got nowhere. In Chungking Chou was kept waiting for days, dealing impatiently with minor functionaries, because Chiang was reported to be sick. "Chou was admitted but once to see the Generalissimo," Teddy wrote, "and then he was treated so contemptuously that he vowed on emerging never to return to Chungking."

Once it was clear that Hurley's attempt to arrange a truce had failed, Hurley committed the United States wholly to the support of Chiang and considered anyone who disagreed with him a troublemaker. Not until twenty years later, when the documents were published, did Teddy learn that the morning after Teddy had confided Mao's position to Hurley, the ambassador sent a classified message to the State Department: "Theodore White, correspondent for *Time* and *Life,* told me that he had just talked to Chairman Mao and Mao had told him that there was not any possible chance of an agreement between him and

Chiang Kai-shek. . . . White's whole conversation was definitely against the mission with which I am charged."

That report, in the dossiers of American intelligence, would plague White in the McCarthy years. Several months later, in a face-to-face argument, Hurley called White "un-American" and "you goddamn seditious little son of a bitch."

Hurley had it in his power to do far more damage to the career of John Paton Davies, the State Department official who had been Stilwell's chief political adviser and had told Hurley the same thing Teddy had. Davies had also argued that the United States should not "indefinitely underwrite a politically bankrupt regime" and should stay out of China's civil war: "the point is not are we for or against Communism, but granting its existence—how best to go about coping with it." Hurley accused Davies of wanting "to pull the plug on Chiang Kai-shek," and in cables to Washington set out to discredit Davies. Joe McCarthy would later quote his false charges on a TV broadcast, blighting Davies's career.

Teddy White glumly summed up the final results of "those lyric fall days in Yenan" in his autobiography: "The Communists, I knew, no longer trusted me. . . . Pat Hurley, the President's man in Chungking, considered me an enemy. The Kuomintang distrusted me, and had since my talk with Chiang on the Honan famine. But I was confident, even arrogant, knowing that I wrote for *Time,* for *Life,* and was Harry Luce's man in Chungking.

"And then Luce, too, repudiated me."

"MORE ALONE NOW THAN EVER I WAS BEFORE"

When Teddy White sneaked out of China his account of General Stilwell's firing, he also got out a letter that he described to Harry Luce as "perhaps the most important letter I have ever written to you." Teddy knew that Whittaker Chambers, the foreign editor, would inflict his own prejudices on *Time*'s Stilwell cover story, but Teddy hoped to go over Chambers's head with a personal appeal to Luce, who would have the final say.

"Stilwell's relief from command," Teddy wrote Luce, "records in black and white the total bankruptcy of our diplomacy, our national policy . . . and our military strategy on the continent." In Teddy's view, the fault was Chiang's, and Teddy was now ready to say to Luce, more boldly (and more dramatically) than he ever had before, that Chiang had "outlived his historical usefulness." He continued: "I have hated dictatorship and cruelty and despotism ever since I began to think about politics. I have hated and denounced Joe Stalin, I have hated and denounced Adolf Hitler; I hate all pinch-penny two-bit dictators of the Balkans and the banana republics. Of all the great despots of our time, the only one I have ever praised in print is Chiang Kai-shek. I shall never do that again."

Expecting Luce to repudiate Chiang was indeed asking a great deal. Though Luce well knew Chiang's flaws, as well as the faults of the privileged Soong family around him and the corrosive corruption of the regime, Luce's attitude toward Chiang was like that expressed in Hilaire Belloc's cautionary tale about Jim, who ran away from his nurse and was eaten by a Lion. The moral was:

> And always keep a-hold of Nurse
> For fear of finding something worse.

Whatever his reservations were about Chiang, Luce never doubted that the Communists were something worse.

On Teddy White's return from his visit to the Chinese Communists in their remote Yenan caves, his first inkling of how different *Time*'s Stilwell cover story was from what he had filed was the summary he had heard of it in a broadcast of a Domei news story. In admonishing Teddy to keep his shirt on until he read the actual *Time* story, Luce wired: "Note that story refers to Chungking as quote a dictatorship ruling high-handedly unquote." And with heavy sarcasm Luce added: "Please remember that President Roosevelt has not yet withdrawn recognition of President Chiang Kai-shek as legal head of the government of China. . . . Remember also that of no Allied government have we published so much criticism."

When Teddy six days later read the printed story, he "hit the ceiling"; it was even worse than he feared, and a "dishonorable lie." The more he thought about *Time*'s Stilwell cover in the years that followed, the more it rankled. In 1952 he wrote to his friend A. J. Liebling, the press critic, that its "inaccuracy, stupidity, deceit was the worst bit of journalism I have ever seen in America."

To anyone reading it today, and unfamiliar with its background, the Stilwell cover story, for all its shifty misrepresentations, has a superficial plausibility. In the story as edited by Chambers, Stilwell was praised as highly as White could have wished. He was shown as a brave, popular soldier, a crack field commander: "Few men have been stouter friends of China." But, Chambers argued, Stilwell had been done in by Franklin Roosevelt's pressing too hard on the "patient" Chiang to make domestic reforms and to come to terms with the Chinese Communists. There was no mention in the story of Stilwell's stubborn fight against the corruption, ineptness, and harshness of Chiang's dictatorship (which was what Teddy thought the story should be about). There was that one-sentence reference to "Chungking" (not Chiang) as "a dictatorship ruling high-handedly," but even such high-handedness was justified, the story argued, "in order to safeguard the last vestiges of democratic principles in China."

Vociferously anti-Communist as Chambers now was, he had as a journalist learned the tricks of the trade when he was a Communist. Whereas young reporters on *The New York Times* were instructed how to present all sides of a situation fairly, Chambers, at the *Daily Worker*, was told how not to. As a skillful polemicist, Chambers was well aware that dishonest journalism is more effective in what it leaves out than in what it says.

As for the Chinese Communists, *Time* said that despite "the tone long taken by leftists and echoed by liberals" about agrarian reform, well-fed troops, and efficient guerrilla operations, the actuality could be seen in a report of harsh living conditions "recently smuggled out of Communist China." This document, far from being something the Communists were trying to hide, as *Time* implied, had been published in full in four articles in Yenan's only daily newspaper—one of those exercises in Communist "self-criticism" whose truth or falseness could never be judged by outsiders since its appearance was intended to serve some propaganda purpose of the party leadership. Since the Communists themselves had disseminated this criticism to their own people, the only "smuggling" involved was the fact that the paper was banned in the rest of China by the Nationalists. But Chambers didn't tell his readers that.

As Teddy White wrote to his friend Joe Liebling: "I don't think Harry Luce ever thought he was doing a wrong thing once. He has this concept of group journalism where every fact is checked and thus any story going into *Time* is factually so. But he has never understood that facts are for use as a builder uses bricks. With bricks you can build a temple to god, or you can make a brick shithouse. And in his China stories he used most of the facts his correspondents sent to build a brick shithouse."

Invited by Luce to list "specific inaccuracies" in the Stilwell cover story, Teddy responded with a long memo "protesting the editorial slant which I know is the prerogative of New York." He objected primarily that Chambers posed the issue as a contest between democracy and totalitarianism when it was really a struggle between two dictatorships—between what Teddy called Chiang's fascism and Mao's Communism. He opposed any "meddling" in China's civil war, particularly on Chiang's losing side. In reply Luce cabled that in supporting Chiang, Luce was no more "meddling" in China's internal affairs than he was in supporting Winston Churchill in England.

The exchanges between Luce and White in the Stilwell crisis represented a rupture, but not yet a break, in their relationship. But as Teddy would candidly acknowledge, "I used him for the next two years and he used me, warily, suspiciously, until we broke."

For the rest of his life Teddy White would "still insist, and know, that I was right and [Luce] was wrong in telling the story of China." History has scored Teddy at least half right—right about the decline and decay of Chiang Kai-shek's regime. And the other half? Teddy had come away from his two weeks in

Yenan, as he wrote Luce, with a "profoundly sympathetic attitude." That view, he said, was shared by all the foreign correspondents who had visited Yenan, by the American military mission, and by the State Department observers based there: "I have never in all my time in China witnessed so unanimous a reaction by men of all shades of political opinion to any political enterprise."

The shared austerity of Yenan seemed to confirm, in the eyes of visitors, the Communists' egalitarianism, though it was Teddy who shrewdly noticed that the leaders lived in better caves. Impressed by the way the Communists had won over the peasants, visitors liked to quote Mao's famous aphorism that the people are the ocean in which the Communists freely swim. These observers had yet to learn the many hidden ways by which totalitarian states can win their plebiscites or how skillfully they camouflage their control. Nor did they foresee how brutal the Communist leadership would be to this same peasantry. Teddy would argue that the Communists changed because power corrupted the leaders; a man like Chambers would say that cruelty was inherent in their character.

The foreign observers "of all shades" who were impressed by the Chinese Communists responded in differing ways. Some, among them journalists of left-wing bent, were starry-eyed; others (Teddy White among them) had arrived in Yenan with skepticism and continued to have reservations but found much to admire; still others, particularly State Department professionals, more dispassionately viewed the Communists as the eventual victors in China and thought that the American interest was to ensure that in coming to power, the Chinese Communists should have an alternative to partnership with a Soviet Union the United States mistrusted. However much these observers differed in their judgments, all would find themselves lumped together by Senator Joe McCarthy as patsies or traitors.

■ ■ ■

Teddy had tried to state his objections to the Stilwell cover story coolly, saving his emotion for an accompanying note to Luce, in which he wrote of his own "very profound and wearying despondency."

> Perhaps because I am ill [he was suffering from diarrhea], I feel so depressed, and perhaps because the monstrous nature of China's tragedy eats me.
>
> I have been toying with the idea of resigning from *Time* for some weeks now—and I love working for *Time* so much that the idea gives me cold chills. I feel that it is so important that America know what is happening out here that if *Time* willfully fails to tell the story, I can't honestly remain.

His problem was that the debate was no longer between Teddy and Luce alone; it had become a triangle. The third party was the foreign editor, Whittaker Chambers, whom Teddy described as Luce's "court favorite at that moment . . . a former Communist *apparatchik* of remarkable literary gifts" and (as Teddy might have added but didn't) an editor with an arrogant disdain for reporting from the field, since he thought his own knowledge and judgment of events superior. Chambers was a formidable antagonist.

Luce now had to cope with the sensibilities of two favorites. Affection and friendship favored Teddy; a shared conviction that an aggressive Communism was a threat to the world favored Chambers. (Luce's sister Beth, asked what Luce thought of Whit, replied simply: "Harry admired his mind.") Whit's vision of a world polarized by Communism—which was his view long before there was a Cold War—had a powerful appeal for Luce.

Teddy wrote in his autobiography, "Luce raised my salary, but would not change *Time*'s policy. I was sad. This man, Luce, had plucked me out of nothing and given me eminence. . . . Now he was repudiating me, and it was as if my father had denied me in public."

Faced with editorial conflicts on his magazines, Luce would often, having favored one side of an argument, seek to compensate the other side. Since Teddy could no longer get his liberal views into the pages of *Time*, Luce published in *Life* a long, sympathetic account by Teddy of his visit to Yenan, "Inside Red China." In it Teddy described how the Communists had won over the peasants by teaching them democracy and reducing their land rents but said he felt less sure about how democratic the Communists would prove to be once they encountered resistance in large urban cities, where "the urban middle class hates and fears Communism."

Time magazine, with its prickly outspokenness, was where Luce's views were most dogmatically reflected. *Life,* as a more universal, popular magazine, tended to be less opinionated. Luce once said that the role of *Time* was to make enemies, of *Life* to make friends. *Time* was Teddy's first home; he wanted to appear there regularly, rather than intermittently in *Life*.

So long as Whittaker Chambers had Luce's ear, *Time*'s views on China were Whit's. In frustration Teddy put up a sign in his bedroom-office on the second floor of the press hostel in Chungking: "Any resemblance to what is written here and what is printed in *Time* magazine is purely coincidental."

He now had a colleague in the Chungking bureau who was just as opposed to Chambers as Teddy was. This was Annalee Jacoby, a spirited young woman who was the widow of Melville Jacoby, a *Time* correspondent killed early in the war. Making the rounds at Kuomintang headquarters with Annalee, Teddy heard one officer say to another: "It's safe to tell them anything. *Time* doesn't print what they send anyway." As Teddy wrote Luce: "That's a wisecrack but it rankles anyway. . . . My position is highly embarrassing."

Almost the only cheery thing that had happened to Teddy was the arrival of Annalee, whom he had known for years, and "with whom I had fallen in love within days of meeting her."* On her return to China as a correspondent, she found Teddy recuperating from diarrhea in the American hospital in Kunming. They flew back to Chungking, where Teddy felt he might use the time he "had earned at the front for a bit of rest and pursuit of romance." But much as Annalee admired Teddy, she was, a little more than a year after Mel's death, too recently widowed to consider romance: "I knew he was in love with me. He was marvelous to work with; he had one of the best minds I ever knew. He was fascinating, but hard to fall in love with. Mel had been tall, good-looking, and elegant." She kept Mel's memory fresh.

In Annalee Jacoby, Teddy had a colleague whose dislike of Chambers's editing equaled his own but who was unwilling to excuse Luce's behavior as Teddy did. Teddy and Annalee both filed stories that *Time* did not publish; Teddy, feeling "chastened," sent dispatches that were "scrupulously neutral" but were still unacceptable to Chambers.

By now the situation had become unsatisfactory for all. A cable to Teddy from the news desk in New York read: "After

---

*This was in Australia shortly after Pearl Harbor; when they met Annalee was the recent bride of Mel Jacoby, who had covered China for *Time* during Teddy's absence in America. Annalee, a classmate of Jacoby's at Stanford, had followed him to Chungking after a spell of writing in Hollywood. The night before Jacoby was transferred to the Philippines, he asked Annalee to marry him. It was to be a short and tragic marriage.

Their honeymoon in Manila was interrupted by the Japanese invasion; General Douglas MacArthur advised them to leave. In the company of ten businessmen they made their way with great difficulty to Cebu in the south, where they were put aboard a cattle freighter bound for Australia, together with their Hermès portable typewriters, cameras, and the revolvers that MacArthur had given each of them. Once in Melbourne they met Teddy White, who outfitted them and took care of them. Weeks later, in April 1942, Jacoby was killed. He was on a flight with General Harold H. George, MacArthur's chief airman. En route they gave a lift to a hitchhiking army officer who asked to be let off at Alice Springs. As George and Jacoby stood on the tarmac, a young pilot crashed into another plane on landing; the propeller flew off, decapitating both General George and Jacoby.

consultation with Luce here's what he (and most emphatically he) would like you to do: stay in and near Chungking for at least four or five weeks to report not political China . . . [but] mainly small indigenous yarns."

Enclosed, as a sample of what was wanted, was an excerpt from the London bureau reporting on England's two-thousandth day of the war: "Yellow crocuses bloomed, daffodils sold for dollar and a half per bunch, Commons passing bill making rear lights compulsory on bicycles . . . in other words, good-fashioned *Time* news. . . . This assignment interesting but not taxing . . . so you've got good chance getting good stories in the magazine. . . . Maybe you should consider coming here for brief refresher. What say?"

Teddy wanted neither a "refresher" trip home nor an assignment reporting on daffodils. It was Annalee, he writes in his memoirs, who "preserved both our jobs" by crafting light, "sun-filled" stories. One of them was her discovery that in the spring the Chinese could make an egg stand on end. The story made front pages all over the United States; when Einstein said this was impossible, Annalee produced a *Life* picture spread proving it true.

Teddy scorned such frivolity when a nation was in agony; but he also had to earn his keep. Finally, "I realized that my only insurance against dismissal would be combat reporting." And so with his usual headlong enthusiasm, his admiration for brave men, and his eye for detail, in the last months of the Pacific war he flew eight combat missions in medium and heavy bombers over enemy-held territory. For this he was awarded the Air Medal.

Two days after the first atom bomb was dropped on Japan, Teddy flew to Manila to interview his "old friend" General MacArthur. Not until the atom bomb had been dropped on Hiroshima was MacArthur finally briefed by Karl Compton of MIT on the revolutionary bomb and its power. When Teddy saw MacArthur the following day, he found him subdued. No longer were wars about valor or judgment, MacArthur said; they were now the property of scientists.

"Men like me are obsolete," MacArthur said, pacing back and forth. "There will be no more wars, White, no more wars." (In just five years MacArthur would be leading American troops and UN allies in fighting a war in Korea. Old-fashioned nasty conventional wars were still possible.)

The Japanese surrender—which war correspondent Teddy White witnessed on the deck of the battleship *Missouri*—soon followed. And with that there was no longer a need for American troops to land on the Chinese coast as a base for invading Japan; no longer a need to bargain with the Chinese Communists, whose guerrillas were best situated to harass the Japanese occupiers of that coast. For the Americans in the Pacific, except for occupying Japan, the war was over. Thoughts turned to bringing the boys back, to their reunions at home and their search for jobs or more schooling under the GI Bill.

But the war was not over in China; after seven years of savage Japanese occupation a new kind of struggle, a deadly civil war, broke out as the Japanese surrendered their weapons and left. Most Americans, weary of war and eager for peace, were ready to celebrate V-J Day as an ending, but as both Harry Luce and Teddy White knew, there was still unfinished business in Asia. Luce decided that the first two postwar issues of *Time* should celebrate victory in the Pacific by putting two heroes on the cover, MacArthur one week, Chiang the next. Teddy, now back in Chungking, was assigned the Chiang story. In a telegram to Luce that Teddy himself later acknowledged was rude, he refused to "legitimize China's somber tyrant yet once again." When Luce then accused him of political partisanship Teddy cabled back, "This office is working flat out under enormous conditions of strain. . . . I resent being called an avowed partisan." But of course he was, at least in his total opposition to

Chiang. Luce was just as avowedly partisan. Each stubbornly thought he had the right of it; both were skilled at infighting when crossed. The crucial difference was that one was the boss, the other not.

Teddy offered to go to New York to make his case; instead, he was premptorily ordered home.

With his influence in the military, Teddy was able to wangle a priority on a flight that got him from China to New York in a week. He returned determined to write a book about China, saying all that Chinese censorship and his editors at *Time* had not allowed him to say. Annalee Jacoby, following him more slowly to New York, would be his coauthor. She, more angry than he at Luce and at *Time,* quit the magazine. But Teddy, who had threatened to quit three or four times, instead arranged a six-month leave of absence. His ghetto upbringing had taught him fiscal caution.

In his autobiography (in which on occasion he curiously shifts from first person to third) Teddy explained: "Because he liked Harry Luce so much, he believed that the justice of his rebellion would be recognized once the book was published, and he would return to some new and glamorous post on the field-correspondent staff. He believed, in all naïveté, he could have it both ways—that he could say what he wanted to say, and yet enjoy the comfort and benefits of the parent organization."

In a sunless apartment on East Twenty-ninth Street in New York, he and Annalee worked with passion and great speed on their book, wanting it to be the first and best book on events in China. Teddy's eagerness to marry Annalee was evident in the generous terms he offered her as coauthor: he would write all but four chapters of the book but would give her one third of the royalties and, more important, a joint byline. Her own research

and knowledge of the scene added to the book; she also persuaded Teddy to delete from the book some of the more purple
patches in his writing.

Thunder Out of China, read forty years later, is an impressive book, a short, highly readable history of modern China,
enriched by the thoroughness of its reporting, the vividness of its
observations, and its shrewd judgments on the characters involved. Its thesis was that only by refusing to take sides could
the United States hope to influence the growth of democracy in
China and avoid the dominance of either of the two contending
dictatorships. To continue to support Chiang was to back the
losing side and could only lead to future tragedy.

Annalee and Teddy had worked well together, but in the
strain of their collaboration their romance came to an end. The
affair, such as it was, had always been somewhat one-sided; in
the end, when Teddy asked Annalee to marry him, she turned
him down.

Just at this low point Teddy received a letter that greatly disturbed him from John K. Fairbank, the Harvard professor who
had earlier been the strongest influence on Teddy's career. From
Shanghai, where he was now working for the United States Information Service, Fairbank wrote: "I miss you out here," then
pressed his attack:

> Why the hell don't you cut loose from Henry and get
> out from under the stigma of being kept by a guy who is on
> the wrong side? I have seen item after item in his publica-
> tions and every time they include a line which is a stinking
> lie and an evil thing to spread to the American people. I
> don't think you should take money from him.
>
> I gather that you have an affection for Luce which is
> personal and based on certain sound associations and
> things in common; but when it comes to policies and prin-

ciples for which he stands, I see no way in which you can reconcile your own views with his performance, and none of your friends can see any way either. You are in every way perfectly competent to cut loose and establish yourself very securely on your own, and no thought of security for your family should enter into it. So I don't understand why you keep on in this equivocal position, which is undermining to your morale and discouraging to your friends. . . . You are capable of being the top man in the world of journalism on China, once you take your stand as you believe, but not until then. If I didn't value you above other people I wouldn't jump on you this way.

John

In some agitation, Teddy replied with a candor not to be matched elsewhere in his personal correspondence:

> I got your very rough letter today, and I guess I ought to answer it tonight, even though I may sound very morbid and maudlin in doing so. I hate like Hell crying to anybody, but you got me where it hurts.
>
> I guess your letter struck me hard because there is nothing you said in it which I haven't said even more bitterly to myself for the past six months.
>
> If I thought I could get back to China again in the next year or so, I'd quit immediately. But, you see, no matter who I work for I can't ever get back to China so long as the present government remains in power. I'm blacklisted—even if I weren't [there is] my book. . . . I decided when I began this book, that it would be dishonest for me to hold back anything I knew which was pertinent just to be able to go back to China again. So I'm cutting my own throat each day.
>
> It hurts like Hell. [China's] all I know, it's been the dominant interest in my life as far back as I can remember. What I've got to do now is to start out in life and build from the ground again. It's pretty hard.
>
> There are several prospects before me—one is to get a

job in New York, on a local paper, if I can, and become a reporter and work from the beginning up. . . . Another is to go out to the South Seas or India and report for someone else if I can get a job doing so. Let me give you the situation: New York is full of guys, ex–war correspondents, men out of uniform, ex-O.W.I. [Office of War Information] people, who all want to be foreign correspondents. There are dozens of people for every job. You may think that my reputation is fairly good stock in trade—actually, I'm just one more of the boys who had a ride during the War, and we all stand even at scratch now.

Now that he was thirty, and had been away so long, Teddy decided that he knew too little about his own country. He wanted to buy a car, the first he ever owned, and travel from coast to coast talking to people:

> If I decide to write about America, I may try to preserve my connections with Time Inc. This may sound like treason to you, perhaps it is; perhaps it is ordinary cowardice. . . . I think it is definite that I will never write about China for them again, nor will they use my name to cover their policy. . . .
>
> There are even other more complicated factors. I wouldn't mind going overseas free-lancing at my own profession of foreign correspondent if I were married. But my love affair with Annalee has blown up after several bitter months, and I am more alone now than ever I was before. I'd hate to rove around a new corner of the world by myself for three or four years, sleeping catch-as-catch-can with the babes I slept with during the past six years, knowing I have no home anywhere, nothing to come back to. . . .
>
> I'm trying desperately to write a good book. I think I am over-trying—everything I write sounds forced and uninteresting even to my own ears. People are fed to the gills with China. . . . I don't give a damn whether the book

is successful or not; I just want people to know what I think so that when I do start looking for a job, my opinions will be known, and I won't have to start by explaining I'm not a Communist, not a Luce-man, not a pen-prostitute. . . .

As you say, there is a real affection between myself and [Luce]. I can't attack Harry with the same bitterness that other people do, because, goddammit, I like him. I don't agree with his point of view. . . .

Well, the Hell with all that chest-beating. This letter is getting to be nauseating. You can see I stand in a mood of doubt and vacillation; I don't know what comes next; personally I'm depressed as hell. . . .

I think it was damned nice of you to write; you're one of the few people who've got the right to dress me down like that, and I guess I deserve it.

Fairbank responded with an apologetic letter trying to soften what he called his earlier "self-righteous blast":

. . . I must say you have done a hell of a lot more to educate the Americans about China than I have, in so much less time, and I don't know why I should toss epithets at you when I have not come into print myself and merely see a few friends from time to time, from the safe vantage point of a "permanent" tenure at [Harvard], and inveigh against the local bastards, who seem to grow hourly more numerous. . . . You should know by this time that you have more on the ball than the rest of the boys, and even if you shift jobs and have a hard year or two you will be able to come out ahead in any field you enter. This is not soap. . . . As for your moral character I am sure I need not worry about it, because you do and that will take care of it.

Teddy's dealings with Luce had become like a mating dance in reverse—the hesitations, the conflicting emotions, of a once-happy relationship coming to a melancholy end. One part of Teddy feared the prospect of being without a job and not on a payroll. Yet along with this was his stubborn insistence on honestly reporting what he saw, heard, and felt. In view of his insecurity, there was a special quality of bravery to this defiance. As Luce confided to one of his top editors with grudging admiration: "A very rugged character is Teddy."

THE REBELLION
OF THE
CORRESPONDENTS

Teddy White, the privileged maverick at the Luce court, was the first to suffer at the hands of the new court favorite, Whittaker Chambers. Teddy had been taken off the political story in China, advised to write about daffodils, finally ordered home. Now it was the turn of *Time*'s leading correspondents in Europe.

Like Teddy, these well-paid journalists understood that their role was different from that of a newspaperman sending dispatches intended to be published exactly as written. It was their job to supply raw material—interviews, color, judgments—for writers in New York to fuse into stories, merging them with details from *The New York Times* and with interpretations of the situation by knowledgeable specialists in Washington or academia, and lightening the mix with poetic wisdom from Yeats or jabberwocky from Lewis Carroll. The resulting story as it ran in the magazine might at times jar or irritate those correspondents, but until Whittaker Chambers became foreign editor, they were used to having their own reporting and judgment at least taken into account.

Precisely because he was a former Communist, Chambers was convinced that he knew the world better than the *Time* correspondents on the scene did; he knew what went on in the dark, and they did not. His path to success at *Time* was not the usual one: After his apprenticeship on the *Daily Worker* in the 1920s, he edited the Communist magazine *New Masses* before going underground to become a Soviet agent. He had been willing to stomach the duplicity of the Moscow purge trials, and much else, before breaking with the party a year before the Hitler-Soviet pact. His parting with Moscow left him not only in emotional turmoil but so broke that at one point his wife, opening her purse, pulled out less than fifty cents and said it was all the money they had.

A year later a friend, comparing Whit's literary talents with those of André Malraux, got Chambers a three-month trial as a reviewer at *Time*. He was then thirty-eight. This is the way Chambers struck T. S. Matthews, the editor who hired him: "I found him unprepossessing but impressive. . . . There was an air of suppressed melodrama about him. . . . He was short and stout, with a large head and a face whose coarse features were enlivened by the intelligence of the eyes and the sensitiveness of the mouth. His dark gray suit, white shirt, and black tie gave him a Quakerish, or perhaps lay brother, appearance. He spoke little, listened with an air of cynical understanding, and sucked a short pipe."

Chambers liked to say that Matthews had hired him because he "began a review of a war book with the line: 'One bomby day in June . . .'" Since Matthews appreciated any unexpected clever touches in writing, Chambers may have been right. Within short weeks Chambers had made his mark at *Time*.

Harry Luce first became aware of Chambers after Harry and his wife, Clare, saw the movie *Grapes of Wrath* and asked who had written *Time*'s review. Told that its author was Chambers, Luce said, "It's the best cinema review ever in *Time*." This extravagant judgment would be superseded a year later when *Time*'s movie reviews began to be written anonymously by James Agee, the best film critic *Time* ever had.

Soon Chambers was not only writing reviews but editing most of the cultural "back of the book" sections. He was a demonic editor, facile and fast; he often worked thirty-nine hours at a stretch, then catnapped on a sofa. Before long he suffered angina pains. He was advised to take it easier, but with a suspiciousness born of his long familiarity with Communist conspirators, he took this as evidence of a plot against him. To Luce he wrote:

> Reports of yesterday's editorial lunch and the attempted putsch there may have reached you. Please do not give credence to the representations that will undoubtedly be made now or later about the state of my health under the "terrible overload" of [editing] 10 or 12 depts. Only your command, sudden death, or a complete editorial flop would make me want to relinquish *any part* of my present responsibility. . . . Please believe that my stubbornness has nothing to do with personal ambition. As I came through Penn Station this morning, I saw the young men lined up on the platforms by hundreds on their way to the army; and at the stair-heads the weeping women trying and failing to look brave. And I will not give up this fight (which is a reflection of their fight) without a fight.

Tom Matthews had only two reservations about the star he had discovered. One was his arrogance. Whit resented even minor editing and would send Matthews "an eloquently despairing note (often quoting Dante, Milton, or some German poet— usually in the original) to the general effect that his story was now . . . completely senseless and not worth publishing. . . . In these and other ways he made it known that he did not feel himself among his intellectual superiors or even equals."

Tom's other reservation was that "on any subject that touched on Russia or Communism he was so biased that he could not be trusted to write fairly." Matthews's solution to this strange "quirk" in Chambers was to keep him from reviewing any such books.

But when Chambers was at last made foreign editor of the

magazine he was ideally placed to indulge his obsession. Harry Luce had found someone as fiercely anti-Communist as himself.

In reply to Luce's "Post War Memo No. 1" to his top editors, asking them what job they would like to have, Chambers wrote that editing foreign news was his first, second, and third choice. He had "spent some 15 years of my life actively preparing for" it and, in an odd reference to his Communist days, noted that some of these were "years spent close to the central dynamo that powers the politics of our time." And so, Chambers concluded, "in dealing with international affairs, I feel like a man in a dark but familiar room: I may bump against the furniture, but I'm usually sure where the door and windows are."

In the corridors of *Time,* where he was seldom seen, Whit was regarded by many on the staff as mysterious, and possibly sinister, brilliant but unbalanced. He darted from the elevator to his office and then locked the door, as if afraid for his life (as he in fact was). *Time* was an open-door kind of place, and at midday some writer would emerge from his warren and bang on neighboring open doors, saying "Who's for lunch?" Then, in groups of three or four or five, they would head for Toots Shor's or Lindy's, or some side-street French bistro. Two among them, admiring Whit's work, separately sought out his company but were informed by him that he was too busy or wasn't hungry. Duncan Norton-Taylor persisted, however, and when Whit finally accepted, he gave Dunc a look that seemed to say, "So you're the Judas who is going to betray me." Dunc followed Chambers out of the building to the nearest subway. The two rode downtown two stops, got off and crossed over to the uptown side, rode one stop back up to Times Square, and then went to the big Automat on Broadway, where Chambers took a seat in the rear so that, in gangster style, he could keep an eye on all entrances. The lunch went well. Dunc Taylor was the most conservative writer in the National Affairs section, which I then edited; he would later become managing editor of *Fortune,* a close friend of Whit's, and the compiler and editor of Whit's papers, published after his death as *Cold Friday.*

Sam Welles, the bulky son of an Episcopalian minister, had a similar experience with Whit. He and Chambers rode the subway to Thirty-fourth Street, entered Macy's and made their way down its block-long ground floor to an escalator at the other end, rode to the second floor, walked back its full length, then strode over to Fifth Avenue, where, at the corner Longchamps restaurant in the Empire State Building, Chambers said, "Okay. Let's eat here." Having decided to trust Welles (who was one of his writers), Whit showed him the pistol he carried in an inside holster and explained the rigmarole he had put Welles through. The secret was never to trust someone else's timing or direction; an enemy often chose a restaurant where, with the help of an accomplice, a person's food could be poisoned.

Usually I saw Whit only at the weekly half-hour conferences where we senior editors met to agree on who should be on the cover of that week's issue—a political figure? an actress? an athlete?—and to choose candidates to be painted for future covers. Rarely saying much, Whit sat in the rear, puffing on his stubby pipe, spilling ashes on his shirt and rumpled suit. But I was not surprised later to read Whit's judgment on his colleagues: "They seemed to know little about the forces that were shaping the history of our time. They seemed like little children, knowing and clever little children, but knowing and clever chiefly about trifling things."

Chambers was a man of predictable judgments and calculatedly unpredictable behavior. Whenever his work kept him from getting back to his three-hundred-acre farm in Maryland, Whit moved to a different inexpensive hotel each night of his stay in the city. This was protection against the unseen enemy without, but he also felt threatened in a different way by those he worked with. "My assignment sent a shiver through most of *Time*'s staff, where my views were well known and detested with a ferocity that I did not believe possible until I was at grips with it." Believing his *Time* colleagues to be leagued against him, he divided the writers, researchers, and editors on the staff into two categories: knaves (serving the Communist enemy) and fools (I think he charitably considered me only a fool). Yet he did have his intensely loyal supporters, one of whom was Henry Grunwald. Henry had come to the United States from Austria in his teens, had finished college, and, while working as an office boy at *Time*, began submitting his writings to Chambers; eventually he was made managing editor of *Time* and some years after Luce's death became head of all editorial operations in Time Inc.

After Chambers became foreign editor, the politically liberal writers in the department got themselves transferred elsewhere as soon as they could. Apolitical writers on his staff also had to be anxious over how long their jobs would last, since hardly a paragraph they wrote would appear in print as they wrote it. Chambers's stamina in rewriting so much in so little time was impressive. Stories that writers had based on files from *Time* correspondents or from material they took from the daily newspapers Whit arrogantly dismissed, for he had his own private cache of material to draw from. Much of it came from fanatic right-wing magazines full of reports of Communist intrigue, some of them true, some false, and most unverifiable. Though much else was happening in the last days of World War II, *Time*'s Foreign News section under Chambers focused relentlessly on the Communist menace in country after country, in what John Hersey, *Time*'s Moscow correspondent, angrily called a "monotony of paranoia."

Hersey himself was about to become, like Teddy White, a casualty of Chambers's reign.

■ ■ ■

As a mishkid from China, John Hersey was not simply modeling himself after Luce in going first to Hotchkiss, then on to Yale. Though not a religious school, Hotchkiss had a tradition of giving scholarships to mishkids. "When I first went to work for [Luce] at *Time,* he seemed a walking wonder of possibilities to a mishkid like me. . . . He was a mishkid who had made good in a big way. He was exciting to be around."

Luce was equally enamored of Hersey and soon came to regard him as the man to succeed him when he stepped down. He told Hersey: "There's something you'll like about us—this is a young man's place." Luce assured Hersey that he intended to retire at forty; but as Luce neared forty, Hersey recalled wryly, the deadline became forty-five. (Luce was sixty-six when he finally retired; he had less than three more years to live.)

Even without Luce's sponsorship the talented Hersey would have done well. After working as a writer and an editor at *Time* and *Life,* he found his true vocation as a correspondent. He covered battles in the South Pacific, North Africa, and Italy, and from these experiences flowed a succession of books, one of which, *A Bell for Adano,* became a best-seller and a Broadway hit play and won Hersey a Pulitzer Prize. Harry, who took pride in Hersey's successes, once showed him without comment a leatherbound copy of one of his books. On the cover, along with the book's title and Hersey's name, was imprinted the message that it had been written "On Harry's Time." As a Christmas present to Harry, his wife had assembled all the books written that year by Time Inc. authors and had had them bound in leather. This would have been a charming present to give the rich man who has everything had Clare been content to leave it at that. (Clare's nasty little dig wasn't even accurate: most of the books had been written after-hours, or on leave of absence.)

As World War II drew to an end and Harry began to make postwar plans for his magazines, he invited Hersey to "come home" to be a senior editor of *Time,* as a step toward taking over the most important editorial job on any of Luce's magazines, that of managing editor. Hersey weighed the offer for weeks. He had long debated whether he should focus his career on writing or editing and had concluded that he would always be a better writer than editor. He cabled Luce from Moscow in the middle of November 1944: "My interests are primarily humanistic rather than political, I am inclined to be more emotional and less tough than a good editor must be, I have insufficient patience with detailed administrative work." And there was one other consideration: "I will never be a Fascist or a Communist but I was last year, and I most certainly am after this experience [the Moscow assignment] confirmed in being politically a democrat, both with and without a capital D. Knowing and admiring the sincerity of your beliefs as a Republican, I am afraid that my stubborn conviction would not help me or *Time* if I were to become an editor."

He concluded, "With considerable regret and not without misgivings, I am afraid that I must decline," while expressing "gratitude for all that *Time* has done for and meant to me and with much personal affection for you as Editor and as a man."

Luce's reply to Hersey's decision was cabled to him at the Hotel Metropole, Moscow:

Delighted to have you carry on according to your present plans and inclinations. *Time* loses a potentially fine editor but Time Inc. keeps a first-class writer and an esteemed associate. . . . As to being a democrat with a capital "D" my only suggestion is that you get a little better acquainted with the joint before becoming a life member. In any case Time Inc. will remain staunchly independent, reserving the right to be fiercely intolerant on just one political subject, namely, the maintenance and promotion of political freedom in America. The years ahead will not be easy. They will be happier for me if we can work together. All regards, Harry Luce

Despite the cordiality of this exchange, Hersey later said, "I don't think Harry was much interested in me after that." Yet, years after they parted, Hersey would say, "I liked him a lot. It was a quasi-parental relationship."

Hersey was now forty years old, tall, lean, and physically fit, with the long neck, trim frame, and easy gait of a first baseman. In temperament he was quite different from Teddy White, being reserved and serious, lacking Teddy's wisecracking wit and amiable adaptability.

In wartime Moscow, Hersey was where he wanted to be, doing the job he wanted to do, but he was increasingly unhappy about what was happening to his work. He was not the only one. All of *Time* magazine's top correspondents in Europe—Charles Wertenbaker in Paris and John Osborne in Rome (both of whom had been foreign editors of *Time* before Chambers), Walter Graebner in London, and Hersey in Moscow—were dismayed by Whittaker Chambers's heavy-handed editing.

Other Luce employees were also troubled. Filmore Calhoun, the cable editor of *Life,* wrote a furious memo he described as "sounding off (thus avoiding ulcers)," objecting to one alarmist story in *Time* that

> bears the mark of a slick writer . . . one who even now says that he has a farm hidden away as a refuge for the day of revolution when I suppose Communist agents take over the U.S. and immediately concentrate on finding and liquidating him. Balls! What's happened to our guts? Are we all frightened to death? I live in a country that is 3,000 miles wide and 1,000 miles deep. It has 130,000,000 people with more ability, imagination and accomplishments than any other in the world. . . . We too can frighten the hell out of everyone if we want to. Certainly there is a leftist trend in the world, but not all of it is inspired by conspirators and bogeymen.

Hell, I read the incoming cables and week after week I am amazed to see how they are either misinterpreted, left unprinted or weaseled around to one man's way of thinking. I like Whit and I admire his slickness, but I wouldn't trust him with any set of facts concerning Russia. . . . The people of this country are told to hide under the bed with such stories as this.

Fill Calhoun sent his memo to Allen Grover, one of Luce's deputies, who was often the go-between and sometimes the mediator in Luce's dealings with foreign correspondents. Grover, who came from a socialite background in St. Louis and had gone to Yale, like Luce, was a gracious and tactful fellow who was on occasion called in by Luce to mend relationships with people who had been offended by Harry's or Clare's imperious rudeness. Interviewed by me when he was ninety, Grover said that Luce "had attractive qualities but was very willful. I know lots of Harry's faults. I never idolized him, never regarded him as a great man. Luce was no hero of mine. In a way, Teddy was."

Looking back on the period when the foreign correspondents rebelled against Whit Chambers, Grover recalled: "There was a real danger of an explosion, breaking up the staff." And so Grover, in sending on Fill Calhoun's outburst to Luce, added his own endorsement: "If Whit Chambers continues to ignore the guidance, opinions, and information from our good foreign news men, we could save a lot of money by replacing them with a few good bird dogs à la the Washington bureau. I'm not saying what I think would happen to the magazine if we did."

Luce impatiently circled Grover's comments and sent them back to him, after scribbling at the bottom: "Yes, yes, of course I know all this. But what is needed is not just reiteration of the point but *constructive* action based on painstaking analysis."

■ ■ ■

After so many of his top correspondents protested to Luce, he ordered his editorial director, John Shaw Billings, to look into their complaints. Having read Billings's report of the staff friction, Luce tried to come down on one side while placating the other. He used one of his favorite devices, an enigmatic memo addressed both to the protesting correspondents and to Chambers.

> In my opinion the correspondents did a fine job. . . . It is also my opinion that the Foreign News Department under Chambers did a fine job. How can these two opinions be held in view of very strong complaints by the Senior Correspondents . . . ? In general . . . the Senior Correspondents wished to convey the information that the rulers of the world, each in their respective capitals, are well-meaning people who are trying to do their best for their own countries and the world. In general . . . the Foreign News Department wished to convey the information that . . . things are not going very well. The posture of events in January 1945 seems to have confirmed Editor Chambers about as fully as a news editor is ever confirmed.

As proof, Luce cited the Soviet occupation of Eastern Europe and Communist gains in China "aided by a world-wide leftist attack on the Chinese government." True, Chambers had

> given a disproportionate amount of space and emphasis to the problem of Russia. Over-emphasis may rightly be criticized but there were good reasons for erring in this direction. . . .
>
> Chambers has to some degree failed to distinguish between, on the one hand, the general revolutionary, leftist, or simply chaotic trends, and on the other hand, the specifically Communist politics in various countries. Chambers fully agrees that this distinction should be sharply made and if this distinction is sharply made, that in itself will, I

think, go far to bring [Foreign News] and the Correspondents in line.

Having made his choice, Luce tried to soften it with some heavy humor:

> I have just been told, in a highly confidential manner, that Stalin is, after all, a Communist. I am also somewhat less confidentially informed that the Pope is a Christian. Some will say: "What does it matter . . . and what does it matter that Hersey advises me that he, John Hersey, is a Democrat?" . . . A good Foreign News Editor, while guarding against the prejudices arising from his own convictions, will not ignore the circumstance that the Pope is a Christian and Stalin a Communist and Hersey, God bless him, a Democrat.

"Cryptic stuff" was Hersey's reaction years later.

At Time Incorporated, where much time was spent mining staff memos for hidden meanings, memos written by Luce were indeed a particularly rich field to quarry. (It was well understood, for example, that the person who got the most fulsome praise and most space in any memo about staff changes was the one being shafted, or at least thrust aside; the winner needed no added recognition.) In the memo about the correspondents' rebellion, Chambers, though cautioned by Luce to guard against "prejudices arising from his own convictions," was judged to be the winner. The victory came to seem less clear-cut, though, when Luce created a new section in *Time* magazine called International, to run parallel to Foreign News, and to be edited by one of the protesters, John Osborne. Readers may have been baffled by two sections seeming to cover the same territory, but the International section enabled correspondents to get stories into the magazine without being subjected to Chambers's whims and biases.

Whit, confined to the Foreign News section, proved that he

didn't need the correspondents, or even a news story, to advance his views. The Yalta conference, in which Roosevelt, Stalin, and Churchill had presumably settled the postwar shape of the world, was just ending. Chambers assumed it would be followed by a blah-blah-blah communiqué heralding a new era in international understanding. Rather than report this, Chambers produced a story of his own. He writes in his autobiography, "I closed my office door for a day and wrote a political phantasy which I put in the mouths of the Muse of History and the ghosts of the late Tsar Nicholas and the Tsarina."

When it was published, the essay, called "Ghosts on the Roof," quickly became notorious. It was illustrated by a touching picture of members of the Russian royal family sunning themselves on a palace roof shortly before the tsar, his wife, and their five children were murdered by Communists, each with a bullet through the forehead, and their bodies were thrown down a mineshaft in Ekaterinburg. In Chambers's satire, the tsar assures Clio, the muse of history, that he has now become a Marxist, because "Stalin has made Russia great again" with victories the tsars could never have achieved, overrunning Latvia, Lithuania, and Estonia, conquering Romania, Bulgaria, Yugoslavia, Hungary, and Poland, and establishing party comrades high in the governments of Italy and France. Soon, the tsar adds, "they will control most of Germany. They already control a vast region of China." Clio disputes the tsar's argument because "all right-thinking people now agree that Russia is now a mighty friend of democracy."

Chambers left his fable on T. S. Matthews's desk, saying he didn't think it something for *Time* to publish, but Matthews might like to read it. Matthews later wrote: "I took it to Henry Luce for his opinion; his eyebrows went up. He admitted that it was a forceful piece of journalism and asked me what I intended to do with it. I said I thought of running it in *Time*. The eyebrows went up again; Luce washed his hands of the affair."

But word of "Ghosts on the Roof" had got around the office, and unofficial delegations of staff members urged Matthews not to print the piece. After all, the war against the Nazis was not yet won; only two months earlier German armies had broken through American lines in the Battle of the Bulge. The Western Allies acknowledged that their own victories had been made possible by the fact that the Russians had earlier borne the brunt of German might, had lived through the dreadful siege of Leningrad, had fought in the largest battles known to man. Now, at Yalta, the Allies had gathered to see whether they could work together in peace. Staff members, protesting Whit's fable, warned Matthews that "it would drive a wedge between the Allies, it was biased and bitter, irresponsible journalism, et cetera." Matthews commented later: "I was sufficiently shaken to postpone publication for a week. Then I sent it to press."

Chambers's own account, characteristically, is more melodramatic: "Feeling ran so high against it, the general malevolence swelled into my office so fiercely, that again I closed my door, this time to edit in a semblance of peace. One of the writers who dropped in described the hubbub outside my closed door . . . as 'like the night of a lynching bee.' "

Readers, too, in great numbers, wrote in angrily. They accused *Time* of trying to sabotage the hope of a peaceful new world. Three years later, in 1948, as the Cold War got colder and Russian troops put down a revolt in Czechoslovakia, *Time* reprinted "Ghosts on the Roof," preening itself on its prescience, but not reminding readers that the story had originally been published at a time when the Allies were still fighting side by side for a victory not yet won.

There is another point to be made about prescience. In *Witness,* his autobiography, Chambers writes: "To get the piece into print, I had to make a common journalistic compromise. I agreed to lop off the end, which described the Soviet Union and the U.S. as two jet planes whose political destiny could be filled only when one destroyed the other." Thus the intended but unpublished moral of "Ghosts on the Roof" was that one nation had to destroy the other; destiny had decreed it. This fanatic attitude would in the years to come spur the United States into needless and costly adventures abroad and would divide America itself in the name of patriotism. Fortunately, the muse of history did not blindly follow that course; fortunately, Chambers's gift of prophecy, so admired by some, in the end proved fallible. A peaceful standoff could be achieved, and was, without one nation's destroying the other.

In Moscow, the publication of "Ghosts on the Roof," Hersey writes, "hit me hard." He had worked for weeks setting up high-level appointments with Soviet leaders, never easy to do in wartime, particularly with sources so wary and secretive. The day that "Ghosts on the Roof" was published in New York, and even before copies of the magazine reached Hersey in Russia, he "got ten phone calls canceling all the appointments—the minister would have to be in Leningrad that day, etc."

Earlier he had cabled Tom Matthews, "In all honor I must report to you that I do not like the tone of many Foreign News stories. I need not itemize. You know what I mean. . . . For this week, and until I cool off, I shall abstain from corresponding with Foreign News."

At one point, Hersey complained, of 11,000 words he had filed from Moscow, Chambers had used, by actual count, 168. Until his tour of duty ended several months later, Hersey concentrated on doing apolitical "back of the book" assignments, found pleasure in reporting on Soviet composers such as Sergei Prokofiev, Dmitri Shostakovich, and Aram Khachaturian, but cabled his editor, "I'm just an extravagance. Why not send me home?"

When he returned to the States, Hersey had a long talk with Luce, his onetime mishkid hero. He then decided to quit his job.

■　■　■

Within six months of the publication of "Ghosts on the Roof" Whittaker Chambers's tempestuous rule as foreign editor of *Time* came to an end. He had persisted in his relentless pace: "Sometimes I found myself writing, or rewriting, a fourth or a third of the Foreign News section. . . . A working day without sleep became my standard practice. . . . One morning coming to work [after a weekend on his Maryland farm] I blanked out on the train. I was unwise enough to speak about it and ask for a week's rest. It was granted and I never went back to editing Foreign News."

It took a while for Whit, always given to mistrust and suspicion, to be persuaded that Matthews was not trying to ease him out of Foreign News but was genuinely concerned about his health. Chambers was given a raise and assigned thereafter to less stressful projects, including writing cover stories, some of them distinguished, about Albert Einstein, Arnold Toynbee, Reinhold Niebuhr, and other intellectuals. He looked back on his days at Foreign News not in triumph but grimly and with a touch of self-pity: "No other editor at *Time* would have stood for a week the insubordination, hostility and insulting behavior to which certain members of my staff treated me."

When three years later Whittaker Chambers became a household name in America, widely admired and widely reviled, his colleagues at *Time* would learn much they hadn't known about why he had behaved so oddly. At the time, though I was strongly opposed to all he stood for, I was aware that men I respected—including T. S. Matthews and Duncan Norton-Taylor—respected him, and later knowledge gave me some sympathy for this complex and tormented man. But I thought then and think now that in his role as a journalist he was a well-poisoner. There is an old Texas prayer that goes: "Dear God, let me seek the Truth, but spare me the company of those who have found it."

A QUESTION OF LOYALTY

During the winter of 1946, while writing *Thunder Out of China* on his leave of absence, Teddy ran into Luce socially several times in New York and, with his old cockiness, needled his boss relentlessly about *Time* magazine's coverage. He did so believing Luce to be "smothered by sycophants" who lacked White's honesty and gall. The fact is that many of those surrounding Luce had as much independence of mind as Teddy; story by story they had to voice their feelings or let Luce simply dominate them. What they lacked was Teddy's privileged status at Luce's court. They fought a number of skirmishes and won some of them, but in winning they sometimes agonized over whether they were only making Luce's transgressions more palatable to the reader.

When Teddy and Annalee Jacoby finished *Thunder Out of China,* Teddy sent the manuscript to Luce, "not for censorship, but for courtesy's sake." This was Teddy's way of reminding Luce that the book was written on his own time and he felt answerable to no one. But how could Teddy have believed, as he said he did, that in writing what he thought of as "the story of the inevitable collapse of Chiang Kai-shek," he would cause Luce to recognize "the justice of his rebellion" and perhaps even be converted to his thesis?

■ ■ ■

Shortly after the war in Europe ended, and while the Pacific war still continued, Luce got his chance to see China for the first time since Pearl Harbor. Luce had been frustrated all during the war by his inability to get to Asia, a situation that he correctly blamed on Franklin D. Roosevelt, whose dislike of Luce was as strong as Luce's dislike of him.* F.D.R. had banned all travel to combat zones by editors, publishers, and news executives— though the correspondents and photographers who worked for them could travel freely and do their jobs. Luce was convinced that the restrictions were directed straight at him and at Colonel Robert R. McCormick, the vituperatively isolationist publisher of the *Chicago Tribune.* To get around the ban, Luce appealed to General George Marshall; he thought Marshall evasive and embarrassed when he explained that no plane transport was available to take him to Asia. Finally Luce took his case to Roosevelt himself, who turned him down.

When Roosevelt died in April 1945, the ban was re-scinded, and in the last months of the war Luce was able to visit the Pacific fleet. (In Guam he asked the whereabouts of the destroyer escort *McGinty*; told that it was anchored in the harbor, Luce got in a five-minute visit with his son, Ensign Henry Luce III.)

In October, after V-J Day, Luce finally returned to Chung-king, at Chiang Kai-shek's personal invitation. Chiang was then in tense negotiations with the Communists, and Luce was able to meet and have a few words with Mao, who "was surprised to see me there and gazed at me with an intense but not unfriendly curiosity." Actually there was little exchange at all. Luce could get only what he described as "polite grunts" from Mao (it takes a grunter to recognize another one). The chairman, Luce noted,

*Long after Roosevelt's death, Luce confessed: "I sometimes pray, 'Forgive me my sins as I forgive that son of a bitch his.' "

was dressed in sloppy blue denims, and "his face is heavier and more peasant-like" than the faces of the neatly dressed generals who were standing around the Generalissimo.

Luce's meeting with Chou En-lai was more memorable. Like everyone else, from Teddy White to Henry Kissinger, Luce came away impressed with Chou: "We had a nice talk," Luce wrote, though it did not start out that way. Their conversation was "completely frank from the moment we sat down. He said we hadn't been very nice to him lately. I said that was too bad because we had a worldwide battle on our hands with worldwide left-wing propaganda—and it was just as nasty as skunk."

After this sharp exchange, Luce told Chou that he longed to visit his boyhood province of Shantung, now in Communist hands. This was the nice part of the talk for Harry. Chou made it possible for him to get to Tsingtao, the German resort town on the North China coast where as a child Luce had spent his summers. To Harry it was "the most beautiful of all places on this earth, where the mountains come down to the sea. Kaiser Wilhelm II called it the fairest jewel in his crown. It was the last grab of European imperialism in Asia. All I wanted was to swim on the beaches of the bay. And I did."

On a second visit to China six months later, Luce saw Chou again. In the memoirs that Harry started late in life but never finished, he described a meeting as memorable as their first one: "I must record the utter confidence as well as the good humor with which Chou En-lai spoke to me. While he didn't say so in so many words, I had the chilling feeling that he expected soon to be in control of all China. At the end of my stay [in China in 1946] I figured he was right."

If Luce really expected all of China to be in Communist hands "soon" (as it would be in three years), he never confided this belief to the readers of *Time*. Luce the advocate continued to champion Chiang's cause, while Luce the realist in his private thoughts was more pessimistic. It was this pragmatic side of Luce that Teddy White had constantly appealed to, with some success until Whittaker Chambers became foreign editor of *Time*.

His leave of absence over, Teddy reported back to work, happy to be with colleagues again after six months of lonely writing. He was after all, he decided, a "born organization man, most comfortable when he had a place in a collective body that would pay him regularly and fairly."

While waiting to be posted abroad again as correspondent, Teddy took on some minor assignments for *Life*, but these did not satisfy him. Impatient about his future, he went to see Charles Christian Wertenbaker, who had become chief of correspondents. A husky, flamboyant war reporter, Wertenbaker had been one of the European correspondents who had protested Chambers's editing. A man of impressive Virginia lineage, and glamorous in a way that Teddy was not, Wertenbaker once posed for a Man of Distinction whiskey ad dressed in a tweed jacket with leather elbow patches in the manner of his hero, Ernest Hemingway. Now, in 1946, with the world at peace, Wert asked Teddy whether he would like to be the Moscow bureau chief. Indeed Teddy would. Neither of them anticipated any objections from Luce.

Teddy thought his relations with Luce still in good order, as indicated by a note he had just received from Luce. Teddy had written him that having so long objected to *Time*'s failure to report the truth about China, he wanted to praise a tough-minded story in *Time* filed by Teddy's successor, William P. Gray, that was critical of Chiang's entourage. Luce replied: "I am, of course, deeply sorry that the Government chaps haven't done better but, at least, says I to myself, Teddy will see that there is no Government which *Time* will fail to kick in the pants when truth and the public weal require. And I know that you and I both wish that we could help China by other means than kicking. It's a sad world."

Less than two weeks after getting this friendly letter from Luce, Teddy was distressed to learn from Wert that the assignment to Moscow was "a matter of debate" in Luce's mind. Teddy thereupon wrote a "rather difficult letter" to Luce, wondering if "you are not quite sure whether I am the person to be sent."

What was the problem? If, Teddy suggested, the question was whether his reporting could no longer be trusted, "then there is no place for me in the organization." If instead Luce believed that Teddy should remain "in the U.S.A. for four or five months to re-acquaint myself with America, I readily agree with you." But the real crux in Luce's mind, Teddy suspected, was Teddy's attitude toward the Soviet Union:

> I shall be frank to say that Russia is a matter of personal importance to me. . . . I need hardly tell you that I have never been a Russian partisan—if you have time to read my manuscript on your vacation I think you will see that; on the other hand I am frank to admit that I am willing to take a more friendly attitude to Russia than the columns of Time, the Weekly Newsmagazine. When it comes to Russia I am swept by great doubts and confusion. My friends—people of the same political beliefs as I—come back either violent sympathizers or twisted enemies. For me it is of cardinal concern to see Moscow first hand; the question of peace or war lies somewhere in the Kremlin. . . . I think the Russian assignment calls for a person of huge curiosity, great energy and an open mind. I am arrogant enough to think that the Moscow assignment is right down my alley; if it is possible to have it I want it very much.

But Teddy's attitude toward the Soviet Union was not what was uppermost in Luce's hesitation. Or at least, it was not the reason Luce gave him that June, when the two sat down to an unforgettably cold confrontation.

■   ■   ■

Harry Luce had long played Teddy White the way a fly fisherman plays a fish whose strength and fighting qualities he respects. Once that fish takes the hook, it begins to thrash about, seeking to break free. The skilled fisherman lets out more line, giving the fish more freedom, and then, as the fish begins to tire, starts to reel it in; if he does so too quickly, while the fish still has fight in him, the line may snap and the fish get away. So the fisherman lets out more line, and pulls it in more slowly, calculating his response by how much resistance he is meeting. Through the years Luce had alternated between giving Teddy plenty of freedom and reining him in. This time Luce was willing to let the line snap and Teddy get away.

The two met in Luce's sunny two-story-high office atop the old Time and Life Building in Rockefeller Center, with its commanding view of midtown Manhattan's skyline—most of the surrounding buildings, like the Time and Life Building itself, being assertive steel-and-granite symbols of corporate ego that reinforced the sense of power of those who had put them up.

Luce was in an angry mood. "The session was highly emotional," Teddy would later write, "a cross-conflict of paternal and professional relations, more personal than political. . . . [Luce] felt that all too many of his bright young men had used *Time* as a personal mount, had galloped to fame on the magazine's back. Young John Hersey, for one. He was breaking with Hersey; it was unclear from Luce's words whether he had fired Hersey or Hersey had quit." There had been harsh words; Hersey, returning from his frustrating experience in the Soviet Union, "had told Luce to his face that there was as much truthful reporting in *Pravda* as in *Time* magazine."

Almost alone among Luce's associates, Hersey and Teddy had broken through the barrier of Luce's reserve, his awkwardness in human relations, his deliberate distancing of himself from the staff. Despite the *Pravda* remark cited by Teddy, Hersey would say years later, "I didn't openly quarrel with him. I simply left," not even trying to negotiate severance pay. If this version is correct, Hersey thereby became a freelancer, free to take assignments from any editor. He went to China on a story for *Life,* and on his way home, at the request of *The New Yorker,* reported the aftermath of Hiroshima. William Shawn, *The New Yorker*'s editor, had proposed a technical report on the damage done by the atom bomb. On the scene, Hersey decided that the human story of the survivors was more interesting, and so he wrote it. Shawn thought so highly of it that he devoted an unprecedented entire issue of the magazine to the story.

Luce was angered by *The New Yorker*'s widely praised scoop, and rejected a seventeen-page *Life* layout on the Yangtze River, beautifully photographed by Dmitri Kessel, because it would have been accompanied by an article that Hersey was to write.

Now, describing in the third person his own confrontation with Luce in his memoirs, Teddy pictured Luce's mood: "Luce summarized, his eyes glowering under the dark brows: White and Hersey were ingrates! Therefore, said Luce, he now had a yes-or-no question for White. He himself was going off on vacation; White could reflect on his answer, but Luce wanted the answer as soon as he came back. Now his voice lacked any affection; it was the voice of the organization, examining an eccentric cog which no longer fit into the machinery. Luce asked: Would the reporter accept, or would he not, any assignment Luce chose to give him in the future—even if it meant drudgery in the ranks, even if it meant serving on the rewrite desk in New York for a year or two? In short: Did White *belong* to *Time* magazine, or was he using *Time* only to advance his personal interests?"

Teddy "flailed wildly," as he put it, objecting to Luce's terms: he was a trained foreign correspondent; he was an outdoor reporter; he could not possibly be useful except as a man in the field; he had already proven his loyalty to *Time* by risking his life in action. Luce was unmoved; he wanted an answer to his question.

Luce left his own account of the seventy-five-minute session in a "strictly confidential" memo he wrote next day to Charles Wertenbaker:

> Teddy has, as he says, a great affection and respect for *Time.* So his general loyalty to *Time* is in no sense in question. Still, the question I raised was and is *the* relevant question in his case—and Teddy answered it, in its various phases, with an honesty for which I like and respect him. At one point, pursuing the question, I said to him: "Are you willing to take any job I assign to you from copy boy to Managing Editor?" His answer: "No."
>
> . . . A very rugged character is Teddy. That's fine. I admire individuality. Indeed I made a speech the other night urging that Americans, as the supposed champions of individual rights, had perhaps ought to display a little more individuality than they appear to be doing in this mass-production age. So anybody who says "By God I'm going to write my own ticket"—I've got nothing against him on that score.
>
> But I have also got an individuality to take care of. By which, in this context, I do not mean one sometimes labeled H.R.L. [the initials Henry Robinson Luce usually scrawled on his memos]. I mean one called *Time, the Weekly Newsmagazine* and another called *Fortune*—and two or three others. These might be called "collective individualities."
>
> . . . *Time* can use the services of a number of people who are not so devoted to *Time.* But the life-blood of *Time* depends on people who are. . . .
>
> And why am I saying all this? Because the issue comes up not only in connection with White but more generally

with Foreign Correspondents. Time Inc. is developing a Foreign News service—and damn proud we are of it and of all that has led up to it. It provides opportunities for fine careers in journalism—and proud we are of that. And we'd like everybody in it to be as happy as larks—to whistle as they work or whatever. But I shall be saying nothing which any parent doesn't know when I say that there'll be no happiness in this family without elements of both devotion and discipline.

. . . we must resist the tendency to think of Time Inc. as a plum pudding from which everyone is concerned only to extract the plums of his choice. All of which implies no criticism of White. While I regret that he feels unable, for technical as well as other reasons, to sign on for general service to Time Inc., he is probably doing the right thing for himself.

Luce had told Teddy that when he had considered Luce's question, he should take his answer to Wertenbaker, who would be empowered to negotiate, based on how Teddy responded. But, as Luce wrote to Wertenbaker, "I have, instead, come to the conclusion that the bases of a satisfactory deal do not exist."

This Teddy did not know. He thought the choice was still his to make, and he agonized for a week. In his autobiography, Teddy writes:

Thus, on Friday, July 12, 1946, with Luce himself away on vacation, [Teddy] gave his answer precisely at noon to one of Luce's deputies. No. He could not continue on Luce's terms, he would not accept any assignment unless it was agreed on in advance. Luce's deputy listened and replied that Harry had expected that answer and left word that if the answer was as expected, the reply must be that Luce felt White had no place in the organization—as of now, and for as long as White persisted in his obstinacy. Although, so ran the reply, at some future time, when they saw the world alike again, Luce would be glad to consider White's return.

Obviously, Wertenbaker had spared White the painful knowledge that Luce had later hardened his decision, so that it didn't matter how Teddy had answered the question. Luce's one-page "Dear Teddy" letter announcing his decision was cold and direct, its blunt message not much softened by its final paragraph:

> . . . After thinking the matter over very carefully, I have decided not to enter into negotiations with you as to a post in Time-Life International's foreign service. I have reluctantly come to the conclusion that you will be more likely to find the kind of career you have envisioned for yourself outside of Time Inc.
>
> Your association with Time Inc. in years past has, as we both know, meant a great deal to both of us. And nothing that happens in the future should ever mar the meaning of the past. On the contrary, I hope that our personal friendship—and our mutuality of purpose—will grow over the years. And for the near future you have all my best wishes for a successful and satisfying career.

That final paragraph of best-wishes-for-the-future sounds like the conventional corporate boilerplate used when a once-valued executive is fired. But Luce, as he would prove, really meant the hope he expressed for a continuing friendship.

Luce had always been terrible at firing people. In the very beginning, back in 1923, when he and Brit Haddon, both fresh out of Yale, were amateurishly launching *Time,* Luce wanted to fire his secretary but had to ask someone else in the office to do it. This man who became a generous and considerate boss, this unrivaled inventor of successful magazines and careful guardian of their fortunes, this employer who sought out unconventional talent and rewarded it with opportunities, this Christian who was as demanding of himself as he was of others and who sank to his knees each night in prayer, was often clumsy in his personal relationships. Even the colleagues who admired him were never entirely comfortable in his presence.

They might sense that something was disturbing him, but he was never good at articulating what it was. They might even know the subject that was preoccupying him, but not what aspects of it were worrying him. At such moments he kept his own counsel and didn't welcome intrusions. Before reaching a painful decision, he had to depersonalize it, to make the case on some higher ground than his own displeasure, even to see it as something that required a sacrifice on his part. In the case of Teddy White, he saw Teddy's longing for "individuality" not as a threat to himself (H.R.L.) but as a threat to "the collective individualities" of his magazines. The phrase was an awkward one, but in using it Luce transferred the issue to a higher, institutional level—the preservation of his magazines, even if that required of him the sacrifice of a talented friend. Once he had worried a problem to the point of solution and convinced himself that he was doing the right thing, he acted swiftly and ruthlessly. All within two weeks, he had written a friendly note to Teddy, subjected him to a severe test, and then cast him off without waiting for his answer.

Teddy, having bravely given his no to Wertenbaker, and "not knowing whether he had quit or been fired, . . . went to lunch with [the photographer] Carl Mydans, one of his dearest friends; and together the two gloomily considered his future. . . . Carl, having seen so many departures from *Time,* had advised making a clean break: when one is fired, get out as fast as possible, don't let them be sorry for you, don't linger, don't mourn. So White went back to his office to clean out files, memos, papers, and decided he would write his letters of farewell to office companions from home."

Then he got a telephone call from his book publisher. The judges of the Book-of-the-Month Club, meeting at lunch, had just chosen *Thunder Out of China* as a main selection. What would that mean? Teddy asked. That he and Annalee would split at least eighty thousand dollars. Teddy was then making ten thousand dollars a year, in those days a princely salary.

"He had been desperate before lunch, abandoned and cast off; now he was free and, in his own terms, rich, rich, rich! So, instead of sneaking out quietly with his packages of papers and notes, he made the rounds of the floors where he had earlier hoped to spend his life, and rather than announcing that he had just been fired, he reported modestly that he was leaving that afternoon—and that by the way, the Book-of-the-Month Club had just chosen his book as a fall selection. It was better to leave with a posture of pride—but he was now on his own again, belonging to no one."

THE REPUBLIC
ENDANGERED

In the postwar decades of the 1940s and 1950s, Henry R. Luce became the most influential magazine editor and publisher in the world. Before him there had never been anyone whose magazines had circulated so widely and exerted the influence his did. And this singular distinction of Luce's is likely to endure: no magazine publisher after him can hope to play a similar role, for television, coming along in the fifties, quickly established its supremacy over the printed word in its power to reach millions.

But just how great was Luce's power? The reach of his magazines was vast. *Time* magazine blanketed the world; foreign offices and public figures everywhere read it. Luce, who loved to travel and to meet important people, had no trouble getting in to see the mighty when he came to call. These were not empty social visits; with that bottomless curiosity of his, he wanted to size up important people and match wits with them; he was properly respectful, but he considered himself their intellectual equal and was ready to set them straight when necessary. Heads of state (as well as movie stars, philosophers, and politicians) welcomed invitations to lunch in New York with Luce and his editors. He never promoted his name in his magazines, and he was too private and introspective a man to be a celebrity like his wife, Clare Boothe Luce, who had the necessary attributes of ambition, a cold beauty, and a quick tongue.

In its heyday the *Life* magazine that Luce invented was as significant an educator as any public school. Its photographers—the best in the business—brought the week's disasters and triumphs into millions of homes; schoolchildren were introduced to nature and science in its pages. The picture-filled Time-Life books, offering potted popular histories of the world's peoples, art, science, and nature, sold in the hundreds of thousands. The University of Chicago's Robert M. Hutchins, a friend of Luce's and the boldest educational reformer of his day, said (or possibly lamented) that "Mr. Luce and his magazines have more effect on the American character than the whole educational system put together."

In art, *Life* introduced Picasso to an audience brought up on Norman Rockwell. (Luce's journalistic eagerness to publicize whoever was number one in every field, even in art, warred with his instinct never to get too far ahead of his audience's taste. Afraid of giving his readers too much Picasso and Jackson Pollock, he would urge his editors to balance that coverage with features about doctors who were Sunday painters. These assignments in banality his editors reluctantly pursued or effectively sabotaged.)

Luce discerned in the American public an itch to be well informed, and with missionary zeal he sought to encourage it. From its beginning *Time* magazine had widened the definition of news by covering fields that newspapers neglected: science, medicine, education, philosophy. Believing that "names make news," *Time* put people like Bertrand Russell, Margaret Mead, and Agnes de Mille on its cover, making popular figures of them, but at the price of subjecting them to the kind of scrutiny of their private lives that only politicians and screen stars had previously had to endure. Sports and entertainment were no longer the only breeding grounds of celebrities; Nobel Prize winners could also qualify. So much of what is commonplace in journalism now was either pioneered by Luce's magazines or exploited most successfully by them.

But when Luce tried to use his influence for other ends his troubles began. The so-called power of the press is greatly exaggerated, and the last to understand this are those in the press who think themselves powerful. Their power is never absolute: they prosper by satisfying their readers and survive by a constant radar probing of readers' reactions.

Luce, like all press lords, prided himself on having the popular touch; he didn't merely echo the readers' wants, he anticipated them. Timing was an essential trait: having provoked reader interest in a topic, he had to know when that curiosity had been sated and it was time to move on.

Luce violated this sensitivity to the readers, and did so consciously, when, on major political issues, he abandoned *Time*'s original pledge to give each side of a question its due. *Time* had always been free with its opinions—that was part of its appeal—but in the 1940s, without shame and without subtlety, Luce injected his political beliefs into news coverage. He was willing to anger his staff, antagonize his readership, and jeopardize the reputations of his magazines in the service of what he regarded as a duty higher than merely reporting the news.

This tendency in Luce had first become evident to a few of his writers and editors years earlier, when T. S. Matthews, then a book reviewer, invited several of his colleagues to a dinner with Luce so that they could get to know the boss better. The guests included, early in their careers at *Time*, Charles Wertenbaker, John Osborne, and a poet, Robert Fitzgerald. Matthews knew Luce only by his reputation as, in Matthews's words, the "plodding, lucky dullard" who had succeeded the brilliant Brit Hadden. Luce countered Matthews's invitation by asking the group to have dinner instead in his suite at the Waldorf Towers. They talked—or rather, Luce talked—until almost midnight.

"We were all much impressed by him," Matthews remembered. They met again, then for a third time, when Matthews engaged a private room at The Players and insisted that Luce be their guest. They still had a few awkward questions to settle, one of them being "Under what circumstances would you consider using *Time* as a political instrument?" Luce by then may have thought that he had exposed himself enough.

> When Luce arrived for this meeting [Matthews wrote in *Name and Address*] he handed us each a copy of the memo he had written. As we read it, we saw that he had anticipated all these final questions and had written his answers. Furthermore he had lifted the argument to a general discussion of journalism, its purposes and possibilities, and ended with a statement of his own journalistic faith. He had cut the ground out from under us. We looked at each other and shook our heads. There was nothing left to say. Luce stared at us inquiringly, read the answer in our faces, and started gathering up the copies of his memo. He said that if we didn't need him anymore he'd be getting uptown; he had a date.

At what point, then, might Luce consider using *Time* as a political instrument? His reply was "If I thought the Republic was in danger." That this presumably sophisticated group didn't question the facile vagueness of that answer suggests either that they were politically naïve (as some of them were), or that *Time* had not yet become flagrant in its abuses. But that little dinner group had witnessed an early hint of Luce's ability to satisfy his Presbyterian conscience by raising to the level of principle his willingness to take the journalistic low road.

In the 1940s Luce was to discover three situations which, he thought, did put the Republic in danger. These, often interacting forcibly on one another, were the menace of Communism, the fate of China, and the moribund state of the Republican Party. For them he would put his magazines at risk, and did.

■   ■   ■

Luce, who found out what he thought by talking it out, often used as his sounding boards a succession of advisers whom we, down on the working floors of the building, used to call, with a touch of disdain, his gurus. Some, like Henry Cabot Lodge or Raymond Buell in foreign affairs, were credible; many were specialists in some cause that had briefly captured Luce's attention before it or they began to bore him. But one slippery fellow had a long run as a Luce favorite.

Willi Schlamm was the character Peter Lorre unknowingly spent all his life learning to play—the insidious, ingratiating man with the Central European accent and the devious, conspiratorial mind. He was a small, bespectacled man with slicked-back hair. Seen from the sidelines, if you were not the target of his charm, he exuded an oily malignance. William F. Buckley, Jr., who later became entranced with him, described Schlamm as "Viennese, volatile, amusing, the soul of obduracy," but that was before they fell out. The son of a Jewish merchant in Galicia, Schlamm joined the Communist party and visited Moscow at the age of sixteen; he was put to editing Communist papers and became a skillful party polemicist, but he missed one of Stalin's political turns and was expelled from the party. When Hitler seized Czechoslovakia in 1939, Schlamm, who was then in Prague, fled to the United States and got a job as an assistant to Luce.

The vehemence of his anti-Communism suited Harry, and his witty malice fascinated both Luces. He dined in their New York apartment, was invited for weekends at their Connecticut home, and was even squeezed into a small dinner party Luce and his top editors gave for Winston Churchill. Like many ex-Communists who made a successful career of their apostasy, Schlamm still held a Marxist belief in the express train of history and was convinced that he knew all the stops along the way. Once Schlamm went too far in lecturing Luce on journalism's duty to lay out that inexorable future. Luce brought him back to earth, remarking: "An editor's job is to stay ahead of his readers by three weeks, not ten years."

Unlike Whittaker Chambers, who after his illness was spending more time on his Maryland farm than in New York, Willi Schlamm was constantly present, with his unctuous charm, to feed Luce's fears that Communism was about to take over the world, at a time when the Communists—in Czechoslovakia, in Berlin, in China—were obligingly doing so much to confirm such fears. He kept the fever of anti-Communism alive in Luce when Whittaker Chambers was not around.

By 1948, Whittaker Chambers had been replaced as foreign editor of *Time* because of concern about his health. He missed the power of that position, where he had regularly been able to smite Communists hip and thigh. After all, he had enlisted with Luce, as he wrote to him, "as the great crisis looms . . . in the task you were destined to perform, that you and you only can perform. All you have achieved is only a preparation. . . . Without it, your work will remain uncrowned. . . . I was sent to assist, however humbly, in this same task . . . and cannot without sinning voluntarily leave *Time* until that destiny is performed."

To free Chambers from weekly deadlines, Matthews had created a department called Special Projects, where two of the best writers on the magazine—James Agee and Chambers— would write cover stories and other major assignments. Agee, *Time*'s gifted film critic, held political views that differed widely from Chambers's, but when Chambers was in town they shared an office and a fondness for working late at night in an all-but-empty building, and they became friends.

Chambers found much less satisfaction in crafting stories on the novels of Graham Greene or the singing of Marian Anderson than he had in alerting the world to the menace of Communism. Moreover, on the Graham Greene story, he and Tom

Matthews had a philosophical disagreement over Greene's Catholic preoccupation with sinners' getting right with God in a final moment of contrition. Matthews gently warned Chambers in a letter to him in Maryland, "You may not like what we do to the piece. But I don't want you to come back to set me straight."

Matthews was the most loyal of Chambers's supporters and had, as Chambers conceded to Luce, borne the brunt of Chambers's complaints with "baffled kindness and restrained exasperation." Matthews, worried about Chambers's health, now urged him to take a leave of absence for two or three months; perhaps, as Chambers had suggested, it was time for him to leave *Time* for less demanding assignments at *Life*. Matthews added, however, "Your leaving will make a gap in our thin red line of 'eroes that will be impossible to fill—and I mean it both personally and professionally."

For Chambers, *Life* was less sympathetic territory. In fact, in a short handwritten note to Luce, he mentioned someone on its staff, whom he did not name, as the "villain in the piece, from whose smiling and malevolent incompetence I have suffered a great deal uncomplainingly." *Life,* hoping to make use of Chambers's erudition, assigned him to write "The History of Western Culture," an ambitious series whose consultant was the scholarly Jacques Barzun, who knew of Chambers's earlier reputation as a brilliant student at Columbia University.

Unfortunately, even when writing about events far away and long ago, Chambers saw them as portents of what he regarded as a disastrous present. To Chambers, the Enlightenment was not an age of liberation but the beginning of what went wrong with Western civilization. His next subject was the Reformation, and, Chambers complained to Luce, the editors ruined it:

> Those clumsy but unerring fingers tore out whatever gave life to the piece . . . and left a mess of lath and plaster that I am ashamed to have had anything to do with. For the

editors understood the meaning of the piece plainly, hated it explicitly and mangled it with knowing love. . . . I could not, in the Reformation piece, and will not in future pieces, rewrite the historical thesis of the Communist Manifesto or any derivative therefrom.

I cannot tell you how much this affair has disturbed me. . . . For it strikes at the heart of my continued usefulness to Time [Inc.]. The increasingly agitated theme among the abler men around here is: Has a man who has something to say and the ability to say it any real place at Time? Do not hacks do the job better . . . ?

Two weeks later he again wrote to Luce, declaring that he nonetheless preferred writing for *Life* than for *Time* with its turf jealousies and antagonisms: "You may say 'You are growing cranky, impatient of restraints, formulas, personalities.' I would not disclaim the charge." He continued: "I am not subtracting myself from the struggle. In fact, I am binding myself closer to it and to you. For only through your concern can I function at all. Apart from you and Tom [Matthews], almost every man here regards me, whatever he may say, as an enemy. And they are right. However we preserve the civilized amenities, I am the intellectual enemy."

Even Chambers's most sympathetic supporters could be forgiven for thinking that not every editorial dispute called for such Wagnerian thunder in the kettledrums, or the onstage clatter of swordplay to the death. The liberals on the staff of the magazines were not such naïfs as Chambers took them to be; after all, many of them were veterans of ugly late-night battles against the Communists in heated and exhausting New York meetings of the Newspaper Guild. But to Chambers, liberalism itself in the end was not much different from socialism, and both, like Communism, were derivatives of Marxism. As he wrote later in a letter to his son: "History is moving with great speed towards a showdown. . . . I am forecasting a world in which Communism may have so far extended its power that the U.S. will be islanded and outnumbered so that the questions of the day will be whether the last fringe war is to be fought in the U.S. and how to avoid it. That is where I am assuming the socialist beachheads come in. They will provide the mediating forces with Communism."

Chambers's battles with his colleagues at *Time* and *Life* seem too apocalyptic for the minor stakes involved, but this would soon change. One day Luce invited Chambers to have a morning coffee with him, side by side at a Rockefeller Center drugstore counter, to discuss whether his future lay with *Time* or with *Life*. Chambers arrived with a more important subject to talk about. He had been tipped off that he would be subpoenaed that day by the House Un-American Activities Committee. Having agreed to testify, Chambers said, "It seems to me you will not want me around here any longer."

"Nonsense," Luce replied, "testifying is a simple patriotic duty."

On August 3, 1948, Whittaker Chambers appeared in Washington, D.C., as a surprise witness before the House committee. He was about to play a role on the world stage where at last the drama would match the dark eloquence of his warnings. Yet as a witness that day he was unimpressive. A freshman member of the committee, Richard Nixon of California, watched him, first as he appeared in executive session, then as he testified at a hastily convened special hearing. "He was short and pudgy," Nixon recalled. "His clothes were unpressed; his shirt collar was curled up over his jacket. He spoke in a rather bored undertone." As Chambers read a prepared statement, his voice constantly trailed off. To Nixon he "seemed an indifferent if not a reluctant witness."

Yet the story he had to tell made headlines the next day, and its consequences spread in ever-widening circles for weeks to come. Chambers, identified as "a $30,000 senior editor at

Time," testified that during the 1930s he belonged to an underground organization of the Communist party which had infiltrated the U.S. government. What made the news a sensation was that he named Alger Hiss as one member of the underground group. Now the head of the Carnegie Endowment for International Peace, Hiss had previously had a distinguished career in the State Department. He had been a member of the American delegation at Yalta and secretary of the San Francisco conference that drafted the United Nations charter. An honors graduate of the Harvard Law School, Hiss had served as a law clerk to Supreme Court Justice Oliver Wendell Holmes on the recommendation of Felix Frankfurter, one of Hiss's Harvard professors.

Though some headlines accused Hiss of being a "Soviet spy," Chambers had carefully not suggested that but had testified: "The purpose [of the group] was not espionage, but penetration of government." And when Chambers was later asked by a federal grand jury whether he himself had been involved in espionage, he lied under oath. In his autobiography Chambers wrote, "My no to the grand jury stands for all men to condemn."

The publicity-conscious Un-American Activities Committee had hardly had time to congratulate itself on the headlines it had made when a telegram arrived from Alger Hiss: "I do not know Mr. Chambers and so far as I know have never laid eyes on him." Hiss asked to meet the committee immediately, formally and under oath, to deny these "fabrications." To Richard Nixon, Hiss's relaxed and confident appearance before the committee was "as brilliant as Chambers's had been lackluster." Hiss's cool assurance even won over John Rankin of Mississippi, an anti-Semitic, anti-Negro bigot on the committee, who had earlier congratulated Chambers. Now Rankin told Hiss: "After all the smear attacks against this committee and individual members on it in Time magazine, I am not surprised at anything that comes out of it." There was laughter, and Rankin rushed to shake Hiss's hand.

Hiss had clearly won the first skirmish. The conservative eastern establishment rallied behind a man with all the correct credentials of dress, speech, and antecedents, who had been maligned by a shabby-looking ex-Communist. Hiss also had the liberals with him. President Harry Truman, up for reelection and standing poorly in the polls, agreed with a reporter who described Chambers's testimony as a "red herring." Later, campaigning on a whistle-stop tour, Truman made a folksy defense of Hiss: "If you work for *Time* you're a hero. If you work for the State Department you're a heel."

At this low point in Chambers's fortunes, Luce invited him to dinner. Chambers arrived to find another guest present, a "nimble, witty European" whom Chambers in his autobiography identified only as "Smetana," after the Czech composer. Presumably, though Chambers did not say so, this was Willi Schlamm, the man from Prague. That night Chambers said little. After all, he was still emerging from the shadows and "bright conversation hurt my mind." Luce turned to Chambers: "By any Marxian pattern of how classes behave, the upper class should be for you. . . . But it is the upper class that is most against you. How do you explain that?"

Before Chambers could reply, Smetana answered Luce for him and, as a man who had lived in this country for less than ten years, did so with patronizing effrontery: "You don't understand the class structure of American society or you would not ask such a question. In the United States, the working class are Democrats. The middle class are Republicans. The upper class are Communists."

After dinner, Chambers got up to leave with Smetana, but Luce drew Chambers back. They sat silently for a while, as Luce studied Chambers's face. "The pity of it is," Luce said at last, "that two men, able men, are destroying each other in this way." Chambers replied, "That is what history does to men in periods like this."*

After another heavy pause Luce said, "I've been reading about the young man born blind." Feeling guilty, as *Time* editors often did when caught out by Luce on something they hadn't read, Chambers answered: "I haven't read *Time* for the last two weeks."

"No, no," Luce said impatiently, "I mean the young man born blind. It's in the eighth or ninth chapter of St. John. They brought Our Lord a young man who had been blind from birth and asked Him one of those catch questions: 'Whose is the sin, this man's or his parents', that he was born blind?' Our Lord took some clay and wet it with saliva and placed it on the blind man's eyes so that they opened and he could see. Then Our Lord gave an answer, not one of His clever answers, but a direct, simple answer. He said: 'Neither this man sinned nor his parents, but that the works of God should be made manifest in him.' "

Slowly, there sank into my mind the tremendous thing that Luce was saying to me, and the realization that he had brought me there so that he could say these words of understanding kindness. He was saying: "You are the young man born blind. All you had to offer God was your blindness, that through the action of your recovered sight, His works might be made manifest."

It was Richard Nixon who rescued Whittaker Chambers. After Alger Hiss's devastatingly confident testimony, the House Un-

---

*Luce's praise of Hiss may seem surprising, but he had seen and admired the way Hiss conducted the San Francisco conference that drafted the United Nations charter. Oddly enough, Whittaker Chambers had earlier complained to a superior at *Time* that he thought his fellow editor John Osborne was a Communist. Why did he think so? Because, said Chambers, Osborne had highly praised Hiss's San Francisco performance in *Time*. Long afterward Osborne explained that he had done so at Luce's urging.

American Activities Committee gathered in executive session in what Nixon called a "virtual state of shock." Most members of the committee, now embarrassed by the impression made by Hiss's appearance, wanted to drop the case. Nixon persisted: he had detected something "mouthy" about Hiss's testimony, and besides resented the way Hiss, with Ivy League condescension, "was rather insolent towards me." If, Nixon argued, they couldn't find out who was telling the truth about whether Hiss had been a Communist, they could at least determine whether Hiss and Chambers had ever met. Chambers was questioned again and displayed considerable familiarity with Hiss's house, his family, and his way of life, and repeated that he knew the Hisses when they and he were in the Communist underground.

Hiss and Chambers confronted each other in a New York hotel room in the presence of members of the committee's staff. Facing Chambers in person, Hiss conceded that he might have known him, but under another name, as a freelance writer who had bad teeth. He asked to look into Chambers's mouth. The request was greeted with derision by the committee staff: Why should it be necessary to examine a denture to identify a man who had once lived in your house, and to whom you had even given a 1929 Ford? Hiss began to lose his aplomb; he rose and loudly challenged Chambers to "make those same statements out of the presence of this committee without their being privileged for suit for libel." That challenge would prove to be Hiss's mistake: Chambers had established only that he had known Hiss, not that Hiss had been a Communist.

Chambers chose to repeat the accusation that Hiss had been a Communist on *Meet the Press,* believing its moderator, Larry Spivak, to be on his side, even though he considered the program itself "fun for the boys but death for the frogs." After Chambers gave up his congressional immunity, Hiss had to be goaded into suing him; when he finally did, Chambers produced the evidence he had saved as his "life preserver": papers and microfilm he had stored in a relative's flat in Brooklyn. He had recently transferred them to his farm; then, fearing that someone might break into his house, Chambers had hidden the evidence overnight in a hollowed-out pumpkin in the field.

The "Pumpkin Papers," along with some rolls of microfilm, included sixty-five typewritten pages of confidential State Department papers and four memoranda in Hiss's own handwriting. Chambers testified that Mrs. Hiss had copied the documents on an old Woodstock typewriter so that Hiss could take the originals back to his office the following day. The documents, mostly about a German-American trade agreement, might have been marginally useful to the Russians at the time but were not a significant betrayal of American secrets; nonetheless they were devastating for Hiss.

When Hiss filed his suits for libel and slander, demanding $75,000 in damages, Chambers became convinced that Hiss was "determined to destroy me," and proceeded to implicate Hiss in a far graver accusation of espionage. Why had he earlier held this back? Chambers testified, "I was particularly anxious, for reasons of friendship, and because Mr. Hiss is one of the most brilliant young men in the country, not to do injury more than necessary to Mr. Hiss." This squares with Chambers's frequent insistence that he was interested in exposing the sin, not the sinner. But in accusing Hiss of spying for the Soviet Union, Chambers was also admitting for the first time that he himself had been a spy. That admission cost him dearly.

Time Inc. had been paying all of Chambers's legal bills, on the grounds that an attack on Chambers's veracity was an attack on *Time*'s. It did so despite protests from a number of its readers, who demanded to know why the magazine was employing an ex-Communist as an editor. Hiring an ex-Communist could be justified; employing a onetime Soviet spy could not. (Clare Boothe Luce later remembered overhearing a conversation in which Harry complained to Chambers that he had never been told about the spying. To this Chambers had lamely replied, "But you knew I was a Communist and all Communists were working for the Soviet Union"—something "a man of your sophistication" should have figured out.)

Chambers was now an embarrassment to Time Inc. He had to go. Characteristically, Luce did not himself ask for Chambers's resignation but left the task to Roy Larsen, the company's president. Meeting Larsen, Chambers quickly agreed to resign; borrowing a typewriter in Larsen's office, he sat down and wrote: "When *Time* hired me in 1939, its Editors knew that I was an ex-Communist; they did not know that espionage was involved. For nine years I have been actively fighting Communism. . . . Now . . . I have been called upon to expose the darkest and most dangerous side of Communism—espionage. . . . I cannot share this indispensable ordeal with anyone. Therefore, with a quiet and firm mind, I am withdrawing from among the colleagues with whom I worked for so many years and whose support has been loyal and generous."

In announcing Chambers's resignation, Time Inc. commented: "Against the admitted disservice to his country of a decade ago must be set the service we are convinced he is trying to perform for his country now." *Time* also made what Chambers called "a settlement so generous that, with what I had accumulated over the years in its trust funds, I did not have to worry about money again during the Case."

The public was not so charitable toward Chambers. Neither were Time Inc.'s enemies in the press, particularly the Hearst papers and their flamboyant gossip columnist, Walter Winchell. At that time, most Americans tuned their radios on Sunday nights to Winchell's breathless staccato delivery of gossip, innuendo, and simplistic judgments on world affairs. Accuracy was never Winchell's highest priority: "Timemag . . . was edited all these years by Whittaker Chambers, self-confessed Communist, accused perjurer and Russian spy! Time botches on!" In one month, after which people at *Time* stopped counting, Winchell delivered, on the air or in print, forty-seven quips and jabs at *Time:* "Gee Whittakers! Time Marxes on."

Attacks by Winchell seemed not to disturb Chambers, who would simply have been contemptuous of him. But there was much else to trouble Chambers in December 1948: the fear of being indicted for lying to the grand jury, a feeling of guilt at having informed on Alger Hiss, a sadness at his parting with *Time.* Drained physically and emotionally, Chambers fell into despondency. One day he bought a large can of cyanide compound in a feedstore in lower Manhattan, then took the train to Lynbrook, Long Island, where his mother lived.

In the evening he wrote farewell messages to his wife and children, as well as another note affirming the truth of his testimony but regretting the harm it would do others. He would now, he added, "spare them the ultimate consequences of my actions and their own, by removing myself as a witness against them."

He opened the cyanide, wrapped towels around the open can so that the fumes of the poison would seep into the room, and then lay on a bed. He awoke in the morning, alive but vomiting. After that harrowing misadventure he made no further attempt to kill himself.

Though, in Chambers's telling, both he and Hiss were guilty of espionage, neither could be charged with the crime because the three-year statute of limitations for treason in peacetime had run out. Either or both of them however could be charged with perjury. At first, the federal grand jury had considered indicting Chambers, but once he produced the Pumpkin Papers and testified freely thereafter, the jury decided not to. Instead, in its irritation at Hiss's evasive denials, the jury indicted Hiss.

It was my responsibility, as the National Affairs editor of *Time,* to organize and edit the magazine's coverage of Hiss's trial for perjury. By then my feelings toward Chambers had shifted somewhat. I could not forgive him the arrogance of his judgments, but I had come to see him as an anguished man. I still thought him a man of warped brilliance who was more of a polemicist than a journalist. With his apocalyptic vision, he regarded the week's news—the downfall of this political party or that—as trivial events, and those who reported them as superficial journalists. When correspondents like Teddy White and John Hersey reported what Communist leaders said and did, he thought of them as carriers—innocently or not—of totalitarianism.

Now that Chambers was revealed as a spy we all took more seriously those melodramatic personal precautions of his that had once struck us as absurd. At this point, however, with so much still unknown about the case, I could not judge whether Hiss or Chambers was telling the truth.

In the weeks that followed, we at *Time* got a thorough education in charges and countercharges. Jim Bell, a skilled reporter, covered the trial, and knowing that everyone in the building—from Harry Luce down—was interested in the case, he filed up to seven thousand words a day: testimony, the lawyers' tactics and motions, the vicious cross-examinations, the courtroom atmosphere. We became familiar with hundreds of details about the Woodstock typewriter, the Ford with the "sassy trunk," the shadowy behavior of FBI agents, the whereabouts of Hiss's maids past and present, the number of occasions when Hiss, a practiced lawyer, just couldn't recall crucial details. As the story unfolded, the writers on my staff—several of them hostile to Chambers, another, Duncan Norton-Taylor, his friend—were equally determined to tell a complicated story straight. We did so without any interference from Harry Luce. In the end, I think, all of us who handled the story were convinced that Hiss was guilty (the first jury split eight to four in favor of conviction and a mistrial was declared; the second jury found him guilty). For years afterward I read numerous articles and books about the case and never found a reason to reverse a conclusion I had taken no pleasure in reaching.

During the two trials, Chambers patronized the reporters

who besieged him after each day's testimony. Not until the first trial ended did he regard any question put to him by a newspaperman as intelligent. Then he was asked, "What do you think you are doing?" Whether or not this question was intelligent, it did give Chambers a chance to lob back theatrically: "I am a man who, reluctantly, grudgingly, step by step is destroying himself that this country and the faith by which it lives may continue to exist."

Chambers's friend Arthur Koestler, the ex-Communist author of *Darkness at Noon,* whose career somewhat paralleled Chambers's and whose talent for bombast matched his, declared that his friend "knowingly committed moral suicide to atone for the guilt of our generation." Less rhapsodically, Alfred Kazin described Whittaker Chambers as "the only American character in *The Brothers Karamazov.*"

In retrospect the Hiss-Chambers case was more a personal tragedy than a national disaster; no great loss of the nation's nuclear secrets had occurred, but the promising career of an intelligent public servant was ended, and the man who destroyed him suffered his own painful decline. T. S. Matthews, who stood by Chambers throughout, believed that in acting as he did Chambers was "trying to make amends for his Communist past." But Matthews did criticize his friend for allowing "himself to become the forerunner of the rascally Senator McCarthy, the tinpot Robespierre who, to the amused disgust of the civilized world, for a disgraceful period became the dominant voice of his half-ashamed, half-terrified nation."

The Hiss-Chambers case was a forerunner, but not the sole begetter, of the McCarthy phenomenon. By the year 1950, when the second Hiss trial ended, the demagogic Senator McCarthy had already succeeded in stirring up public hysteria over Communism. Chambers, a private figure living in unwelcome notoriety, was now jobless, living hand-to-mouth on his Maryland farm, and (despite considerable financial help from Time Inc.) facing heavy legal bills.

Persuaded that the Hiss verdict had vindicated Chambers, Luce and Matthews thought the time had come to rehire him. As Matthews once remarked, "Whit's no saint, but he *can* write like an angel." Chambers was invited to New York to discuss a job, but before the train reached the city, Luce changed his mind; he had run into almost unanimous resistance from senior executives in the company. It was left to Matthews to greet Chambers, who had taxied up from Pennsylvania Station. Matthews reported to Luce: "I've seen Whit and told him it was no go. I did not go into the various reasons; it wasn't necessary. It was apparently not a surprise to him. . . . I also took the liberty of apologizing to him, in both our names, for having broached the matter before we were sure we were willing to go through with it."

The parallels between Chambers's treatment by Luce and Teddy White's experience six years earlier are not many. In Teddy's case, Luce broke with a friend whose reporting he disagreed with; in Chambers's case, Luce felt unable to support a controversial figure whose politics he did agree with. But Luce's responses to both were remarkably similar. They exemplify the difficulty Luce had in cutting himself off from people he admired, and the awkward evasions he felt driven to make. To Whit, as to Teddy, Luce wrote, confessing to vague misgivings about the situation; then he went off on a trip, giving each man a chance to think things over. This time, Luce frankly admitted to Chambers that he was going away on a trip *because* of the problem:

Dear Whit:
    I have got to the point where it seems that the best thing that I can do not only for myself but for all concerned is to take a vacation. And so I'm heading South tonight.

But there's one matter on which I'd like to express myself before leaving. That is the matter of whether you should want to or should work for Time.

My feeling on this is that it ought to be possible to arrive at a "right" answer to this question—that is, one on which we mutually agree for mutually agreed reasons.

I'm not sure whether Tom and you did arrive at the right answer in this sense. . . . Perhaps it was too soon to do so.

However, I guess for my part I will not be satisfied that a right decision is made unless I have an opportunity to talk with you myself. I shall be getting back [in a month] and hope we can have a talk soon after that.

Luce's letter has the sound of a man assuaging his conscience while prudently giving no encouragement to the notion that the "right" answer would be to rehire Chambers. More than a month elapsed before Chambers's handwritten response arrived from Pipe Creek Farm, Maryland. Chambers's rejection of an ambiguous overture from Luce was more final than Teddy's had been.

It was also vintage Chambers. Calculating in its assault on Luce's conscience while denying any such intention, his letter nonetheless has a certain nobility about it in its refusal to paper over the situation he was in:

Dear Harry:
    Never, as a child, did I believe in the happy ending. And to that extent I never could wholly believe in the American Dream, to which the happy ending is the essential tag.
    You are the only person who has ever made me believe in the happy ending, and that only for a few hours. When Tom made his proposal [of taking Chambers back] I said to him: "I didn't believe this was possible." Not that I should return to *Time* but that there can be a happy ending. For a few hours, you must take

the credit for allowing me a kind of euphoria. Then, quite suddenly, my sense of the worst took over again, and I said: "No, it is not true." Thus, I was quite prepared for Tom's reversal of his offer. That did not spare me hours of a bitterness such as I trust life will spare you—a bitterness that I cannot wholly shake off, a natural and justifiable bitterness. But that now lingers only as a privilege of amusement at the world.

What is there, kind friend, for us to talk about? The facts need no laboring: 1) the man needs a job; 2) if a man has "done more for the country than anyone else in five years" do you let him sink?; 3) the editorial and economic rout of W. Chambers is a considerable victory for the Leftists and will teach any other upstart stalwarts the reward of valor. Do not misunderstand me: I am writing this with a smile.

And with a smile, I say: Harry, in the end, you will decide that it all hinges not on what you will but on what you can. That little "can" can shrivel us all. Nor should the slightest reproach brush you in consequence.

But why should we worry it with talk? I recently wrote Tom in this connection: "Our enemies can never do these things to us. . . . Only our friends can drive the knife through our vitals."

But I do not think that we are then required to turn the knife in the wound. And that, it seems to me, is what a talk between us would amount to.

Surely, my last letter to you said all that was needed: for your many kindnesses, I am grateful; we shall not meet again. I am very tired.

Faithfully,
Whittaker

"I CAN FIRE ANY OF YOU"

I f, as Lord Acton proclaimed, power corrupts, the *absence* of power corrodes. In the early 1950s such a corrosion of spirit was very evident in the Republican Party. After being denied the White House for twenty years, the party was ready to employ desperate means, wrapped in patriotism, to get back in. To help them, Henry Robinson Luce was just as ready to use dubious journalistic tactics, similarly wrapped in red, white, and blue.

The Republicans had been driven from office in 1932 because Herbert Hoover had responded only with a principled inertia when faced with the desolation, joblessness, and shantytown Hoovervilles of the depression. A buoyantly confident Franklin D. Roosevelt, taking office, restored the nation's spirit by spending freely and experimenting boldly. Even Harry Luce, later so determined a critic of Roosevelt, was at first favorably impressed. Roosevelt was reelected easily in 1936. Four years later, when war seemed close at hand, Roosevelt won a third term from an electorate unwilling to gamble on a change of leadership. Then came a fourth term in 1944. World War II was nearly over and Franklin Roosevelt was visibly ailing; nonetheless he prevailed again. He lived only eighty-seven days into his new term before Vice President Harry Truman inherited the office. To the out-of-power Republicans, Roosevelt's unprecedented run in office reflected not only the dominance of his personality but the unusual circumstances of back-to-back emergencies, a depression and a war. But to make sure that the same thing couldn't happen again, Congress passed the Twenty-second Amendment not long after Roosevelt's death, limiting future presidents to two terms, an example set by George Washington and followed by the thirty other presidents before Roosevelt.

By Truman's day the momentum and the mission of the New Deal were both gone. The enthusiastic and idealistic reformers of the Roosevelt era had either settled in as weary jobholders or prospered on the outside as Washington lawyers or lobbyists. By all rights, with Roosevelt no longer around, 1948 should have been the Republicans' turn at last. Certainly Republicans thought so. To Harry Luce, Truman was "the *reductio ad absurdum* of the Common Man."* At a time when Truman had sunk dangerously low in the polls, Clare Boothe Luce, by then a congresswoman from Connecticut, assured the Republican convention that Truman was a "gone goose." Acting on that assumption, Governor Thomas E. Dewey campaigned as if waiting only to be coronated. Truman's come-from-behind victory over Dewey in 1948 had not been anticipated by any pollster, nor predicted by commentator or columnist. All of these discredited experts glumly swallowed their breakfast of crow but by nightfall were dining out again as authorities. A gloating Truman waved aloft the *Chicago Tribune* election issue with its banner DEWEY BEATS TRUMAN, though as an example of egregious forecasting, he could as easily have displayed the photograph of Dewey in *Life* showing the "future President" crossing San Francisco Bay.

Devastated at losing the prize that should easily have been theirs, the Republicans—divided on so much else—were united in vowing "Never again." Next time, in 1952, they would cast

---

*Luce later changed his mind and in his memoirs, unfinished at his death, ranked Truman as one of the great American presidents.

aside all restraints. It was not as if their earlier conduct had been particularly forbearing: Dewey, with his prosecutor's ways and his deep baritone voice, may have sung his theme song too softly, but there was little temperate about the words: Truman was a political hack whose administration was rife with corruption, and as the Hiss-Chambers trials had shown, he was "soft" on Communism too. (For his own part, "Give 'em hell" Harry Truman, in his simplistic and strident attacks on the "do nothing" Eightieth Congress, had done nothing to elevate the tone of the campaign.) What more could the Republicans possibly do, casting aside all restraint, to win back the White House in 1952?

They found one answer in the scurrilous roughneck demagoguery of Senator Joseph McCarthy. At a time when concern over Soviet expansion was genuine and well founded—the Communists had lately seized Czechoslovakia and blockaded Berlin—McCarthy found his target: The Democrats had not just been "soft" on Communism; they harbored Communist traitors in their midst—the State Department was crawling with them. To put his message across, Joe McCarthy instinctively exploited the vulnerable spot in the working habits of the daily press. Unlike the Luce magazines with their insistent pontificating, most newspapers and most newspapermen prided themselves on laying out facts, accusations, denials, scrupulously, without rendering any judgments of their own. To get the press's attention you had to do three things: say something that would get attention; have recognizable credentials ("After all, he's a United States senator, isn't he?"); and make any accusation sound specific, even when your "facts" were spurious. In a Lincoln's Birthday speech in Wheeling, West Virginia, in February 1951, McCarthy, waving a piece of paper, announced that he had in his hands the names of 205 "known Communists" in the State Department. In the days that followed, he changed the charge to 57 "card-carrying" Communists and then, in a lengthy speech in the Senate, made it 87.

By the time the press realized that McCarthy could not back

up his wild charges it was too late to deflate the monster the press itself had created. By now McCarthy was a front-page figure who could not be ignored. Many of his fellow senators despised him but feared to challenge him. McCarthy had touched a public nerve; it became fashionable to deplore his methods but to acknowledge that he was on to something—perhaps just what was needed for the Republicans to win in 1952. At first considered on the loony fringe, McCarthy now had powerful supporters in the Senate leadership, among them, surprisingly, "Mr. Republican" himself, Senator Robert A. Taft. Though back in 1946 Taft had been the first to raise the "soft on Communism" issue against the Democrats, his dour, cautious conservatism had seemed the starchy embodiment of responsibility and respectability. Now he was urging McCarthy to "keep talking and if one case didn't work out, to bring up another."

This McCarthy now did: as charge after charge was refuted, he airily deflected criticism by making a new accusation. His charges often made page one; the denials usually came later and were buried inside the paper. McCarthy was living proof of Mark Twain's adage that a lie could circle the earth while truth was putting on its shoes.

Harry Luce had long ago persuaded himself that it was all right to distort the news in the service of a "higher" cause; he had convinced himself that electing a Republican president was in the national interest. He set as his goal a Republican victory in 1952 and was ready to support "almost any Republican" who could win. He was aware of *Time*'s "tremendous political power"; as he wrote to his longtime partner, Roy E. Larsen, the president of Time Inc., "I don't particularly like it, and I know you don't, but there it is."

He had put that "tremendous political power" to use before, not just in the magazine itself but by injecting himself into the choice of Republican candidates. In his first try in 1940, the

Luce publications had succeeded in getting Wendell Willkie nominated but could not elect him.

Willkie, a burly and appealingly midwestern businessman, had never been elected to any office, but he satisfied Luce's chief criterion—that of being an internationalist when most Republicans were isolationists. His candidacy was born on a weekend visit to the Connecticut home of Russell Davenport, the managing editor of *Fortune*. Davenport was so entranced by Willkie that he became his biggest advocate, his speechwriter, and his campaign manager. Together these political amateurs triumphed over the Republican Old Guard to win the nomination, but in the finals they were no match for the wiles and popularity of Franklin D. Roosevelt.

In the next election, in wartime 1944, Luce was less keen on his party's nominee, Governor Dewey, but this did not stop him from twisting the news columns of *Time* in Dewey's favor. That was my first exposure to *Time*'s political distortions. I spent forty days crisscrossing the country on Dewey's campaign train and reporting his lackluster performance while *Time* was applauding him and proclaiming his coming victory.

After Dewey's defeat, Luce threw an elaborate dinner at one of his private clubs for *Time*'s unhappy editorial staff (with the usual amenities—cocktails before dinner, wine during the meal—before Luce spoke). He was conciliatory, almost apologetic. He admitted that the magazine had fudged on its coverage, a venial sin that he likened to "cheating at cards." I remember asking myself at the time, Who—except in a casual game of solitaire, when one is playing alone and is too lazy to reshuffle the deck—ever cheats at cards?

Four years later, when Dewey in 1948 again displayed his talent for losing elections he might have won, Luce resolved to involve himself from the beginning in picking a Republican winner in 1952. That meant rejecting the party favorite, Senator Taft, which he did with regret but ruthlessly: "I respected Taft— as who did not? . . . and not so incidentally, I knew him personally as a Yale man. His brother Charlie and his cousin David Ingalls, who was his campaign manager, were two of my closest friends. But I decided that I must go for Eisenhower. . . . I was sure that Eisenhower could win. I was not sure that Taft could."

In January 1952 *Life* published the editorial "A Case for Ike," and the following week, Senator Henry Cabot Lodge—friend of both Luce and Eisenhower, and a useful go-between—announced that Ike's name would be entered in the New Hampshire primary. Ike, writing to Luce, thanked him for *Life*'s editorial, which "erred grossly on the side of generosity" toward him, but had "been one of the factors that influenced me." Calling on Eisenhower in Paris, Luce urged him to resign as supreme commander of NATO and return home as soon as possible, and finally persuaded him that he should do so.

Luce left his talk with Ike, as he later wrote, "under the agreeable spell of a great personality and with the sense of confidence that the Republican Party had a winner." But this hardly seems equal to the spiritual lift he had once felt in the presence of General Douglas MacArthur, when he was moved to tears. Luce's response to MacArthur was emotional, to Eisenhower pragmatic. Luce wanted a winner.

After twenty years of Republican exile, and twenty years of subjection to Democratic oratory, Luce thought "the American people should have the experience of living under a Republican administration and discovering that they therefore were not reduced to selling apples on street corners."

Two events during the Truman presidency, each involving American generals, reinforced Luce's Republican sympathies. The first concerned America's most respected general in World War II, George Catlett Marshall. He had been retired for only six days in 1945 when President Truman asked him for help to get out of a political jam. Pat Hurley had just assured Truman that everything was under control in China, and then, without

warning Truman, had gone before the Press Club in Washington, D.C., that same day to announce his resignation as the president's special emissary to China, and to accuse the State
Department of siding with the Chinese Communists.

To offset the embarrassing headlines from that "son of a
bitch" Hurley, Truman telephoned the man he regarded as the
greatest living American: "General, I want you to go to China
for me." Marshall, answering at his Virginia home, said only
three words: "Yes, Mr. President."

Marshall's job was to bring Chiang Kai-shek and the Chinese Communists back into coalition, an impossible assignment
at which Hurley had already failed. Marshall's year in China—
until he was brought home by Truman to become secretary of
state—was a bitter interlude in his career. "I hate failure," he
told a friend. The general, who had been *Time*'s Man of the
Year that year, was unable to budge either side; he came away
with a dislike of the Communists but also with a distaste for the
corruption in Chiang's regime and with a low opinion of
Chiang's generals. When Chiang was beaten two years later and
retreated with two million followers to Formosa (known now as
Taiwan), Luce blamed the loss of China on American policy and
a "political atmosphere which destroyed the judgment of such a
noble man as George Marshall."

Luce thought he knew the origin of Marshall's prejudice
against Chiang. As he later wrote to Edward K. Thompson, the
managing editor of *Life:* "When the great five-star Marshall
stepped into his magnificent four-engine aeroplane to glide
across the Pacific he was carrying in his hand a book [*Thunder
Out of China*] by a very clever correspondent, Theodore White,
one of the best newshounds we ever had. . . . I know Teddy. He
is very intelligent and on decisive issues very wrong." In this
private, offhand explanation of the failure of Marshall's mission, Luce did not blame Chiang Kai-shek and he made excuses
for General Marshall; he saved his toughest criticism for White.

■ ■ ■

The second event to stir Luce's Republicanism was Truman's firing of General MacArthur. At first, when the North Korean Communists invaded South Korea in 1950, Luce had enthusiastically backed the president's committing United States forces to a "police action" in Korea (never a declared war, though fifty-four thousand Americans would lose their lives) and in winning United Nations support. A *Life* editorial said: "The reaction of the plain man seems to have been, 'At last, it's the only thing to do.' " In endorsing the president's bold decision, *Life* seemed to overlook one prudent precaution taken by Truman. Hoping to keep Communist China from entering the war being fought on its doorstep, Truman ordered the U.S. Seventh Fleet to patrol the straits between Formosa and the Chinese mainland. This would keep Chiang's forces from seizing the moment to invade Communist China—or, as Secretary of State Dean Acheson said, vice versa.

After initial losses, General MacArthur, commanding the UN forces (including troops from fifteen other nations) pushed the invaders back toward the 38th parallel, the boundary between North and South Korea. At this point, Chou En-lai, Communist China's foreign minister, issued a warning. He had not conspicuously objected to the UN's limited objective of repelling the invasion, but now he warned the world that if UN troops crossed the 38th parallel into North Korea itself, Communist China would intervene. Not only MacArthur but the Pentagon and the White House as well dismissed Chou's threat as bluff. Before long MacArthur's troops, having crossed the parallel, were in "hot pursuit" of the North Koreans, heading north toward the Chinese border on the Yalu River.

In a chesty atmosphere of approaching victory, President Truman flew halfway around the world in mid-October to Wake Island to confer for an hour and thirty-six minutes with his victorious general. MacArthur and Truman, who had never met, got along well, to the surprise of both. (This was the man Truman in his diary had described as "Mr. Prima Donna, Brass Hat," and "God's right-hand man.") They even discussed politics amiably. Truman asked MacArthur whether he had any political ambitions. "None whatsoever," MacArthur replied. "If you have a general running against you, his name will be Eisenhower, not MacArthur." (Truman, who liked Ike and regarded him as a friend, laughingly dismissed this possibility: "Eisenhower doesn't know the first thing about politics.")

MacArthur confidently predicted that "formal resistance" by the North Koreans would end by Thanksgiving and American troops would be back in Japan by Christmas. The president asked what were the chances of a Chinese or Russian intervention. "Very little," MacArthur replied.

But on the day after Thanksgiving, more than a quarter of a million Chinese troops—"hordes," as the American press described them—began crossing the Yalu River. MacArthur was taken by a surprise so complete that his troops, which he had incautiously divided into two groups, suffered heavy casualties as they beat a disorderly retreat in snow, wind, and subzero temperatures. "We face an entirely new war," MacArthur grimly announced; it was one that would continue for three unhappy years.

MacArthur, hero of the war in the Pacific in World War II, now found himself criticized—even in the admiring pages of *Time*—for a military disaster. He became depressed and defensive. Pleading that his own soldiers were "mentally fatigued and physically battered," MacArthur urged that they be reinforced with eight hundred thousand of Chiang Kai-shek's troops on Formosa. Widening the war in this way, he all but guaranteed, would not bring on an intervention by the Russians, with their nuclear weapons.

In a fatuous editorial, *Life* magazine seemed undaunted by that possibility: "World War III moves ever closer. . . . The Chinese forces assaulting our forces are as truly the armies of the

Soviet Union as they would be if they wore the Soviet uniform. . . . We do not 'want' war with China. The Communists force war upon us."

A week later a *Life* editorial put it even more plainly: "*Life* sees no choice but to acknowledge the existence of war with Red China and to set about its defeat, in full awareness that this course will probably involve war with the Soviet Union as well."

These two inflammatory editorials (written by John Osborne) got such an angry reaction from readers and from Osborne's colleagues in the corridors of *Time* and *Life* that he tempered his jingoism with another editorial, "This Way to Peace."

Fortunately for everyone, by spring American troops commanded by General Matthew Ridgway had ended their retreat and retaken the offensive, diminishing the sense of impending catastrophe. With fewer troops than the enemy, but with superior firepower, Ridgway drove the Communists back to the 38th parallel. At this point Truman was ready to propose peace talks and a cease-fire, but before he could do so, MacArthur on his own issued a taunting ultimatum to the Chinese, belittling their performance in Korea and threatening to extend the war to their seacoasts and interior bases.

Truman was outraged at MacArthur's unilateral ultimatum and his calculated defiance of American policy. With the full support of his Joint Chiefs of Staff and of his new secretary of defense, George Marshall, Truman dismissed MacArthur for insubordination. In the uproar that followed, Senator Taft was among Republicans calling for Truman's impeachment. Much of the American press, however, sided with the president— except for Luce's magazines. In an overwrought two-page editorial (though it was not labeled an editorial) *Time* defended the general.

MacArthur, looking like a conquering hero, returned home to a dramatic appearance before both houses of Congress, an event watched on television by an estimated thirty million

Americans. He made a movingly grandiloquent and maudlin speech ("Old soldiers never die. They just fade away"), pleading to be allowed to go all-out to defeat the Chinese Communists. In war, he declared, "there is no substitute for victory."

The American public was in no mood for so risky and costly an adventure. As Truman had predicted, MacArthur soon did begin to fade away; the public began to tire of his pomposity, his high-flown rhetoric, and the prospect of a seemingly endless war with China. Sensing this shift in public mood, Luce's managing editors on both *Time* and *Life* urged him to get off the MacArthur bandwagon, or at least to modulate the banging of the editorial drums. Luce, who had an editor's intuition when not to push his readership too far, agreed.

But Luce had found the themes his magazines would continue to strike: that merely trying to contain the Communists was not enough; anything less than all-out confrontation was appeasement. In MacArthur's readiness to use Chiang to continue the war with Communist China, and in the determined opposition of Truman and Acheson to any such action, Luce saw his two earthly obsessions—the futures of China and of the Republican Party—conjoined.

Luce's next step was to prepare his magazine for battle. To ensure a Republican victory in 1952, Luce wanted to have sufficiently partisan editors in key places on his magazines to propagandize for his candidate and to smite the opposition. As always, he did not reveal his intentions until ready to strike. He decided he had to replace the managing editor of *Time*, T. S. Matthews.

Tom, about the same age as Luce, had joined the magazine in his twenties, an example of Luce's capacity for spotting talent. He had not set out to be a journalist and was never comfortable in being one. To make him managing editor was one of Luce's most audacious executive choices.

The most literarily gifted editor *Time* ever had, Tom Matthews was handsome, patrician, and reserved. He was also apolitical ("I have lived among historical events without noticing them," he once acknowledged). He disdained politics as a vulgar, irrelevant game played by hacks and people with uninteresting minds; economics was a boring subject pursued by self-important experts just as confused as everyone else about the subject. These were two very large areas for the managing editor of a newsmagazine to treat with an amateur's disregard. To Matthews a nation's arts and literature were its real news.

Matthews was a child of privilege but not of luxury. His father was the stern Episcopal bishop of New Jersey; his mother was a Procter, an heiress to the Procter and Gamble fortune. Tom descended to *Time* after Princeton, Oxford, a spell at Mallorca under the tutelage of his friend the poet Robert Graves, and a literary apprenticeship at *The New Republic* under Edmund Wilson. When young Matthews joined the upstart newsmagazine Wilson all but disowned him.

From the outset, Tom was not happy at *Time*. At *The New Republic*, the young Matthews had felt himself in the company of "scholarly, distinguished men"; at *Time*, of "smart ignorant boys." Of his first years at the magazine he once commented, "On every piece of copy I wrote, I could have written with truth, 'I do not like my work.' "

Matthews couldn't get the hang of writing in *Time* style—which he characterized as "this ludicrous, exhibitionistic but arresting dialect of journalese"—until he decided that the trick was to parody it. Once he became an editor, Tom's great achievement at the magazine was to abolish its hackneyed and irritating mannerisms, replacing them with a straightforward colloquial English informed by his admiration for Fowler's *Modern English Usage* and the cadences of Yeats's poetry.

He stayed at *Time* for nearly twenty-five years. If he disliked it so, why did he stay? "I had become so used to *Time*'s ways . . . that I hardly noticed them any longer—as I suppose a worker in a glue factory becomes impervious to the smell of glue." But as he also came to take *Time* more seriously, he was put in charge of editing *Time*'s cultural coverage, the "back of the book," and succeeded so well that he grew in Luce's favor. If this was so, Tom believed, it was because of his performance, "not because our personalities matched." In his autobiography, *Name and Address,* Matthews drew this portrait of his boss:

> Luce was a good-looking man: just under six feet, with strong, regular features, unusually bushy eyebrows, shapely, tapering but hairy hands. His physical endowments were certainly above the average, and yet the sum total was disappointing, the general effect cold. Perhaps it was his small eyes, whose normal expression ran a narrow range from the noncommittal to the suspicious, peering out at you from under the thicket of his eyebrows; perhaps it was the set of his face, which he could manipulate into quizzical amusement, mock surprise or wary attentiveness, but which always settled again into a severe, poker-faced, almost Oriental impassiveness.

The two men sometimes got on each other's nerves; there were occasions when Luce thought Matthews was being snobbish or morally superior, or when Matthews was irritated by Luce's "bad manners and devious secretiveness." Yet, Matthews wrote, "men who work together long enough get to know each other pretty well, and sometimes even develop a kind of attachment to each other that is no less real for being the result of a chance association. In this sense at least, Luce and I were friends. As far as he was concerned, I don't think he had any other kind."

Luce's "devious secretiveness" was much in evidence as the 1952 election approached. He wanted to move Matthews out of his influential job as managing editor of *Time,* yet he didn't want to lose him. Luce might be famously clumsy at getting rid of people, but he could be most adept at shuffling them about.

Two years before the 1952 election he invited Matthews to lunch in his apartment, where for forty-five minutes Luce was at his "disarming best," Matthews later wrote, before he "casually let drop the fact that he had given my job to my deputy. Well now, what were we going to do about me? That seemed to me his problem, not mine, and I said so."

Finally Luce indicated "that he might be willing to vacate his title of editor of *Time* in my favor." That post meant something when Luce himself was called the editor, but, as Matthews quickly discovered, the title was an empty one when given to anyone else. Traditionally on the magazine it was the *managing* editor—"one of the toughest and most exacting jobs in America," Luce called it—who ran the staff and sent each issue to press, as Matthews had done for six years. Put out to pasture as the editor, Matthews had to be given suitable responsibility. He would edit the magazine's cover story each week. This would pose no problem, since Matthews was so politically indifferent. But in the year 1952, when his Princeton roommate Adlai Stevenson became the Democratic candidate, Matthews suddenly discovered that the distasteful world of partisan politics, with all its flagrant misrepresentations, rabbit punches, and nasty tactics, really did count. Luce's lightly taken decision to have Matthews edit cover stories would have consequences unforeseen.

Luce's choice as the new managing editor, Roy Alexander, was in marked contrast to Matthews: he was easygoing, matey, and politically savvy. In *Time*'s aviary, a congeries of poets with their wings clipped and a number of other colorfully plumed eccentrics, Roy was that rare bird, a seasoned newspaperman. A Marine in World War I, he was an ardent military buff who during World War II, after long hours at *Time,* spent his weekends test-flying new warplanes, until Roy Grumman discovered that Alexander had seven children and grounded him. A popular, unpretentious man, Roy Alexander felt conscious of his "peasant complex" whenever he ate at expense-account watering holes like 21; he was more at home in Toots Shor's, a brassy plebeian bar where, like Frank Sinatra, he was always assured of a head table.

A devout Roman Catholic,* and once a strong believer in Franklin D. Roosevelt, he gradually, without admitting it to his colleagues, defected from the Democrats on the issue of Communism. He was a forerunner of the Catholic voters who became known as Reagan Democrats; he was ideally suited to carry out Luce's 1952 campaign plans.

Luce's next task was to choose someone sufficiently partisan to produce the kind of National Affairs section he wanted. That meant moving me out—though it was not put to me that way. I was told that Max Ways, the foreign editor, was tired of his job and wanted to trade places with me. I was assured that the move would be lateral—that the job of foreign editor was "just as important." This in fact proved to be the case in the nine years I spent in that job. Events such as the upheavals in the Soviet leadership, the rebellion in Hungary, Nasser's seizure of the Suez Canal, war in the Middle East, and turbulence in Africa proved "just as important" to me too. I later came to see, though I did not think so at the time, that in moving me in 1952, Luce had wanted to spare me, as well as himself, much anguish, since he was determined to cover the 1952 election in a way I could not have lived with.

Max Ways, who succeeded me, was an intense, dogmatic, and well-read Catholic intellectual, a heavy-handed editor who allowed his writers little more freedom than had Whittaker

---

*A phrase that Roy would not tolerate in *Time*. To him this suggested that Baptists, Jews, Arabs, and Episcopalians were less devout. Instead, to make the same point about faithful Catholics, he would describe someone like General de Gaulle as a "daily communicant."

Chambers. But after hours, at the racetrack, this onetime Baltimore newspaperman could be a congenial companion. He was the polemicist who had written *Time*'s heavy-breathing attack on Truman's firing of MacArthur.

Ways's next big moment came at the Republican convention in Chicago. Though Eisenhower with his friendly grin had drawn big crowds on his return to the United States, it was Taft who was the favorite among convention delegates. Out on the hustings Ike had shown himself ignorant and evasive on the issues; the party faithful knew where Taft stood, and most shared his views.

To challenge Taft's lead among delegates, Eisenhower's political strategists decided to make a moral issue out of Taft's control of delegations from the deep South. There, where white Republican voters were few, the handpicked delegates, most of them black, were traditionally delivered to the highest bidder. The Eisenhower forces challenged the seating of eighty-eight delegates from Georgia, Louisiana, and Texas. They did so with help from *Time* magazine. The magazine had gone to press in Chicago several hours earlier than usual so that at each seat in the convention hall delegates would find a specially delivered copy of the magazine, detailing the accusations of corruption, along with a handy chart, devised by Ways, showing that in states where Republicans had a real chance of winning, Eisenhower was more popular than Taft. With this crucial assist from *Time,* Eisenhower overcame Taft's lead and won the nomination. Many of Luce's friends among Taft supporters never forgave him for the magazine's role in destroying Taft.

Having picked a candidate whose genial naïveté might make him a weak campaigner, the convention chose Richard Nixon as vice president, knowing that Nixon could be counted on to do whatever rough campaigning was needed—a man who would take partisan advantage of the unpopular war in Korea, raise a fuss about corruption in the Democratic Party, and denounce, with the innuendo he was a master of, "Dean Acheson's Cowardly College of Communist Containment."

Once Eisenhower was nominated, *Time* turned with practiced skill and long experience to denouncing the Democratic ticket. As managing editor, Tom Matthews had acquiesced indifferently in those earlier distortions, acknowledging in his autobiography that he "might have taken politics more seriously." He was serious enough this time. As he wrote: "In 1952, when it sniffed victory in the air at long last, there was no holding *Time*. The distortions, suppressions and slanting of its political news seemed to me to pass the bounds of politics and to commit an offense against the ethics of journalism."

For Matthews the issue was joined when, two weeks before the election, *Time* put Adlai Stevenson on its cover. (With a subtlety probably wasted on most readers, Luce liked to put the *Republican* candidate on the newsstands the week voters went to the polls, hoping this would influence voters.)

Under the new arrangement, it was Matthews's job to edit the Stevenson cover story. One of the magazine's top editors, himself politically conservative, volunteered to write the story. Aware that Matthews would edit the story, the writer knew that he would have to sneak his own point of view past Matthews. Presumably he took as his model the wily oration Shakespeare's Mark Antony delivers at Caesar's funeral, in which Antony, while seeming to praise Brutus ("For Brutus is an honorable man"), stealthily denigrates him. In similar fashion the *Time* writer praised Adlai Stevenson's eloquence but gave an uninspired example; and in celebrating Stevenson's wit quoted a lame, unfunny remark. It was, as Matthews put it, "a clumsy but malign and murderously meant attack." Matthews took his scissors and paste and inserted a genuinely eloquent passage and a genuinely witty one, and gave the rest of the story a going-over. In the ensuing argument, Max Ways joined in on the writer's side. (Ways, in a fury, had once shouted at Matthews:

"The trouble with *Time* is, it's too fucking fair, and you're the one that does it." Matthews considered this a tribute and treasured it.)

As the result of so much bickering over the Stevenson cover story it was no literary gem, nor was it a model of political journalism, but at least it did not demonize the candidate. Now it was Luce's turn to be furious. He sent Matthews a curt note saying that he personally—and not Matthews—would edit the final week's cover story on Ike.

As Luce had predicted from the beginning, Eisenhower won the election, and by such a landslide in both the electoral and popular vote that Luce must have wondered whether it had been so necessary to compromise *Time*'s integrity to elect him. Perhaps, after twenty Republican years in the wilderness, Luce wanted to take no chances. But it was a costly price to pay, in terms of public trust and staff morale. The Eisenhower campaign was the high point—or low mark—of *Time*'s distortion of the news.

Once again the editorial staff was invited to a conciliatory dinner in the luxurious precincts of the Union League Club. It was Matthews who suggested it. Most of the staff arrived expecting an apology from Luce for *Time*'s campaign misbehavior and believed it would come easier for Luce now that the Republicans had won. Luce spoke without text, which always encouraged his tendency to ramble, as he did that night, wandering from Marx to Nietzsche. It also brought forth from him some ill-considered off-the-cuff remarks taunting Matthews. Luce was anything but apologetic. "Though it has never been said to you before," he told his dinner guests, "I'm your boss."

Some in the room, recognizing in the occasion a side of Luce they had never seen before, began taking notes, and afterward they gathered to coalesce their scribbles into what became a kind of authorized text of the evening: Luce, to a questioner: "I told you I was your boss. I guess that means I can fire any of you." Looking over at Alexander, the managing editor, Luce added: "I don't know anyone here who has a contract, have they, Roy? So I could fire any of you. . . . But I don't know anybody who can fire me. Sometimes I wish there were."

It was the worst public performance by Luce that any of us had ever seen. Perhaps it was the bad behavior of a man who, having overruled his conscience, was still troubled by it. Afterward, a half dozen of Tom Matthews's friends joined him at the nearby Polo Bar for a postmortem. The mood was mutinous. "I've got to resign," Tom kept repeating to us, "I've got to resign."

Any writer who tries to join together the professional lives of Harry Luce and Teddy White soon discovers that Teddy has most of the best lines. Teddy spent a lifetime recording his feelings about what he saw. Harry, except for outbursts like that at his Eisenhower victory dinner, rarely went public with his feelings. They must be deduced from the reactions of his colleagues. No one saw him more closely and with more clarity than Tom Matthews, who once made a catalogue of all the contradictory adjectives that could be applied to Luce: *suspicious, devious, cold, rude, crude, sensitive, flinty, generous, exciting, boring, enthusiastic, exhausting, inspiring, appreciative, shrewd, quick, prejudiced, shy, complex, simple, brilliant, ambitious, remorseful.*

Matthews is an ideal witness to explain the attraction of working for Luce and *Time* because the usual assumption made by unfriendly critics that the staff was seduced by big money did not apply in his case. Matthews was so well-off that his salary was an added tax burden to him.

Once, when Matthews was managing editor, he got so mad at one of Luce's brusque memos that he wrote Luce:

No decent human being would answer your memo by accepting it. . . . You have written it as if to dogs, not to human beings. And you thus make a great mistake.

If you're really degenerating into a barking boss, you'll soon have behind you only the anxious, stupid, dishonest subservience that kind of boss can command. But you will no longer command either my respect or my services.

Matthews would later conclude, "As I look back on those days, I can see now that Luce must have put up with a great deal from me. . . . I can't imagine Beaverbrook, or McCormick, or any press lord you can mention, tolerating that kind of talk from one of his subordinates." Since both of the men were, as Matthews reminded Luce, "preacher's sons," they often in their political arguments irritated each other by claiming to have seized the higher moral ground. In one such tussle Luce wrote to Matthews:

> For years & years liberals thought it was their privilege to hound and inquisit others. Practically every businessman was a villain, in their book, until proved innocent. . . . And how about Journalism—it is a villain in your book, isn't it, which barely on occasion shrives itself? But the liberal was never a villain. He might be at worst an alcoholic. It was his privilege to seek out villainy, he being immune to it.
>
> Look, Tom, we are all sinners and all have "fallen short" as St. Paul says. . . . Men judge each other and society from very narrow biases. Both yours and mine are doubtless narrower than they ought to be.

The differences between Luce and Matthews are to be found in the files, a matter of record; what is not to be found there is their more routine daily satisfactions: the stimulus of working out together a fresh response to complex events, the craftsman's pleasure in a job well done, even admiration for each other's talents. I know that such satisfactions were there, for I was present through most of those years.

When Tom Matthews submitted his resignation after the unpleasant staff dinner that followed Eisenhower's election, Luce (who knew of Matthews's fondness for England) persuaded him instead to go to London to look into the possibility of an English edition of the magazine, to be called *Time-in-Britain*. Tom worked hard at his assignment for several months, devising a magazine in three parts—news, views, and reviews. (His secret ambition, he told me years later, was to design on a modest budget an English *Time* that would put to shame its wayward American sister.) When Luce offered to invest a million dollars in the experiment, Matthews took a three-year lease on a London flat. But Luce quickly reversed himself when the business managers of the company, taking a colder look at the budget, said no.

Hiding his disappointment, Tom wired New York: "Why did you keep me standing on tiptoe so long if you weren't going to kiss me? Ah well." On that blithe but bitter note, Tom Matthews left *Time* for good.

Matthews came to think of Luce as torn daily (and nightly) by a struggle with apocalyptic beasts, between the miserable sinner of his Presbyterian creed and his constant competitive striving to be a success. "I finally decided that what most drew me to Luce and made me feel that we had something in common—and has kept me fond of him, even when I didn't like him—was his guilty conscience."

After Luce died, Matthews summed up his ambivalence about his former boss in these words: "Luce was not a likeable man, but he was in some ways a lovable one."

Chapter 14

THE DARK AGE
OF JOE McCARTHY

Midway in the twentieth century the sky was darkened over the United States, as an eclipse might blot out the sun, by the phenomenon of McCarthyism. But unlike a solar eclipse, which quickly gives way to sunshine, this despicable era in American history persisted for years. The phenomenon of McCarthyism, which helped sweep Dwight Eisenhower into the White House, grew even stronger after his victory, eventually tarnishing Ike's own reputation before McCarthy himself could be brought low.

During this demonic period a public swept by fear believed liars, demagogues, and charlatans; a miasma of suspicion seeped through government, journalism, and the halls of academia. People who had earlier joined some worthy cause whose letterhead bore the names of left-wingers found their innocent act branded treasonable. Colleagues who had once worked together agreeably on campuses, on newspapers and magazines, in the theater, or in Hollywood now suspected one another of disloyalty and informed on others to save themselves. Those who "took the Fifth," refusing under oath to name names to a congressional committee, were themselves subjected to calumny and sometimes lost their jobs.

Joe McCarthy, a cynically ambitious star-spangled brawler, had chosen as the targets of his twentieth-century inquisition those who "lost China to the Reds." Anyone who had anything to do with China before the Communists took over that country in 1949 was particularly vulnerable. McCarthy waved his shotgun so wildly and recklessly that Harry Luce and Teddy White, so far apart in their judgments on China, were both caught in the crossfire. Of the two, Teddy White suffered more. He was driven to exile in Europe. McCarthyism blighted Teddy's personal and professional life for a decade.

Luce found the era of McCarthyism perplexing: Though he deplored McCarthy's methods, many of the senator's victims had earlier been targets of Luce himself. Furthermore, Luce's two most influential advisers on foreign policy, Whittaker Chambers and Willi Schlamm, both ex-Communists, had made careers out of being anti-Communist long before the possibility occurred to Joe McCarthy. That Chambers and Schlamm differed sharply in their response to McCarthyism is one indication of the complexity of the turmoil the senator created.

TEDDY WHITE AND JOE MCCARTHY

Teddy's great success with *Thunder Out of China* not only established his reputation as a journalist but also contributed to his undoing. On page one of *The New York Times Book Review* his old Harvard teacher John K. Fairbank gave the book a rave review, but in the Middle West most of the major newspapers criticized it.

As Teddy wrote later, at first he enjoyed the public attention his China book got "without realizing that its longest-lasting effect would be to list him as a leader among those who 'lost China to the Reds';* [he was] completely unaware that with the

---

*In view of what later became known about the Communists' brainwashing of their people, perhaps the most vulnerable misjudgment by White in *Thunder Out of China*

publication of his book, the FBI was instantly on his trail, noting his speeches, his actions, the meetings he attended, scrutinizing his private life for detail running back to the war years."

But, for the moment, Teddy joined the convivial company of a Manhattan crowd of journalists, many of them former correspondents, liberal in their politics, who drank together and traded war stories. With the royalties from his book, he could afford to pursue the kind of career he wanted.

He turned down the middle-of-the-road *Saturday Evening Post*, which wanted to hire him as a correspondent, to take a job that paid half as much as an editor at *The New Republic*. There, he figured, he would be at a magazine whose liberal political views he shared. Its new editor was Henry Agard Wallace, who had been vice president of the United States during Roosevelt's third term. Wallace had earlier made his fortune in Iowa developing hybrid corn. As a professional geneticist he was precise; as a politician he was woolly-minded and gullible. In his personal beliefs he was something of a mystic: to his admirers a guru, to his detractors a "bubblehead."

White was surprised at the depth of Wallace's loathing of Roosevelt, who, by abandoning Wallace and choosing Harry Truman as his running mate on the Democratic ticket in 1948, had put Truman in the White House, where Wallace thought he himself belonged. Wallace, White wrote, had become "a bitter man; eccentric, ambitious, self-righteous." Still longing to be president, Wallace had fallen under the influence of Communists and other left-wingers. They flattered and counseled him, and persuaded him to head the ticket of the new Progressive

---

is this passage: "Yenan's unanimity of spirit could be judged as you wished. . . . The Kuomintang claimed that Yenan's unity was totalitarian, that Yenan operated with secret police, with concentration camps, with all the other apparatus that the Kuomintang possessed itself but denied possessing. I could find no evidence of any such machinery of oppression in Yenan; I was there for only a few weeks, but other Americans who were there for months were equally unaware of any such Communist apparatus of dictatorship as Chungking had mastered." He wrote this in 1946.

Party. In China, White had admired Communists ready to die for their cause, but American Communists he found to be "an unpleasant breed of neurotics." Within six months, White quit *The New Republic* in disillusionment. He had learned that " 'liberalism' in politics does not always extend to personal courtesy or intellectual tolerance. There was less freedom to deviate from the line of the *New Republic* than from the line of *Time* magazine."

Teddy's next enterprise, undertaken in admiration and friendship, added to his journalistic reputation—both favorably and unfavorably—and also to his future problems. General Stilwell's widow, wanting to see her husband vindicated in history after his humiliating dismissal, asked Teddy to make a book out of the general's diaries and papers. Stilwell's scorching denunciations of Chiang Kai-shek were set down in a neat legible hand, though often written in anger and fatigue after hours in the field. White's commentary was balanced and temperate, but though *The Stilwell Papers* got good reviews from those whose opinions he valued most, Teddy himself was sometimes unfairly denounced for "having distorted, violated, clipped and cut the private thoughts of a great American war hero, to make a left-winger's political point in the debate about China." Such was the political climate of the day.

In his autobiography, White noted: "Thus evaporated all the offerings and jobs he had rejected a year earlier to join the *New Republic*—all the major magazine assignments, all the staff posts, all the opportunities. The McCarthy years were about to close in," and he would be caught in its spotlight.

White was concerned about his future, the more so since he had just fallen in love with Nancy Bean, whom he described as "one of the beautiful researchers at *Time* magazine. She was young, gay and loving." She had been assigned to work with him on a story about the Yangtze River, and when she entered his office, where he sat with his feet up on his desk, he greeted her with "What do you know about gorges, gorgeous?"

She came from a conservative Connecticut family; her father, an executive in a metal company, was president of the local chamber of commerce. But after Sweetbriar and war service in India with the Office of War Information, Nancy had become, in Teddy's words, a "flaming liberal." She was lively, intelligent, gregarious, and fascinated by politics.

She was Protestant, he Jewish, and because of objections from their families, neither a synagogue nor a church seemed an appropriate place for their marriage. But in New York City, where judges were political and religious distinctions mattered, arranging a quiet civil wedding proved difficult. It would be politically awkward in those days for a Jewish judge to marry a young Jewish man to a Gentile; no Protestant judge was available. Finally they found a Catholic judge who, upon learning that the groom was Jewish and the bride Protestant, fortunately concluded that both were pagans in the eyes of God, so he was free to marry them. He recessed a murder trial over which he was presiding to marry Teddy and Nancy in his chambers. A few correspondent friends were present; Nancy's parents stood on one side of the chamber, but not, Nancy insists, "glowering," as Teddy wrote. Teddy's mother and his younger brother Robert were there, but his sister refused to come.

Teddy would later decide that the differences in temperament between the newlyweds had to do not so much with religion as with a "sense of class." Though Teddy seemed the hearty, cocky one, fast on his feet and funny, popular at office gatherings and friendly to everyone, he was also given to melancholy self-doubts. Nancy had a confident sense of belonging. She was, Teddy wrote, "full of gaieties; her presence made any gathering a party, and parties became a way of life for them, until, too late, he realized he hated parties almost as much as she loved them." Teddy worried about his money giving out; she, confident in herself and confident for him, was fearlessly prepared to take chances. He was anxious to get back to reporting, though at this point he needed a job, and a fresh start, more than money.

He worried about staying on in America: his celebrity as a best-selling author and his reputation among fellow journalists did not reflect his true circumstances. He had, "in effect, been blacklisted by the mass magazines that had only months before sought his copy and his by-line." He had already been summoned to appear before one congressional committee and could foresee being called by others. Some of his friendships with old China hands were fraying; he found them living too much in a past he was trying to escape from. He saw no future in writing for small left-wing magazines, with the dubious distinction of being revered as a martyr. Nor did he want any part of the sectarian quarrels of Manhattan's politicized literary intellectuals. He was meant to write for large magazines with mass audiences, good salaries, and generous expense accounts. None of these magazines, and no big newspaper, would send him abroad. Finally, "after seeking, telephoning, groveling," he landed a one-year job in Paris for a small, nearly bankrupt service called the Overseas News Agency. It paid little but gave him the journalist's credentials he needed.

Teddy and Nancy loved Paris. The years immediately after the war were a golden time for a convivial pack of American journalists stationed there, among them Don Cook, Frank White, Ben Bradlee, Art Buchwald, and Teddy. They could live cheaply and eat well. Drawing on his New York bank for royalties from *Thunder Out of China,* Teddy in the spring of 1948 was able to buy five hundred French francs for a dollar on the black market (a skill he had perfected in Chungking). At that rate, a fine meal in a top Parisian restaurant cost him two dollars; he and Nancy rented a fashionable apartment on the Rue du Boccador off the Champs Élysées for one hundred dollars a month, living a little more grandly than their colleagues, and partying on champagne and caviar. They hired a servant, bought an automobile, then a second one. In that first year of the Marshall Plan, with the United States sending millions of dollars to help Europe recover, Americans were popular and enjoyed special perks. With U.S. passports they could buy a car in a few days; Frenchmen had to wait a year. Correspondents enjoyed semidiplomatic privileges at a commissary, where they could buy American luxury goods denied to the French.

Best of all, for the journalists, they had a succession of exciting news stories to cover. Europe was beginning to recover from defeat, but each step of the way was contested, in strikes and street battles between the left and the right. After the cold and hunger of 1945 and 1946 and the crop failure of 1947, France's exhilaration over the Liberation had given way to unrest. The Cold War had begun. Paris was the international capital of Communism—thuggish demonstrators in the streets, arrogant literary lions in the salons, eager to gain for Stalin the dominance in Western Europe he had already won in the East. To resist these efforts, NATO was born. Teddy White, who had once begged Harry Luce to send him to Russia to find out for himself whether Russia's critics were right or wrong, now had no doubts. With the Korean War, the coup in Czechoslovakia, the blockade of Berlin, Teddy "passed my own divide": he was now a Cold Warrior, ardently welcoming NATO.

Teddy had meant to stay in Europe only a year or two before finding his way back to China. Instead he stayed for five and a half years. In 1949, the year Chiang fled to Taiwan and the Communists gained control of the mainland, Nancy White was pregnant with their daughter, Heyden; the next year, when the Korean War broke out, she was pregnant again. "Our son David was born in January 1951," Teddy wrote, "but I no longer regretted being kept away from war and revolution in Asia. That story was now part of my past, too far away to seek again."

He was enjoying Europe's good living and its story opportunities too much. He found American leaders he could enthusiastically support, and as an outsider traveling with meager credentials, Teddy set out to cultivate them. He was always good at getting to people at the top. With cheeky charm, and adroit flattery when needed, he ingratiated himself with men who became his news sources. Paul Hoffman, an ebullient midwestern businessman who headed the Marshall Plan, came close "to being a saint, in the secular sense." Hoffman's partner in administering the Marshall Plan was the wealthy Averell Harriman, who in government service was hardworking, single-minded, and a bit dour. A special favorite of Teddy's was Ambassador David Bruce, who was an elegant amateur of the arts and a smoothly professional diplomat.

These men became his tutors, giving him a crash course in international economics and European politics. He would fill pocket-sized spiral notebooks with facts and numbers and explanations. When he made fact-gathering trips to other countries he would check out his impressions with Jean Monnet, the brilliant French planner known as Mister Europe. Monnet, quick of mind and tart of tongue, had an irritating way of suddenly asking a crucial question. "You would open your mouth to answer; he would snap Don't explain. Just answer yes or no. We both know your reasoning either way. I just want to see how you add things up."

Though happy in Europe, Teddy could not escape his Chinese past. One day in 1952, while reporting a story in Germany, Teddy got a frantic cable from his younger brother Robert, a junior technical researcher at MIT, working on a secret weather-forecasting project for the air force. Robert's security clearance was being lifted "because he was the brother of the well-known subversive Theodore H. White"!

To Teddy the situation was Kafkaesque. Teddy held NATO press card No. 6, "which meant clearance, re-clearance, and over-again clearance by every security agency of the U.S. Army. . . . Could the Air Force fire, for brotherhood, a man whose brother the Army had cleared?" Teddy White appealed personally on his brother's behalf to David Bruce, by then undersecretary of state. Robert's clearance was quickly reinstated; he went on to create and to head the National Oceanic and Atmospheric Agency.

The following year Senator Joe McCarthy's two rascally young assistants, Roy Cohn and David Schine, junketed to Europe and visited USIA libraries, looking for subversive materials, and headlines for themselves. In Berlin they found copies of *Thunder Out of China* and ordered them removed and burned. Teddy's friend Ben Bradlee, then a press attaché in the American embassy in Paris, got up a letter to be signed by his boss, Ambassador Douglas Dillon, listing all the credentials and security clearances Teddy had, including one signed by the new president, Dwight Eisenhower. This was sent to the new secretary of state, John Foster Dulles, who, while not noted for standing up for members of his own department when their past views on China became controversial, supported Dillon in this case. *Thunder Out of China* was restored to USIA bookshelves, against the dictates of Joe McCarthy and his roving thought-policemen Cohn and Schine.

Although he was receiving royalties from *Thunder Out of China* Teddy was not earning enough otherwise to pay his expenses. The Overseas News Agency, just a step from bankruptcy, was several thousand dollars in arrears in the salary it owed him. In desperation Teddy set out to market his own stories on any subject on which he could find an interested editor. He wrote about Paris fashions, the Irish birthrate, the best restaurants of Paris, the plight of German women, who outnumbered German men by six million. But American editors, buffeted by the winds of McCarthyism, often found him "too 'controversial' to print—except on gourmet food and Roman ruins." Only two men—Lester Markel, the powerful editor of *The New York Times Magazine,* and Max Ascoli, editor of the magazine *The Reporter*—had the courage to print signed pieces on political subjects by Teddy White. "Of the work I did for Markel and Ascoli I was proud; of all the other work I felt like a rug merchant, proud not so much of the product as at having closed the sale."

The dreary hours spent in journalistic hackwork, the continuing concern about his fading reputation, and the fact that he and his family were living beyond their means troubled Teddy. "In four spendthrift years," he wrote, "we had eaten up all the savings of *Thunder Out of China*." His wife, Nancy, ever the more optimistic of the two, had a simple solution: Teddy should write another best-seller.

Teddy decided to write a book about how, with wise and generous American aid, Europe was recovering its health. While he was writing it, Teddy and Nancy decided, they would live in style with what funds they had left. They splurged on a seven-bedroom villa on the Riviera, with nine acres of vineyard and orchard leading down to the Mediterranean, in the fishing village of Le Lavandou. They took along two servants to cook and care for the children. Teddy worked at his typewriter every morning from seven to eleven, then went for a swim, his writing done for the day.

The family lived among lemon and orange trees, and in the evenings they sat on the terrace watching the sunset, often in the company of visiting friends and overnight guests. Teddy worked there on his book in the spring of 1952, and in the summers of 1952 and 1953. Weeks after he sent his manuscript to New York, the telephone rang. It was his publisher calling; in New York, the Book-of-the-Month Club judges had just chosen *Fire in the Ashes* by Theodore H. White as a main selection.

As Nancy had confidently anticipated, it became a best-seller. The *New York Times* review called it a "challenging and well-reasoned book." His publishers, the book club judges, and the book-buying public had restored his reputation and his self-confidence. He and his family returned to the States; he was in the money, a celebrity. His patriotism had also been reaffirmed—or so he thought. But the forces that had been unleashed by Joseph McCarthy were not yet through with Teddy White.

HARRY LUCE
AND JOE MCCARTHY

Though *Time* and *Life* were from the outset in the forefront of journalistic opposition to Senator Joe McCarthy, Luce himself was slow, as his sister Beth acknowledges, to recognize the evil of McCarthyism. He and McCarthy were too much in agreement on who were the American villains in the "loss" of China to the Communists.

Yet as early as 1950 Luce had sent a memo to his editorial writer on *Life:* "It's about time to hit [McCarthyism] hard. 'Communism' has become too much the . . . scapegoat of everything that's wrong with us. The fact is, Communism is no longer a real issue, even indirectly, in America."

Time's first cover story on McCarthy, in October 1951, was captioned "Demagogue McCarthy." It treated the senator with distaste and disdain as a "burly, ham-fisted . . . two-fisted drinker" who had designated himself a sentry for the Republic, a sentry "who maliciously cries wolf, shoots up the coconut trees and keeps the camp in a state of alarm and confusion."

Behind the ridicule was a touch of embarrassment that such a lout should vulgarize the very case Luce himself was trying to make. The cover story tried to make this distinction clear:

1) His antics foul up the necessary examination of the past mistakes of the Truman-Acheson foreign policy.
2) His constant imputation of treason distracts attention from the fact that patriotic men make calamitous mistakes for which they should be held politically responsible.

3)   There are never any circumstances which justify the imputation of treason or other moral guilt to individuals in or out of office.

After the cover story was published, Senator McCarthy, who had previously ignored criticism by the Luce publications, wrote Luce a letter rumbling with menace, suggesting the line of attack he would later use against *Time:* "As you know . . . the Communist *Daily Worker* has led a vicious personal smear attack against me, which has been gleefully joined in by a vast number of the camp-following elements of the press and radio. You, of course, are fully aware of the extent to which *Time* magazine has joined in this campaign."

The angry reaction by many readers to *Time*'s cover story convinced the editors that it was too late in the day to destroy McCarthy and McCarthyism by mere ridicule. McCarthy had touched a sensitive nerve: the public was alarmed by the fall of China to Communism and by the Soviet Union's continuing military threat to Western Europe; it was weary of the Korean War, in which Communists were killing Americans. McCarthy fanned this discontent by arguing that the United States was being destroyed from the inside by traitors. This charge gained credence when Klaus Fuchs, a Communist scientist who had held high-level atomic posts in the United States, was arrested in London as a spy, and the United States learned, as *Time* put it, that it "had been playing the game of survival with the enemy looking over its shoulder at all its top-secret cards."

Yet *Time* persisted in pointing out that McCarthy had not proven his case that the State Department was riddled with traitors; not one Communist had been found there. "Loud-mouthed Joe McCarthy had been irresponsible all right—and worse," *Time* said. "His charges were so completely without evidence to support them that he had probably damaged no reputations permanently except his own."

One of McCarthy's strengths was knowing how to play the

press, which by now generally despised him but hungered for headlines. As soon as the State Department accusation was discredited, McCarthy proclaimed that he had unearthed the "top Soviet espionage agent in the United States." This charge proved to be against a Johns Hopkins professor, Owen Lattimore, an Asian scholar who had once worked for Chiang Kai-shek, before turning against him. McCarthy's accusation dumbfounded J. Edgar Hoover. Though Lattimore's name was to be found on the FBI's voluminous lists of subversives, Hoover didn't regard him as important, or a spy. Hoover, no more anxious than anyone else to take on McCarthy, kept this knowledge to himself.

Time, in reporting McCarthy's charge against Lattimore, agreed that in speeches and books and in his influence at the State Department, Lattimore "undoubtedly contributed to Chiang's downfall and the triumph of Chairman Mao," a belief strongly held by Luce. But again *Time* insisted on a distinction: In the tangled ugly period of free China's last years, "he was not alone in his judgment. He may have made enormous errors of judgment—but that was a long way from proving him a Communist, let alone a 'top Russian espionage agent.'. . . McCarthy had said he would stand or fall on the case of Lattimore. It looked as if he had fallen."

Early on, Luce had been convinced that Communism would be a "phony issue by 1952." But this time the editor who prided himself on his gift for prophecy and his ability to read public opinion was decidedly wrong. McCarthy, with a demagogue's touch for exploiting public concern, became increasingly a political force to reckon with after he helped the Republicans score heavily in the 1950 off-year elections. A lonely operator with no talent for organization, McCarthy nonetheless attracted a motley army of supporters, ranging from veterans groups, professional patriots, religious people who saw Stalin as the anti-Christ, opportunistic politicians, mercenary informers, and millionaire right-wingers.

In a climate where fear and suspicion flourished, a new cottage industry of character assassination was born. The more commercially astute of these volunteer vigilantes assembled blacklists of presumed subversives and threatened Hollywood, the networks, advertisers, and publishers who dared employ anyone listed. Typical was a "newsletter" called *Counterattack,* which told its readers early in 1950 that *Life* magazine had given Marsha Hunt a million dollars' worth of free publicity by putting her on its cover and had also dared write admiringly about Judy Holliday, though both of these actresses had supported causes *Counterattack* considered unpatriotic. Furthermore, *Fortune* magazine, in celebrating its twentieth anniversary, had put a "proud American eagle" on its cover, though it had been sculpted by William Zorach, "who [had] carved himself a niche in the Communists' Hall of Front Supporters." It urged its readers to put pressure on both Luce and the head of *Look* magazine (which had offended by putting Leonard Bernstein on its cover) for helping build Communist power in the United States, actions "incompatible with the anti-Communist stand both men have taken in their publications."

That was too much for Luce. In a letter to the publisher of *Counterattack,* one J. G. Keenan, Luce offered to match his record of anti-Communism against Keenan's, adding sarcastically: "We have not yet adopted a policy of suppressing all news of purely artistic achievement by people who are deficient in political understanding. . . . Also, we have not yet engaged or organized a private FBI to check up on all painters, sculptors or other artists before any of our Art Directors may give them any assignments. Do you think we should?"

Yet there were times when *Life*'s editorial page seemed to echo McCarthy. It described Secretary of State Dean Acheson as the man "who befriended Alger Hiss and was mixed up with the Owen Lattimore crowd in the State Department who stupidly or deliberately played into Communist hands in Asia." At best, this malicious passage is no better than a drawing-room re-phrasing of McCarthy's earthier street version.

In the daily blizzard of informal memos Luce rained down on his editors from his aerie atop the Time and Life Building—these were meant to be indications of his state of mind, not to be taken as instructions—he would complain that readers knew of the magazines' opposition to McCarthy, but did they also know of the magazines' opposition to Owen Lattimore? Privately Luce took a harder line than his magazines; he nagged and nudged his editors but did not overrule them.

Time and *Life* were clearly getting under Joe McCarthy's thin skin. In January of the election year of 1952, McCarthy sent a registered letter to Luce, simultaneously releasing it to the press, in which he advised all *Time* advertisers "of the type of publication" they were supporting: "The policy of *Time* magazine to throw pebbles at Communism generally, but then to parallel the *Daily Worker*'s smear attack upon individuals who start to dig out the dangerous secret Communists, is rendering almost unlimited service to the Communist cause and undermining America."

Even newspaper editors who didn't like Luce disliked still more the notion of stirring up advertisers against someone's editorial policies; they rallied to Luce's side. McCarthy's threat failed: a few small advertisers did withdraw their ads, and Andrew Heiskell, the publisher of *Life*, had to throw one major advertiser out of his office for objectionable behavior, but that was all. Nor was McCarthy any more effective when he hired an ex-Communist investigator who said that *Time* and *Life* had "76 hard-core Reds" on its staff. (The credibility of this amateur prevaricator declined when he also found "126 dues-paying Communists" on the Sunday staff of *The New York Times*, which had only 93 employees.)

The Luce publications earned their battle ribbons, or at least their Purple Hearts, in the campaign against McCarthy. Luce himself, however, wasn't sure how much he prized the honor. As the 1952 election campaign warmed up, he sent a memo to his editors: "I think we should seize every opportunity to remind ourselves and our brethren and sistern that Communism is still infinitely more dangerous than McCarthyism. McCarthyism is offensive; Communism is dangerous."

To Luce the Democrats seemed to be gaining a propaganda edge by denouncing McCarthy while the Republicans were denouncing Communism. Luce tried to make his case on journalistic grounds in a memorandum to Tom Matthews: "The Ship of Public Opinion, or of Man's Emotion, including Mass-Intellectual opinion, is always lurching to one side or the other—and often it lurches into the sea of disaster. . . . In my judgment as a skipper, Public Opinion, especially among the Upper Middle Class (much of our audience), has lurched to anti-McCarthyism. So we need to counter that lurch."

But stability for the ship of state in this sea of disaster was hard to achieve as Senator McCarthy became ever more reckless in his accusations. He had already called Truman and Acheson traitors and had demanded their impeachment. Then, in a three-hour speech to the Senate, he added General Marshall to his list of villains, as a man who had joined Acheson in a Communist conspiracy unparalleled in history; it was "the mysterious, powerful" Marshall, McCarthy insisted, who created the disastrous China policy and set the military strategy that was causing American boys to be slaughtered in Korea. Before McCarthy finished his harangue, all but three of his fellow senators had walked out on him.

What did candidate Eisenhower think of this attack on General Marshall, the man to whom he owed so much, the man who had picked Eisenhower to command the invasion of Europe? Ike wasn't saying. Finally his staff let it be known that when he got to Wisconsin, where the senator was seeking reelection, Eisenhower would speak out. A passage paying tribute to Marshall had been included in a speech Ike would deliver in Milwaukee.

Then Eisenhower reneged. As his campaign train neared the Wisconsin border, McCarthy boarded it and rode into Wisconsin pleading with Ike to omit the tribute. Eisenhower is said by his aides to have responded with "red-hot anger," but when the train reached Green Bay, Eisenhower publicly thanked McCarthy for meeting him and said that he and the senator disagreed only on methods. In Milwaukee, with McCarthy seated on the platform behind him, Eisenhower said that for two decades the nation had been poisoned by a tolerance of Communism, which had created "a government by men whose very brains were confused by the opiate of this deceit." No mention of Marshall. Among the many disappointed Eisenhower supporters was Arthur Hays Sulzberger, the publisher of *The New York Times,* who wired the campaign train, "Do I need to tell you that I am sick at heart?"

President Truman was even more upset. He considered Marshall—who had faithfully executed every assignment the president had given him, including the ill-fated mission to China—the greatest living American. Earlier, when Eisenhower had first announced that he would seek the Republican nomination, Truman told a press conference, "I'm just as fond of General Eisenhower as I can be. I think he is one of the great men produced by World War II." Truman's first reaction to Eisenhower's performance in Milwaukee was sadness: "I wish for the sake of history, and for the sake of future generations who will read about him in the schoolbooks, that he had not so tarnished his own bright reputation as a commander of men. And I mean that with all my heart."

As days went by, Truman got angrier at what he considered Eisenhower's betrayal. After all, the president told friends, it was Marshall who three times had given a crucial push to Ike's career, as Ike was advanced from lieutenant colonel to general;

it was Marshall who had agreed that Eisenhower should be made the supreme commander, a post that Marshall had wanted for himself. In a speech in Utica, New York, Truman's bitterness toward Eisenhower came out: "He knew—and knows today—that General Marshall's patriotism is above question. . . . He knows or ought to how completely dishonest McCarthy is. . . . Now, in his bid for votes, he has endorsed Joe McCarthy for re-election—and humbly thanked him for riding on his train. I can't understand it. I had never thought the man who is now the Republican candidate would stoop so low."

Now it was Eisenhower's turn to take umbrage, though he had less reason to be offended. In a rage at Truman, he vowed that if elected, he would not ride down Pennsylvania Avenue with the outgoing president. Once Eisenhower was elected, the two did make the ride together, but only after Eisenhower had behaved with petty rudeness. Following tradition, the president and the first lady had invited the Eisenhowers to lunch at the White House; Ike declined. On Inauguration Day Ike and Mamie drove up to the White House but refused an invitation to join the Trumans inside for a cup of coffee, remaining in their limousine in the driveway until the Trumans emerged.

Eisenhower had won in a landslide, which makes his refusal to defend his friend Marshall and his abject surrender to McCarthy even more lamentable. That incident was the most serious blemish on Eisenhower's candidacy, and it ensured that McCarthy would still be around to make trouble after the election. It is no excuse that Eisenhower, as a political amateur, deferred to more experienced and cautious advisers. Of course politics entered into his calculations, but his behavior in Milwaukee, if it can be defended at all, has to be defended on other grounds: Eisenhower, for all his contempt of McCarthy, thought that the senator had identified the right enemy, Moscow. In leading the West's victorious armies in World War II,

Eisenhower had behaved with scrupulous professionalism toward his Russian allies, ignoring political advisers who urged him to take Berlin before Soviet troops could get there. His reasoning was moral: he could not ask troops to die in such an enterprise. The Russians did not reciprocate: they swiftly jettisoned the agreed-upon four-power occupation of Germany, making East Germany their own, and broke a promise of free elections in Eastern Europe. When Russia's behavior brought on the Cold War, Eisenhower was called back into uniform to head the NATO alliance to defend Western Europe. Such a history explains the depths of Eisenhower's feelings about the Communists, but it does not explain how Eisenhower, after participating closely with Truman and Acheson in formulating and carrying out the Western strategy in Europe, could leave unchallenged McCarthy's attacks on the two men, which questioned the ardor of their anti-Communism and the sincerity of their patriotism.

Like Eisenhower's, Harry Luce's feelings about Joe McCarthy were an uneasy combination of political calculation (Luce's determination to elect a Republican president) and a deeply felt hatred of Communism (instilled in him by his religion and sharpened by his distress at the fall of China). For both Eisenhower and Luce, dealing with a scoundrel as popular as McCarthy, and one so vicious when crossed, was never easy. Their revulsion at his scurrilous style was compromised by its usefulness to them.

In victory Eisenhower owed a great deal to Luce, who had even lent Ike's campaign the services of one of Luce's top writers, Emmett Hughes. As a speechwriter, Hughes crafted Eisenhower's most effective campaign line: "If elected, I shall go to Korea." The only job in Eisenhower's administration Luce would have liked to have, he once admitted, was secretary of state, for which he did not feel sufficiently qualified. Some surmised that he would have been flattered to be offered an ambassadorship to the Court of St. James's, if only to have the pleasure of turning it down. Instead Eisenhower made Clare Boothe Luce ambassador to Italy.

In Rome Luce spent the next two years, ever the curious tourist, exploring Rome's history, taking a daily walk in the zoo, and enjoying lunches and dinners in the embassy residence, Villa Taverna. He kept in constant cable touch with his magazines, guiding their policies and appointments. Without diplomatic status, except as the ambassador's spouse, Luce was by protocol seated at the lower end of the table at state lunches and dinners. He accepted this arrangement uncomplainingly. It enabled him to keep his New York editors informed not only about Italy, but about Sri Lanka, Indonesia, and Belgium, based on crumbs he industriously gathered from diplomats from second-rank powers at his end of the table.

The assumption among respectable Republicans was that Joe McCarthy, having helped them regain the White House, would gradually fade away once the Eisenhower administration got under way. McCarthy was not so obliging; he thought he had earned status in his own right. Like all bullies, once he had savored the pleasure of having someone give in to him, he was eager to reassert his dominance. Having campaigned against "twenty years of treason" under the Democrats, McCarthy within months was sounding a new cry—"twenty-*one* years of treason"—suggesting that even under Eisenhower, the government was still infested with traitors. Eisenhower vowed he would not descend into the gutter with that fellow, leaving it to members of his cabinet and administration to deal with him, and to be badgered and humiliated when summoned to testify before McCarthy's committee. Opinion polls showed McCarthy more popular than ever.

The unhealthy atmosphere of McCarthyism spread even to Rome. In a letter from Rome to one of his colleagues in New York, Luce described "an extremely pleasant occasion," a luncheon at the Villa Taverna with two couples, the Cabots and Lamonts ("as you know, they are practically Mr. and Mrs. Harvard"). He continued:

> Then last night I went to a small dinner for them at a restaurant and Cabot and I found each other at the end of a table. We got into a hell of an argumentative fight. Without giving a blow-by-blow account, some of the items were: Cabot thinks Dean Acheson one of the greatest of all U.S. Secretaries; he also thinks Hiss is probably innocent and, of course like other Harvard characters, he is hysterical about McCarthy—"the end of U.S. liberty."
>
> I was very rude—said that what annoyed me most in the U.S. was not Commies but these Park Avenue and Cambridge muddleheads. I guess I got pretty offensive. You can imagine the argument.
>
> After an hour of hammer-and-tongs, we came to sort of a gentlemanly agreement. But—what the hell—it's when I run into a Paul Cabot that I almost become pro-McCarthy. . . .
>
> Why do I bother you except as a means of upchucking my nausea? Because—I guess all our serious brethren will agree—we still have a two-front war on our hands: one against McCarthy, one against that complacent upper-class Achesonianism. Our task: to walk the middle ground with an equanimity *not* displayed by me.

In the States, McCarthy continued to terrorize an unresisting Eisenhower administration until his Senate colleagues, who disliked and feared him, finally decided that he had for too long taken advantage of the excessive tolerance allowed all members under what is picturesquely called senatorial courtesy. In December 1954, the Senate summoned the will to condemn McCarthy formally for "conduct which tended to bring the Senate into dishonor and disrepute." To be censured in this way by his colleagues, to have his bluff and his bullying called at last, was the beginning of McCarthy's end. Disgraced and abandoned, he died three years later of acute alcoholism at the age of forty-eight.

WHITTAKER CHAMBERS, WILLI SCHLAMM, AND JOE MCCARTHY

After parting with Harry Luce, who wouldn't take him back on the staff, Whittaker Chambers was still burdened with heavy lawyers' bills; he and his family were living "as poor as rats" on their Maryland farm. He sat down hoping, like Teddy White, to craft a best-seller that would deliver him from debt.

He knew there was a huge market waiting that would have been satisfied with the spy thriller story he could tell, full of intrigue and betrayal, but his aspiration was greater: to write a memoir that would rank as literature. *Witness,* his autobiography, is a brooding, ambitious book that begins with moving scenes of a scarred childhood, then evolves into the tale of a brilliant but lonely college student who becomes radicalized, enlists in the Communist party, and is ordered to go underground, where, under a variety of aliases and identities, he gathers information about the American government for Soviet intelligence. At last comes the break with Communism and his resolve to expose its threat. It is a story of idealism perverted and loyalties betrayed, told with a melancholy fatalism that suggested to many readers and reviewers the tone of a Russian novel. But *Witness* is flawed by inflated, apocalyptic prose, by mawkish self-pity, by patches of dishonesty, and by a readiness to score, fairly or not, on those who crossed him. It remains a valuable work but is overly colored by the heightened emotions of its era, and history has not been kind to its excesses.

Luce was eager to publish excerpts from the book, perhaps in part to atone for his evasive treatment of Chambers. But before he could even submit a bid for the magazine rights, they were sold to *The Saturday Evening Post,* then the favorite weekly magazine of Norman Rockwell's America. Instead of publishing Chambers in *Life,* the repository of the memoirs of Churchill, MacArthur, and Truman, Luce had intended to serialize it as news in *Time.* He offered to top *The Saturday Evening Post*'s bid but was turned down; as Chambers wrote to him, *Witness* might be an embarrassment to *Time.* When the first installment appeared in the *Post,* the magazine sold an extra half million copies on the newsstands.

Among the scores Chambers had to settle was one with Teddy White. He also got even with John Hersey and the other European correspondents on *Time* who had written a protest against Chambers's heavy-handed editing of their dispatches: "Let me list the signers of the round-robin . . . [who] continued to feed out news from the viewpoint that the Soviet Union is a benevolent democracy of unaggressive intent, or that the Chinese communists are 'agrarian reformers.' . . . Foremost among them were: John Hersey, John Scott (son of my old teacher of the law of social revolution, Scott Nearing), Charles C. Wertenbaker, the late Richard Lauterbach, Theodore White. These are the top names; there were others."

This is a preposterous misrepresentation of the reporting done by correspondents like John Hersey, who filed his cables from wartime Moscow through a dictatorship's censorship and was under no illusions about the absence of democracy in the Soviet Union; or of Teddy White, who explicitly reported that the Chinese Communists refused to regard themselves as agrarian liberals but proudly styled themselves Communist.

In 1953, the year when *Witness* was published, the frenzy of McCarthyism was at its peak. As Whittaker Chambers well knew, dozens of vigilante outfits were roaming the countryside, gathering signatures, besieging congressmen, threatening advertisers, publishers, and filmmakers, and circulating blacklists of writers and performers. By his unjustified innuendos against White and his colleagues, Chambers guaranteed their continued harassment.

Yet during that aberrant period in American history, when many people acted unpredictably—equivocally, courageously, or cravenly—one of the most surprising reactions was that of Whittaker Chambers. How did he feel about the man who claimed to be continuing Chambers's mission to expose Communists in government? Chambers despised Joe McCarthy.

Chambers had become a hero to a man he hadn't met, a remarkable young gadfly named William F. Buckley, Jr., who after his graduation from Yale published a book, *God and Man at Yale,* denouncing his alma mater for ungodliness, which became a minor literary sensation. Years later when Ronald Reagan spoke at the twenty-fifth anniversary of the *National Review,* the magazine that Buckley founded, the president predicted that eventually it would be acknowledged that "Bill Buckley is perhaps the most influential journalist and intellectual in our era—that he changed our country, indeed our century." This is a banquet eulogist's exaggeration, delivered with Reagan panache. A more accurate judgment would be more modest: in the 1950s Buckley, as a sharp-tongued debater and an ornately erudite polemicist, almost single-handedly made right-wing conservatism intellectually respectable.

Before launching the magazine that made it so, Buckley read *Witness* and "was shaken by that book." He decided that he wanted Chambers to be one of his editors and was encouraged to hire him by Chambers's old comrade-in-arms in the service of Henry R. Luce, Willi Schlamm.

Schlamm had been out of a job, and without a sponsor, after Luce decided not to start a new intellectual magazine called *Measure,* with Schlamm as its editor. Looking around for another rich man to sponsor him, Schlamm discovered the twenty-nine-year-old Buckley, whose father had made an immense fortune in oil in Latin America. Schlamm helped Buckley plan the *National Review*. Confident that Buckley was young enough to need instruction, he advised Buckley to keep full power for himself as the editor and to retain all voting rights in the stock. This was advice that Schlamm would later regret.

Together Buckley and Schlamm drove down to the Maryland farm to recruit Chambers as an editor. Things did not go as well as expected, because Buckley failed to recognize a subtle ingredient in the relationship between Schlamm and the man Buckley called Schlamm's "old pal Whit." Though Chambers and Schlamm had been colleagues in schooling Luce on the sinister secrets of Communism, they had learned in their years in the movement to trust no one, including each other.

Chambers, who had recently suffered two heart attacks, could not be persuaded to join the staff. His health was not the only problem; there were also fundamental differences in outlook: Chambers was showing signs of the heresy of liberalism, a development that would have startled Chambers's old antagonists and victims on *Time,* who had suffered from his antipathy to all things liberal. Chambers found his visitors too radically right-wing for him.

Buckley confided to Chambers that by the third issue of the magazine, once it was successfully launched, he intended to read President Eisenhower and Richard Nixon out of the conservative movement. Buckley, a zealot of narrow and rigid convictions, thought Eisenhower "a man unguided and hence unhampered by principle. Eisenhower undermines the Western resolution to stand up and be counted." Buckley was equally dismissive of Vice President Nixon, who at a crucial time in Chambers's life had rescued him by arranging the public confrontation between Chambers and Alger Hiss.

Buckley left the Maryland farm much impressed by Chambers and so eager to hire him that he later proposed to make

Chambers the editor of the *National Review* instead of himself, a surprisingly generous offer from a man with so highly developed an ego as Buckley's. He and Chambers became lifelong friends, though he seemed not to have understood why Chambers refused to join him: "Chambers gave as his formal reason the matter of his health. His true reason was his fear of association with a journal whose editors entertained doubts about Richard Nixon's fitness to succeed Eisenhower."

Buckley also seriously misjudged Chambers's attitude toward Joe McCarthy. Buckley had written a book called *McCarthy and His Enemies* (it had been edited by Willi Schlamm), which he hoped Chambers would endorse. In it he fastidiously disdained McCarthy's vulgar excesses while championing his cause. Chambers wanted nothing to do with McCarthy, "a heavy-handed slugger who telegraphs his fouls in advance." He expanded on the point later: "For the Right to tie itself in any way to Senator McCarthy is suicide. . . . He can't lead anybody because he can't think. He is a rabble rouser and a slugger. . . . This issue touches you and me closely. McCarthy as a man, a man of pathos, maimed and crippled in spirit and career by men no better than he—that man I would gladly comfort—as a fellow man. Of McCarthy as a politician I want no part. He is a raven of disaster, and an irresponsible, headstrong bird, to boot."

Nor would Chambers join a magazine which in its first issue proclaimed that it "stands athwart history yelling Stop." Chambers believed, with Disraeli, that conservatism could prosper only if it constantly changed, accommodating "itself to the needs and hopes of the masses"; merely to block change was, Chambers wrote, to foredoom the movement to "futility and petulance."

Chambers had still another, though unacknowledged, reservation: he could not, would not, work with Willi Schlamm, whose capacity for infighting and intrigue was creating turmoil at the *National Review*. When Buckley ordered Schlamm to work at home, Schlamm objected and demanded a staff meeting to discuss the order, saying, "The *National Review* is as much my creation and my life's central concern as it is yours." Buckley consented to the meeting, which turned tumultuous and teary. Schlamm announced, "You can't fire me," but it turned out that Buckley could and did. Schlamm eventually departed for Europe.

Chambers was at last willing to join the magazine. Had Schlamm been the real problem all along? With a wide, toothy grin, Buckley acknowledged to me: "It *did* cross my mind." Chambers had earlier written to Buckley: "Willi was heaved out of the Communist party. I broke out. . . . I have known a dozen minds of the general size and shape of Willi's. He has no surprises for me. He cannot think for me. . . . He cannot raise any 'moral' stakes which I have not topped."

Yet even with Schlamm gone, Chambers did not breathe freely in the intensely claustrophobic air of the *National Review*. When President Eisenhower invited Nikita Khrushchev to the United States in August 1959, Buckley in a fury organized an anti-Khrushchev rally at Carnegie Hall and threatened to dye the Hudson River red so that Khrushchev would enter the United States on "a river of blood." When the magazine in the same spirit described Khrushchev as merely a reincarnation of Stalin, Chambers protested. He wrote Buckley, "[Khrushchev] is no monster in the sense that Stalin *was* a monster; and it does much disservice to say he is. It blurs where we need clear window-panes."

The logic of the *National Reviews*'s position would lead to war, Chambers added: "If gentlemen hold that war is what is necessary, I, for one, wish they would say so simply, clearly, courageously, stating their reasons for believing so. . . . But short of this forthrightness, shouts of 'Russkies go home!' and the like lack coherence, meaning, gravity."

Within a month of writing that letter, Chambers resigned from the magazine. His challenge to the rigidity of Buckley's

Cold War views represented an evolution in his own thinking. Teddy White's thinking was changing too, so that his views and Chambers's could almost be said to be converging. Teddy supported the Cold War; before long the man who had been mildly Marxist at Harvard would turn conservative in his politics, even become a luncheon companion of Bill Buckley's.

Whittaker Chambers continued to live with Quaker-like simplicity. With the investment advice he got from a friend from his *Time* days who had become a stockbroker, Chambers and his family were financially comfortable in his last years. After a succession of heart attacks Chambers died in the year that John F. Kennedy became president.

Willi Schlamm deserves a final note. He had left Europe when, as a Jew, his life was in danger, at a time when Hitler, having seized power, was preparing for war. Schlamm returned to a Europe at peace, and in a war-weary, defeated Germany he quickly established himself as a controversial public figure. Having become an American citizen in 1944, he warned Germans, "The United States will sell you out [in a deal over Berlin with the East Germans and Russians] if you let them." He insisted that the Americans were duty-bound to restore Germany to its 1933 pre-Hitler borders, driving the Russians back. His inflammatory speeches to German crowds led to violent disputes, heckling, picketing, and near riots; there were demands in the parliament that he be expelled as a warmonger and demagogue. *Der Spiegel,* the German newsmagazine modeled after *Time,* put him on its cover and said of him that "since Hitler and Goebbels there has been no one in Germany who could use the stimulant of national mass hysteria as audaciously and cleverly as he has."

Fanatic to the end, he argued that the Germans should keep steady military pressure on the Russians, even at the risk of war. He assured his audiences that this was the best way to prevent war, claiming to speak with the authority of an ex-Communist who was privy to the way Communists thought: the Russians, he said, would give way, as they always did when threatened with war. On another occasion he declared that it would be "morally just to deny that world to Communists even if the defense of the West would cost 700 million human victims." Eventually, Germans tired of his rant and rejected his arguments; his hold on a significant segment of the German public, like McCarthy's on the American public, gave out.

With the help of history and hindsight, it is now possible to render a judgment on three people whom Harry Luce listened to on foreign affairs in the 1940s—Teddy White, Whittaker Chambers, and Willi Schlamm.

White was a friend whose reporting and liberal sympathies became unacceptable to Luce. The other two did not so much convert Luce to their views as confirm and buttress his own anti-Communism, while also warning Luce that the nation and his own magazines were honeycombed with untrustworthy people. Chambers was a man whom Luce respected (as his sister, Beth, has said) "for his mind." Schlamm, quick-witted and clever, knew how to play Luce like a courtier.

White in every way differed from the other two. He acquired his views, as journalists generally do, by reporting and interviewing, absorbing new impressions constantly. He came to conclusions and wrote articles and books expressing them, but they were always snapshots of the time, subject to correction by subsequent events or new evidence. Chambers and Schlamm were polemicists, not reporters. They dismissed as superficial assessments that had been made, as Teddy's were, by an eyewitness to events, living in a country, talking to its people, and interviewing its leaders. Intellectual condescension was a favorite weapon in the world Chambers and Schlamm came from. Theirs was a deeper, "scientific" knowledge of history, as defined by the system they had broken with. Impersonal forces were more powerful than individuals. In that bizarre time, men like Chambers and Schlamm, who had spent years doing reprehensible deeds in the service of Satan before repudiating Communism, were seen as true-blue American patriots, valued for their insider's knowledge of Hell.

The Marxist interpretation of history didn't much interest Luce, though it guided the thinking of Chambers and Schlamm. Chambers was so much a captive of the "scientific" validity of the onward march of Communism that in repudiating Communism he melodramatically announced that he was consciously joining "the losing side." As he put it, "I felt that the cause I fought for was so powerless to help itself that even God had given up."

Philosophically, Chambers and Schlamm were passengers on Marx's express train of history. Even after passing through the dark tunnel where they lost their faith, they continued to ride into a new landscape with the blinds drawn. Only in his later years did Chambers at last seem to rid himself of his obsession.

The "scientific" laws of history in which both had believed had been proven false. Without even having to pass through a river of blood, the side that Whittaker Chambers had chosen with dark foreboding turned out to be the winning side.

OUT FROM UNDER
THE CLOUD

After spending more than five years in Europe, Teddy White found his reentry to New York City a jarring contrast to the memory of the country he had left behind in 1948. One of the significant differences was the pervasiveness of television, which, for all its sterile hours of mediocrity framed by commercials, could rise to highs in drama, music, and sports. When it covered some major disaster—a flood, a plane crash, a riot—it did so with a vividness that Teddy White's words could not improve upon and Harry Luce's still photographers could not hope to match.

Teddy White got his first exposure to television's new way of packaging reality from his friend Edward R. Murrow, the CBS war correspondent whose resonant greeting "This . . . is London" became the most famous radio signature of World War II. Murrow had just started a new television show called *Person to Person,* interviewing celebrities in their homes. Would Teddy appear on it, to talk of his return to the United States? Of course, Teddy said, seeing a chance to plug his new book, *Fire in the Ashes,* but wishing he had been asked to talk instead on Murrow's radio show, which he mistakenly thought would have a wider impact.

He expected to see his friend Ed Murrow arrive at his home on the night of the telecast. Instead, two huge vans drew up outside the Whites' rented apartment on Central Park West; cables were strung down the exterior of the building while a producer and fifteen other people rearranged the furniture in the Whites' apartment to fit the script, emphasizing empty packing cases to show that the Whites had just returned from abroad. Murrow himself was somewhere downtown in a CBS studio. Teddy and Nancy could see him on the monitor, his lean face wreathed as usual in cigarette smoke (Murrow would die later of lung cancer). The cross-cutting by camera that an audience of eight million people had gotten used to as a "person-to-person" encounter between people who were not even in the same room came as such a surprise to Teddy that he responded a bit stiffly to his absent host. But White received more mail from fifteen minutes on television than he had from the book itself; strangers recognized him on the street; *Fire in the Ashes* began its ascent on the best-seller list.

Outside his apartment, on Central Park West in the mid-eighties, another new reality imposed itself. Teddy had been pleased to find so large an apartment with a fine view of the park and a low rent; unknowingly the Whites had moved into a "neighborhood in transition." Friends had warned them "to know the block" before deciding, but as enlightened liberals, the Whites felt no objection to blacks and Hispanics moving into the area. That generous attitude lasted less than a year. As Teddy wrote in his autobiography, "for the first time in all his life—in Irish Boston, in warlord China, in darkling Germany—he was afraid to walk the street outside his own house at night . . . his wife felt unsafe going to the delicatessen on Columbus Avenue by daylight . . . his children were not safe going to play in Central Park" across the street. (Nancy remembers the experience less starkly, and also remembers a favorite saying of Teddy's: "Hyperbole is the garment of truth.")

Before the year was up the family joined the "white flight," not to the suburbs, but crosstown to a more fashionable and safer enclave of brownstones and apartment houses. A friend from Harvard days, the historian Arthur Schlesinger, owned a brownstone across the street from the Whites' house. Teddy called his new neighborhood "the perfumed stockade," inhabited, as he saw it, by brokers, bankers, publishers, and advertising men, dominated by social hostesses: "In Upper East Side New York, no family pedigree was required for admission to the Round Table of Celebrities—money, or achievement, or passing notoriety would do. If one had such money, or solid achievement, or this year's publicity, the Court invited one into its best parties, its best dinners, its best weekends."

The Whites enjoyed the social bustle and their inclusion within a circle of snobbery, though Teddy, as usual, professed not to. Eventually itching to get back to work, he went to see Max Ascoli, the editor of *The Reporter,* who had published Teddy's political reporting from Europe when most magazine editors would not. And so *The Reporter*'s former chief European correspondent became its national political correspondent. But, grateful as Teddy was for Ascoli's support in the worst of the McCarthy days, he found Ascoli hard to get along with. Ascoli became one more portrait in a gallery of editors Teddy had worked for, each of whom could be compared for better or worse with Harry Luce.

As a professor of law at the University of Genoa, Ascoli had bravely fought Mussolini's dictatorship; then, fleeing Italy without any money, he found a teaching job in New York City at that ingathering of distinguished European exiles the New School. Ascoli married one of his students, Marion Rosenwald, a Sears, Roebuck heiress, and when World War II ended, she set her husband up as editor and publisher of his own magazine, *The Reporter.* As Teddy noted, most of the country's great liberal magazines had always been "subsidized by conscience-smitten heirs to great fortunes," including the oldest of them, *The Nation,* and *The New Republic,* where Teddy had gone through his first disillusioning experience with Henry Wallace. The publishers were usually noble in their aims, Teddy observed, but "frequently abusive of their staff, pinchpenny in pay, intolerant of political deviation."

Ascoli was one more variant: a man brilliant and learned but vile of temper, with a "histrionic brutality" of manners, capable of screaming in rage and tossing a writer's copy in the air "like a child kicking leaves into the wind." Ascoli's strength lay in his serious-mindedness; he believed that institutions, not individuals, guided society. This meant a different writing discipline for Teddy. Ascoli privately enjoyed listening to political gossip as much as did Harry Luce, but stories about personalities had no place in his magazine. *The Reporter*'s sober and thorough examination of the issues won a small but loyal audience in academia and government.

For *The Reporter,* White set out to explore the role of the American scientific establishment and found himself covering a public hearing on the loyalty of the nuclear scientist J. Robert Oppenheimer. He also learned of a loyalty hearing that was being held in secrecy and that involved his old friend from the China days John Paton Davies. It was a season in which mendacious men sought to rewrite the history of the previous decade by portraying widespread treason in high places.

After his service in China Davies had gone on to a distinguished career, as first secretary of the U.S. Embassy in Moscow, then to the sensitive post of director of political affairs in the U.S. Embassy in postwar Germany. But after he was singled out by Senator Joe McCarthy in a radio broadcast, Davies was being subjected for the *ninth* time to a secret investigation by the State Department's Security Hearing Board.*

It is hard to know what prompted Teddy to do what he did next—whether he acted out of hubris or guilt. He called up Davies's attorney and offered to testify in Davies's behalf. "You

---

*Clearing such hurdles was not enough to save Davies's career. "When I refused to resign under attack, John Foster Dulles, secretary of state, fired me in 1954 as a risk to the security of the United States," Davies wrote, adding with quiet satisfaction, "In 1969 the State Department reexamined my case and granted me security clearance."

mean you'll volunteer to do that?" the attorney asked incredulously. Certainly Teddy felt guilt: Nancy remembers that one of the reasons Teddy had wanted to move to Europe was to escape the "opaque eyes" of his diplomat friends, who were stunned to see their careers in ruins. But in an oddly self-deprecating passage in his autobiography, Teddy suggests that he also felt a cocky desire to play hero:

> [He] felt invulnerable. He was a well-known author. . . . He knew President Eisenhower and was friendly with the White House staff. And his friend Davies was being assailed.
>
> White testified sharply, intemperately. He tried to make one principle clear: A State Department officer, he insisted, must report the truth to his government no matter how unpleasant the truth. White reached back across the years to China days. If Davies had reported that the Communists were going to win in China, which turned out to be correct, he merited praise, not purging. The government must be informed correctly at all times; that's what we paid these men for.
>
> White was thus feeling very noble, very effective, a detached but able master at this game of loyalty inquisition.

He was testifying in a darkened basement room in Washington, D.C., with the window blinds drawn against the July heat; he could not make out the faces of the five inquisitors, who sat, shadowed, with their backs to the window. The man in the center, a general, now closed one folder before him and opened another.

> It must have been the White folder; and almost instantly White realized that this was not a judicial hearing—it was a lynching party. Davies was to be lynched; and if White had to be gotten in the process, why, so be it.
>
> "Mr. White," came the first question, "isn't it true that

you made a speech to the Negro troops on the Burma Road urging them to a revolt during the war?"

With that question, White's composure cracked.

Caught by surprise, Teddy tried to piece together a memory of a time ten years earlier when he ran into a childhood friend from his Boston ghetto neighborhood. The friend, a lieutenant in the Engineers, was the only white officer in an otherwise all-black labor battalion that was hacking its way through jungle to cut a trace between the Ledo Road and the Burma Road. His men were demoralized; they might as well be in a Georgia chain gang. Many suffered from malaria, but they were not even allowed, like white troops, into the forward base at Myitkyina. Would Teddy, as a big-shot war correspondent, come out to eat in their mess and "tell them why it was so important for them to build this road through to China"?

Teddy told his inquisitors that he couldn't remember what he said that night, but when he spoke to troops on similar occasions in his war correspondent's uniform, his pep talks would combine a few facts and figures and dollops of patriotism with some appropriate profanity to show that he was not an officer but a cynical correspondent they could trust. His speech, he testified, went like this: "The Japanese were the worst racists in the world after the Nazis, and we had to help the Chinese knock off the Japanese; [then] we would all go home and knock off racism in the United States. So lift that ax, girdle that tree, bulldoze that road."

The prosecutor broke in: "Is it true, Mr. White, that your wife is a member of the Communist Party?"

Teddy writes in his autobiography: "I can still remember my squeal. My voice tends to rise in anger or argument, and I squealed out in astonishment: 'My wife, Nancy?' 'I don't know what your wife's name is.' "

After that ordeal, Teddy got a further shock a few weeks

later when he went to the Fifth Avenue passport office in New York City to pick up a passport he had left to be renewed. The man behind the desk searched for a few minutes and then blandly told White that he could not have his passport back or get it renewed because he fell under the "legislation." "It was like the click of unexpected handcuffs," Teddy remembers.

He knew that he had already been blacklisted by amateur vigilantes in the newsletter *Counterattack*. As one result, he was banned from working at CBS or even being interviewed again on any of its programs—despite urgent protests by Edward R. Murrow to his boss, Bill Paley.

A passport was crucial to Teddy; *The Reporter* had given him a two-month leave of absence on loan to *Collier's* magazine, to fly to Germany to write a special report, "Germany Ten Years After Defeat." Unless he could get his passport restored, he would have to tell both magazines that he was now officially branded subversive and indefinitely prohibited from reporting overseas. He requested a hearing, and this time, instead of swaggering and huffing and puffing, he resolved to follow some advice by Ernest Hemingway he had read somewhere: in dealing with bureaucrats, never argue with them but "meet them meekly and correctly within their narrow rules."

Teddy arrived at the office with a nine-page answer to the charges and a copy of *Thunder Out of China*. Some accusations were easily met: it was said a Russian agency had taken him on a tour of the Near East or the Far East in 1948 or 1949; if they looked at his passport they would see that this could not be so. His hearing officer, a thin, pale-faced man, asked Teddy what he had been writing about since. About Europe. Teddy was startled to learn that a State Department officer had never heard of *Fire in the Ashes,* which by then had sold a quarter of a million copies. "Gulping," Teddy writes, "I went into the degrading act of describing both my own book and my support of the American cause in Europe. I groveled." The hearing officer was still bothered: "Some people wrote about Europe only to take Americans' minds off the Far East," where the Reds were killing millions.

Gradually the man thawed as he examined Teddy's credentials. Teddy would be given a passport "valid for travel to Germany, France and Germany" for two months. Then he decided to extend the passport for a full year and apologetically said it wouldn't be necessary to get supporting letters from important people Teddy knew: "It might be embarrassing." Teddy went off to Germany to report his story and performed so well that *Collier's* offered him a full-time job. All through the trip, however, he felt insecure in carrying a "dirty" American passport, stamped as it was with a time limit suggesting he had not yet cleared himself. Then Teddy and Nancy were asked back to Washington to answer more questions under oath, but this time—after their ten-week ordeal—the mood was friendly and the questions perfunctory. It was two days before Christmas, 1954. Three weeks earlier, on December 2, Joe McCarthy had been condemned by the full Senate. The hearing officer said that perhaps Teddy and Nancy would like to have clean new passports when they flew back to New York for Christmas. Why didn't they go out to lunch and when they got back everything would be arranged. With relief Teddy and Nancy took possession of their passports, respectable American citizens again, free to travel everywhere.

Teddy saw his clearance as his chance to break free from Max Ascoli. If he had not won back his passport, he knew, Ascoli was "so flamboyantly brave he would have insisted on keeping me on his payroll, as a known subversive, if only to taunt the primitives." But Teddy also knew that he would then have been an indentured servant to a man capable of subtle cruelties and impulsive rages. He decided to make his exit grandly; he invited Ascoli to a "fine French lunch," to thank him, to tell him of his new job at *Collier's,* and to quit. As he left the lunch, Teddy felt that the long years he had lived under the cloud of McCarthyism had at last come to an end.

"It was years before the McCarthy experience faded from my sleep-tossing self-catechisms," he writes. "No amount of self-reproach will reconcile me, even today, to the self-doubt that followed my clearance. From 1954 to 1972, I never wrote another article about the China I knew so well; and only four articles on Vietnam. It was not so much that I was afraid; I had stood up when I had to and the fear passed away in time." At this point in his autobiography the emotions he writes about are plainly genuine, though the self-reproach borders on the excessive, and he almost flaunts the garment of hyperbole. He would never feel as sure of himself as he did in his China coverage, he writes, and unless he felt that sure, "I would never again want to be a polemicist or an advocate in a national debate. I recognize now that I also consciously withdrew from a reportorial area of intense past interest to me—arms and defense, weaponry and combat. . . . A self-censorship, imposed not by government but by prudence, circumscribed me—as it circumscribed countless others." He thinks it would have been "nobler and more heroic," to have fought the "faceless men"; he harbors a sense of shirking in going on to other things.

But now the eclipse was over; the sun shone; he was happier at *Collier's,* surrounded by a talented group of journalists, than he had ever been before or would be again. He was back in the big time: *Collier's* had a circulation of 4.3 million, compared with fewer than 200,000 at *The Reporter.* As the national political correspondent, he got to cover Washington in the last Eisenhower years, when a capital without McCarthy again became a pleasant place to work. Alas, *Collier's* was losing so much money that the owners of the Crowell-Collier company concluded they could prosper again (as they did) only if they folded the magazine. Directors of a corporation large, pragmatic, and soulless—and with little of Luce's moral commitment to journalism, or his loyalty to his staff—decided to gather in all the advertising pages they could during the crucial Christmas season, then close the magazine abruptly just before Christmas. Teddy, though he had been at *Collier's* only sixteen months, helped organize a campaign of pressure and publicity that shamed the company into paying a million dollars in severance to the staff. But he too, like everyone else, faced the holiday season without a job. He felt a hatred toward the television camera crews ghoulishly recording the event, the tears, the drunken farewells.

He was only forty-one. As the winner of numerous awards and as the author of two best-sellers, Teddy expected that he would shortly receive many job offers. He got only two calls. One was from Edward R. Murrow, who offered him a reporter's job in CBS's Washington bureau, but Teddy thought that a nightly ninety seconds on the air would be too confining for someone like him, who needed space to tell his stories. The second call, as surprising as Murrow's, was from Harry Luce, who invited him to dinner and told Teddy it was time to come "home."

But Teddy declined that offer too.

FRIENDS AGAIN

U sually when Harry Luce broke with someone the break was permanent. What began as a difference of opinion became in time, as it worked its way through Harry's conscience, a moral justification for ridding himself of the person involved. At that point he was no longer open to argument; the closer the earlier relationship had been, the more unforgiving was Harry. Those scorned in turn became bitter. Once Luce and John Hersey had quarreled, these two stubborn mishkids, each the product of China, Hotchkiss, Yale, and *Time,* could achieve no more than a wary politeness whenever they met. Each nursed an unrelenting grievance.

With Teddy White, after his bitter quarrel with Harry over China, the friendship was interrupted for a time but never fully severed. This was mostly Teddy's doing. He was—as he once described himself—a hustler; since Luce was the dominant employer in the magazine business, Teddy was not one lightly to ignore a potential meal ticket. But the crassness of his opportunism does not explain everything; after all, Teddy had earlier been courageous enough to break with Luce rather than give in to him. Teddy wanted to become friends again with Luce and concluded that this was possible only by resolving never again to be on Luce's payroll or beholden to him.

In February 1952, Teddy had heard that Luce would be in

Paris—Luce (though Teddy didn't know it) was on a mission to urge Ike to run for president on the Republican ticket—and dropped him a note. Would he like to come by Teddy's apartment for a drink? When Luce agreed to, Teddy proposed one condition: no discussion of China. Then Teddy called his wife, Nancy, who was working in the Paris office of *Life;* he told her not to come home until she got word that Luce had left.

The reunion went well, though gingerly. Afterward each had reason to keep the rendezvous private. After all, around *Time* and *Life* Teddy White had been declared a nonperson. The situation was much like that in the Soviet Union, where once Lavrenty Beria, the secret police chief, fell from favor, his name could no longer be found under the letter *B* in the *Soviet Encyclopedia.* For Luce, meeting Teddy was like trafficking with the enemy. As for Teddy, among his fellow correspondents he had a reputation to sustain as the reporter who wouldn't cave in to Luce.

Luce liked to operate in secrecy. He felt a private satisfaction whenever his nosy journalistic bird dogs, trained to detect secrets, missed the scent and failed to sniff out what he was up to. It was some time before Frank White, *Time*'s bureau chief in Paris, took me aside (I was then the foreign editor of *Time*) to confide that when Luce came to Paris he would ask Frank to line up the public figures Luce wanted to see, then would sneak off for a private visit with Teddy. (In the gossipy intimacy of the Paris bureau, perhaps it was the office chauffeur who gave Luce's secret away.)

Much as both Teddy and Harry might long to resume their intellectual swordplay, they dared not feint and parry with their previous abandon for fear of reopening old saber wounds. Even five years after they had resumed their acquaintanceship, Teddy in 1957 became alarmed when the liberal *New York Post,* doing a series on the Luce empire, quoted Teddy at length about Luce, violating the *Post* reporter's promise to read what Teddy had said back to him for approval before printing his words. "An intellectual love affair sprang up between us immediately," Teddy was quoted as saying in describing his first meeting with Luce in Chungking. But later, when Teddy concluded that Chiang's cause and his government were hopeless, "there was a definite coolness" between Luce and Teddy: "He acted literally as if I had betrayed him. . . . I believe he was largely responsible for the dead end our policy has reached in the Far East. He's more than publisher, or editor, or journalist. He's a sovereign; he has enormous power, a power uncontrolled, unchecked and thereby dangerous." After their split, Teddy told the reporter, "Harry had said some damned harsh things about me," though they had since had "a long friendly drink together."

When the *New York Post* series appeared, Teddy wrote Luce:

> Few things have distressed me more in many years. . . . I can only apologize for whatever hurt it may have caused you. . . . This story . . . violates the privacy of our friendship, which I cherish. . . . I have been plagued for years—as you must have been, too—by all manner of people who want to investigate our old relationship. I have always refused to make it public. It was something between us. . . . I am equally upset by my own folly in giving even an off-the-record confidence.
>
> The world has moved a long way since the days of our old differences; there are many exciting and important things happening around the big globe now. We both realize how far we were apart on China. I know your position to have rested on the deepest conviction; so did mine. But this never affected the respect and affection I have for you, personally. This abides.

Fortunately this letter gave Harry the chance to ease his own conscience with a belated apology for an indiscreet interview he had given to the *St. Louis Post-Dispatch* years earlier—in fact three years earlier than Teddy and Harry's long, friendly drink in Paris in 1952. In the interview Luce had described how he and Teddy "once saw eye to eye on Chiang Kai-shek and the whole Chinese situation," but then Teddy "went all the way over to the side of the Communists in China." Their much-publicized disagreement, in which Teddy was widely seen as the hero, still rankled Luce, the *Post-Dispatch* reported. Luce said he had cabled Teddy that "he should not write anything more about the political situation in China but should confine his writing entirely to the war itself. Perhaps I made a mistake and should have fired him immediately but it was difficult at that time to get good men."

That embarrassing interview in St. Louis could now be put behind him. Luce's reply to Teddy's apology illustrated how deep, despite their disagreements, was the affection between them:

> Fortunately, I hadn't seen the Saturday [New York] *Post* story, so my weekend wasn't spoiled. . . . Your good and generous letter had already extracted the poison and the sting.
>
> I share your feelings entirely—too bad that some personal relationships aren't allowed a little "right of privacy." And also, if you felt "folly" in finding yourself quoted extensively when you had not intended to be—so did I in the case of my alleged interview.
>
> We both feel similarly embarrassed but, speaking for myself, no damage has been done between us. On the contrary I treasure the good opinion of me which you expressed; against that, your adverse opinions weigh, in the scale of friendship, like a feather.
>
> . . . Could you perhaps have dinner Wednesday or Thursday night?

This amicable exchange emboldened Teddy, less than two months later, to make a cheeky, audacious proposal to Luce:

. . . the sounds coming out of Washington seem to indicate that some day, sooner or later, the State Department is going to validate American passports for China again.

China has been too much of my past for me not to itch to report it once more. . . . Certainly among all the quick and hasty dispatches and stories that will come out of the opening rat-race, there ought to be some written by people who knew China before, who speak the language, who have the feel of the country.

I've reflected long and searchingly on how much I want to do the story and for whom. And I want to do it very much. And, preferably, for *Life*. We both know there has been a past; and for me, personally, this past need have no bearing.

What I want to do is not a quickie, three-week, in-and-out trip with the Potemkin tour of Peking, Shanghai, Hankow and Canton; but something rather slower, in which—if Peking permits—I can get on a bus in Canton and travel slowly north to Peking, sleeping at Chinese inns, and talking to people I once knew in places where I had friends. Then, on this basis, I should like to brace the crowd in Peking with what I learn of the country and there try to get into the personalities, politics and power structure.

. . . I'd be happy if you'd turn the idea over in your mind and, if possible, let me call you Friday morning to see whether it's an idea which should be explored seriously. . . . I certainly hope you'd have no hesitation in telling me flatly that you're not interested. I get excited when I think about China again; and so must you; it might, finally, turn out that we can get excited on the same frequencies again.

Since there seems to have been no written reply from Luce to Teddy's proposal, Harry must have had "no hesitation" in telling Teddy that he wasn't interested when Teddy telephoned Luce that Friday morning in April 1957. On the subject of China, Luce was neither "on the same frequencies" as Teddy was, nor excited by any such possibility.

Yet at Christmastime a few months earlier, when *Collier's* folded and Teddy found himself without a job, there was "the familiar, gruff halting voice on the telephone, stammering an invitation to dinner at the University Club." In his autobiography Teddy writes that over dinner he and Harry "found themselves on agreement on almost everything but Eisenhower and China—particularly China, over which they argued violently, furiously and enjoyably." They adjourned the argument to Teddy's town house, where Luce broke it off with his remark that it was time for Teddy to come "home" to the magazines where Teddy had begun.

After this "act of generosity and peace-making" by Luce, Teddy could explain "neither to himself nor to Luce why—sitting there together in warmth, under his own roof with his children sleeping upstairs, and knowing he must support a family—why he could not accept Luce's invitation to be safe." He confessed to Luce that he never again wanted to be caught on Christmas Eve without a job. But, as Teddy wrote later, what he "wanted Luce could not give. He wanted both security and freedom. He wanted to go where and when he wished . . . and yet to command the weight and support of an organization, too."

At that point, in a very shrewd assessment of Teddy's character, Luce called him an "impossible combination of born organization man and born malcontent." Teddy had to concede that Harry had it about right. Yet in the years to come, Teddy would make that impossible combination work—doing what he pleased, going where he pleased, writing what he pleased, with the help of an organization to support him in style.

Teddy White had cavalierly turned down the first two jobs he had been offered after the demise of *Collier's*—invitations from his friends Edward R. Murrow and Harry Luce—only to discover that no one else was knocking at his door. He was jobless at forty-one; he had made a lot of money but had spent a lot too.

He considered starting a political column and went to see Walter Lippmann, the oracular dean of Washington columnists, for advice. Lippmann, so loftily Olympian and philosophical in his writing, was hardheaded and practical in his answer: Unless Teddy could get a Washington or New York newspaper outlet, which wouldn't be easy, his economic prospects would be dim.

Teddy gave up the idea after a few practice columns in which he was unable to find the range; he "could scarcely clear his throat in eight hundred to twelve hundred words." Then—almost as a finger exercise at his typewriter, wanting Nancy downstairs to think he was busy at work while he avoided going out to look for a job—he began to toy with a novel. He was trying to get down on paper what had troubled him in Asia in his twenties, when a well-intentioned United States had spread destruction over a wide swath of China in 1944 as its retreating army skillfully dynamited everything in sight—highways, bridges, and dumps—to keep them from falling into Japanese hands. Nancy was sure he could write a novel; all their friends did.

To get some of the technical details right Teddy relied on an old army manual on demolition that he had saved. With that and his memories to go on, Teddy left his family in the city so that the children could finish the school year, and took off for Fire Island, a fashionable sandbar in the Atlantic that was desolate and deserted during a cold and rainy spring. There, a lonely bachelor, for three months he wrote for long hours, fixed his own meals, and shivered.

He finished all but the last chapter of the novel; the story reached its climax in a fury of explosions at the ammunition dumps of Tushan, after which, in a berserk rage, the Americans destroyed a nearby village—a fictitious scene that would later become a reality at My Lai.

It took him almost as long, close to three months, to do the last chapter, containing the "message" of the book. He learned much later the reason for his difficulty when, not for the first time, he went to see the movie made from *The Mountain Road.* In a sleazy second-run theater in Times Square he was seated in front of a pack of teenagers who were enjoying all the violent explosions. But then the leader of the gang, who had seen the film before, stood up to leave. "The hell with it," he told his gang. "That's the best part of the picture. The rest of it's crap." Teddy could only agree; his ending had failed to speak to conscience, to acknowledge American error or guilt, and thus was fuzzy and hesitant. He should have been more forthright with his message, Teddy concluded, but he hadn't been so sure of it at the time: "Asia was a bloody place; we had no business there."

Still, *The Mountain Road,* his first novel, remained Teddy's favorite of all his books. It sold to a book club and to Hollywood and freed him from debt. It took him another year to write his second novel, based on his experiences at *Collier's,* called *The View from the Fortieth Floor.* It, too, sold well.

He could see ahead a new career as a novelist, "making money as he learned the sales tricks" of crafting best-sellers. He had read no how-to books on writing fiction; he didn't need to. But with sales to book clubs, paperbacks, and Hollywood, he was already earning more than "the best-paid reporter in China, Paris or Washington."

He thought of his particular turf in the literary field as the storyteller's patch; he was writing "reportorial novels," along with Herman Wouk, James Michener, and John Hersey. It was big-income, low-prestige territory. Teddy was alarmed to detect in his friend Hersey a desire to defect from the group, to court serious literary criticism instead of writing best-sellers. For himself, Teddy scorned the pretensions of literary academia just as much as those solemn people scorned his novels.

Aware that he would never be considered a great novelist, Teddy eventually decided that he would rather be known as a good reporter than as a minor novelist. But he also liked to live well. At this moment, Gary Cooper came galloping to Teddy's rescue. Cooper had read and admired *The View from the Forti-*

eth Floor and wanted to buy the film rights in order to star in it. As Teddy describes it, "Cooper was tired of the 'yup' and 'nope' parts other producers offered him." What appealed to Cooper was that the novel's hero was, as Teddy puts it, "loquacious, eloquent, almost incontinent of mouth."

Cooper wanted a fast answer to his offer of eighty thousand dollars (an impressive sum at that time), with an escalator clause if a book club chose the book. This was something that Teddy, who shamelessly romanced book club editors, was able to arrange.

One reason that Teddy's books became best-sellers was that he worked as hard, and almost as long, selling his books as he did researching and writing them. He endlessly toured the country, giving interviews, visiting bookstores, signing autographs, and plugging his books. He wrote buttery thank-you letters to reviewers (the notes were almost all alike, varying only in the sentence in each critic's review singled out for praise, and always congratulated the reviewer's perception in recognizing what Teddy was trying to say).

Teddy's answer to Gary Cooper was a fast yup. Though Cooper died before he could make the picture, his money gave Teddy the freedom to do what he now most wanted to do: write a reporter's book on his favorite subject, politics, using a novelist's techniques.

As a novelist Teddy had learned how to make the reader turn the page: "The way to tell a story is to locate a hero in the middle of trouble; then to increase the trouble; complicate the trouble; bewilder the hero; and have him emerge with the stroke of decision or direction that resolved all."

But instead of writing about imaginary people with imaginary problems, Teddy would describe real people in real trouble: "The idea was to follow [the 1960 presidential] campaign from beginning to end. It would be written as a novel is written, with anticipated surprises as, one by one, early candidates vanish in the primaries until only two final jousters struggle for the prize in November. Moreover, it should be written as a story of a man in trouble, of the leader under the pressures of circumstances."

Teddy now had the money to finance the months of expensive travel he would need to follow the candidates around the country. He knew that 1960 would be a good political year, rich in characters, all of whom Teddy knew and many of whom he admired. On the Republican side the cast included Teddy's friend Nelson Rockfeller; Dwight D. Eisenhower, "the great presence"; and Richard Nixon. On the Democratic side were John Kennedy, whom Teddy liked; Adlai Stevenson, whom he "cherished"; Averell Harriman; and Hubert Humphrey. As he sketched out the book he intended to write, he saw that Richard Nixon, whom he disliked, was "critical to the story—White had cast Nixon as the villain, as in a novel," before even beginning to report the campaign.

To Teddy's surprise, his book proposal, which he enthusiastically outlined to whoever would listen, found a cool welcome. His wife, Nancy, said, "It's probably a good book if Kennedy wins. But if Nixon wins, it's a dog." His own publishers didn't think the public would be interested in going back over a campaign six months after an election but said they would be willing to publish the book in gratitude for the money Teddy's novels had earned them. Two other publishing houses indicated they would risk losing money on it if Teddy gave them the rights to his future commercial novels. Finally Teddy found a responsive listener in his friend Michael Bessie, a Harvard contemporary of Jack Kennedy's. Bessie was starting a new publishing firm, Atheneum, in partnership with Pat Knopf, the son of America's most respected book publisher, Alfred A. Knopf. Bessie was in the market for new manuscripts and new ideas. *The Making of the President 1960* became Atheneum's first best-seller, and for the next twenty years its successors every four years became the firm's bread and butter.

Teddy, speaking of the great success his book was to win,

borrowed a line Speaker Sam Rayburn used to describe a rich and lucky Texas oilman friend: "He was playing the bass tuba on the day it rained gold."

That 1960 campaign—so close that it was decided by 112,000 votes out of 68 million ballots cast—was also the election in which Harry Luce gave up distorting the news to elect a president. Eight years earlier, he had willingly jeopardized *Time*'s journalistic reputation to elect Ike. Now the Eisenhower era was coming to an end.

Perhaps a change of parties in the White House every eight years is beneficial to the nation's good health, to prove to the outs that not everything wrong can be blamed on the ins: too many of the country's problems are either intractable or insoluble. The Republicans had denounced the Democrats for being weak against Communism, but once in office, Eisenhower had shown himself cautious in deploying American power, and had the advantage as a war hero in not needing to prove his manliness.

Luce's Presbyterian friend John Foster Dulles made holy speeches as secretary of state about "liberating" Eastern Europe, but when the Hungarian people revolted against Soviet rule, Ike refused to send troops to help. When French soldiers were surrounded by the North Vietnamese at Dienbienphu, Vice President Nixon and Admiral Arthur Radford, chairman of the Joint Chiefs, urged a carrier strike to relieve the siege; Eisenhower said no.

In later years, after the war in Vietnam had dimmed the American enthusiasm for foreign adventuring, historians who had once dismissed Eisenhower's do-nothing presidency came to appreciate that only once in eight years had Eisenhower, with great prudence, committed troops to battle. In 1958, after first assuring himself that the Russians would not get involved, Ike sent Marines into Lebanon in a landing so uncontested that the

American ambassador went down to greet them in a limousine, accompanied by his two poodles.

If Ike had been a tepid Cold Warrior and slow to act in domestic affairs, he had an additional failing in Luce's eyes: as president, Eisenhower had done too little to ensure the future of the Republican Party. As a military man, Ike disdained politicians; when he was given the Republican nomination, Eisenhower—as Luce grumbled—had "reaped what he had not sown."

Luce had been cured of wanting to be a kingmaker. Though he still liked Ike, he had been disappointed in his presidency; Richard Nixon, Ike's heir, was a man Ike himself found useful but not endearing. Luce spoke of "Dick" Nixon not in terms of dislike but with a noticeable tone of condescension. On the other hand, Harry had a liking for that tough old bird Joe Kennedy, Jack's father. At the Democratic convention in Los Angeles, Joe Kennedy had rented Marion Davies's former mansion but stayed out of sight; either he or his family reckoned that his presence would have an adverse effect if the press discovered him. On the day of his son's acceptance speech, Joe Kennedy flew back to New York. Rather than watch his son in some lonely hotel room by himself, he called Harry Luce from the airport. Harry, who was having dinner with his son, Henry, invited Ambassador Kennedy to join them. Together around the television set in Harry's Waldorf Towers apartment, the Luces, father and son, and Joe Kennedy watched Joe's son accept the Democratic nomination.

Luce's declining fervor for the Republican cause was matched by changes in the editorial structure of his magazines; he was grooming Hedley Donovan as his eventual successor. Donovan, the managing editor of *Fortune,* was a taciturn man of conservative instincts who did not believe that the magazines should be partisan. Roy Alexander had been replaced as managing editor of *Time* after ten years in the job. But right after the 1960 Republican convention the new managing editor suffered a serious cerebral incident (from which he completely recovered within four months) and it fell to me, as the assistant managing editor, to edit *Time* magazine during the Nixon-Kennedy campaign.

Having long objected to the Republican tilt of our political coverage, I had no desire to replace it with a Democratic bias. I simply wanted to restore *Time*'s trustworthiness in election years. In this I would have the powerful backing of Hedley Donovan and the willing cooperation of Louis Banks, who as national affairs editor supervised our election coverage. But it was Luce's own attitude that fascinated (and concerned) me. In his book *The Powers That Be,* David Halberstam quoted Luce as calling me the "loyal opposition," which suggests a favored status I did not enjoy. I sometimes lost a step in promotions to someone more in tune with Luce's thinking; to me, the independence I valued was not a work benefit but something I expected to pay for.

One day Luce called a lunch of a dozen or so of the top editors of *Time, Life,* and *Fortune* to discuss *Life*'s editorial-page endorsement in the approaching election. Knowing how deep was his Republicanism, I assumed the choice was a foregone conclusion. Instead, he opened the meeting by saying we were gathered to discuss who our choice would be. Though caught by surprise, and having no argument prepared, I decided to speak out. In that savvy crowd there was no need to talk issues; we all knew one another's views; instead I spoke to the character of the two candidates. (I didn't like Nixon and admired Kennedy but had reservations about a ruthlessness in the Kennedys and deplored their coziness with Joe McCarthy.)

As a lawyer would, I pitched my argument to the jury I faced: Nixon presented himself as a resolute fighter, but Kennedy was the man with the stronger, tougher character. No one challenged me on the point. But no one else said a word in Kennedy's favor, either, though I had the strong feeling that some around the table were closet Kennedy supporters. A kind of consensus by osmosis was reached without any fiat from Luce. *Life* would favor Nixon, with the understanding that Kennedy would be praised too. On *Life*'s editorial page, where such opinions belonged, that tepid endorsement seemed to me fair enough.

Friends and colleagues warned me that as the campaign heated up, Luce would end *Time* magazine's brief flirtation with even-handed coverage and insist on the usual blatant Republican bias; this would have been a real problem to me if it had come up, but it never did. Luce stayed out of my way. He would come by my office to chat about the campaign, fascinated, as he always was, by the great game of politics. But when I outlined our plans for the next issue, he scrupulously withheld advice. Was this rectitude his own idea, or had he pledged neutrality to Donovan? I never learned.

When we put to bed the last issue before the election, too late for anything he said to affect the magazine, Luce telephoned me from his home in Phoenix to praise the magazine's campaign coverage and to ask me to convey his congratulations to the staff. (He then told me to order myself a case of champagne. Why didn't he have his secretary order it? I couldn't see myself ordering a case and indicating on an expense account, "Approved by Mr. Luce." So I didn't.)

Professionally, I thought we had achieved coverage that was neither mealymouthed nor partisan. Personally, I was pleased when the historian (and Roosevelt biographer) Arthur Schlesinger, no great admirer of the magazine, said, "This is the best *Time* political coverage since 1936, the best and the fairest."

It must have been a puzzle to critics who believed Harry Luce a man set and predictable in his dogged convictions. "I don't know what you tell your friends," he said to me in one phone call from Phoenix during the campaign, "but when my scientific friends out here ask me what has happened, I just tell them that times have changed." He enjoyed leaving them with a mystery. He was always more complicated than his reputation and, in his way, as much a maverick as Teddy White. There was a contrary streak in him that never wanted his response to anything to be taken for granted.

In *The Making of the President 1960,* Teddy wrote as a journalist, not as a novelist or as a partisan. Teddy could chum up with sources but describe their actions candidly, and he could write neutrally about what he deplored. In the gathering of a story, he was capable of dissembling and flattering his sources, saving his honesty for the telling of it. In making this separation Teddy acted much as did the Soviet composer Dmitri Shostakovich, who in much more dangerous circumstances was forced into servility to the party line, to deviousness, and to humiliation, but could nonetheless say, "I never lie in my music."

Though Teddy was personally partial to Jack Kennedy, both candidates are seen in his book as able and ambitious politicians determined to win, each marked by his origins, each with his individual strengths and weaknesses.

The roundness of character that eluded White as a novelist he was able to achieve as a reporter. His method was to set the scene for each of the candidates, describing his circumstances, studying his handicaps and opportunities, and then telling how each set out with a plan, concentrating on states he had to win and ignoring those where he had little chance. As a young correspondent in China, Teddy had been hampered by his unfamiliarity with the country, by language difficulties, and by the sheer size of the place; in Europe, he arrived with an ignorance of the languages and of international economics as well; but in reporting the United States he had a natural feeling for the country's diversity and divisions and rhythms, as well as an easy understanding of the basic drives of politicians, whom he liked as a breed. *The Making of the President 1960* became a handbook for future correspondents and for future politicians alike.

The most memorable chapter in the book is the story of the

pivotal West Virginia Democratic primary. In a state where 95 percent of the voters were Protestant, the Kennedy strategists decided they had to win to prove to convention delegates (including several worried Catholic governors) that Kennedy's religion would not drag down the national ticket.

The man Kennedy had to beat was Hubert Humphrey, a warmhearted, garrulous soul whose efforts in the Senate on behalf of unions entitled him to the heavy support of West Virginia's coal miners; his own humble origins and folksy manner had a special appeal to West Virginians. But he was outgunned, outorganized, and outspent by Kennedy. Humphrey's campaign was deeply in debt, and the candidate had to write personal checks on his own household account to buy half an hour on television. Kennedy, with his money, had all the television time he wanted. And in West Virginia politics, where money notoriously talks in other ways, no one will ever know how much Jack Kennedy's rich father paid out to clinch the election. That money advantage mattered, but Kennedy won because, despite the caution of some of his advisers, he also faced the religion question head-on. He went before television cameras in West Virginia to declare: ". . . so when any man stands on the steps of the Capitol and takes the oath of office of President, he is swearing to support the separation of church and state; he puts one hand on the Bible and raises the other hand to God as he takes the oath. And if he breaks his oath, he is not only committing a crime against the Constitution, for which the Congress can impeach him—and should impeach him—but he is committing a sin against God. A sin against God, because he has sworn on the Bible."

On election night, fearing he would lose the state, Kennedy stayed in Washington. He went to a movie with his next-door neighbor, Ben Bradlee, the Washington bureau chief of *Newsweek*. When they got home they learned that Kennedy had won. He broke open a bottle of champagne and then, in his private plane, flew off with Bradlee to West Virginia. Hubert Humphrey, expecting to win, had ordered up a frugal victory party of liverwurst sandwiches. As the returns rolled in, a gallant and beaten Hubert Humphrey conceded and, downcast in spirit, withdrew from the presidential race.

Before the 1960 campaign began, Teddy's connection with the Kennedys was not significant. Teddy had been a Harvard classmate of Kennedy's older brother but didn't know him: they were at different ends of the social scale. Jack Kennedy was two years behind Teddy at Harvard. Teddy first became aware of Jack Kennedy in reading a *New Yorker* article by his friend John Hersey describing Kennedy's wartime exploits as the skipper of a PT boat. When Teddy got to know "the dashing, impeccably tailored, handsome Boston Irishman with the Harvard gloss," Jack Kennedy struck him as a charming dilettante, a man who regarded politics as a game, was curious about personalities but not about issues. "He was by nature stylish, by twist of mind ironic, by taste a connoisseur of good prose. These qualities combined to convert the newsmen who followed him from reporters to a claque, of whom, I admit, I must be counted one."

But Teddy's real conversion did not come until the campaign reached Montana, Kennedy's last stop before the Democratic convention. Kennedy invited Teddy and Blair Clark of CBS, who had been a Harvard classmate, to make the long night flight back to Cape Cod with him on his private plane (just the kind of intimacy with the candidate that in the days of rat-pack journalism any reporter would have envied). Teddy and Blair drank whiskey; Kennedy contented himself with tomato soup, into which he dropped gobs of sour cream. After the three had talked a while, Teddy, falling under Kennedy's spell but exhausted and "slack-tongued with drink," blurted out that he just didn't like Jack's father, Ambassador Joseph P. Kennedy, and told why. Kennedy leaned forward and said, "Teddy, you must meet my father someday; he's not like that at all," but he made no further effort to persuade him.

> Then I said that another thing I didn't like was what he had said about my teacher John Fairbank. In his first term as congressman, Kennedy had joined the pack and proclaimed that both John Fairbank and Owen Lattimore, another friend of mine, had been part of the Communist influence in the State Department which lost China to the Reds. Kennedy had no answer to that. But he put his head down into his hands, shook it, then said, as I recall, "Don't beat up on me. I was wrong. I know I was wrong. I didn't know anything then—you know what a kid congressman is like with no researchers, no staff, nothing. I made a mistake." His remorse was so real I could not press the matter.

Teddy then discovered within himself that he had just crossed the barrier of reportorial neutrality. His doubts satisfied, he now committed himself "to the loyalty of friendship" with Kennedy.

Yet in Teddy's treatment of Richard Nixon the reader will look in vain for an unfair characterization, a cheap shot, any animus. Nixon's handicaps are treated as White treated the handicap of Kennedy's religion, as problems that the candidate and his advisers had to face. For Kennedy the suburban and the Protestant vote were worries, for Nixon, the farm vote and the Catholic vote. As the challenger, Kennedy ran all-out from the beginning; Nixon, confidently ahead in the polls, believed in pacing, and in not peaking too soon. Nixon began in low key because, as one of his strategists put it, "We have to erase the image of pugnacity first." His campaign would stress peace and prosperity as the legacy of Eisenhower, then contrast Nixon's experience with Kennedy's lack of it. It seemed a winning strategy.

Once Nixon was nominated, he headed for the Democratic South and drew surprisingly large and enthusiastic crowds in Atlanta. But, as Teddy wrote, "there was always an element of sadness about the Nixon campaign, from beginning to end, and a sequence of episodes that wrung sympathy for him even from his most embittered opponents."

Nixon struck his kneecap on the door of his car in Greensboro, North Carolina, and for a crucial ten days in September lay out of action in Walter Reed hospital, his leg held in traction by a five-pound weight. That should have been reason enough to cancel his rash promise to campaign in all fifty states. Instead, while Kennedy concentrated on the heavily populated states, Nixon further wearied himself by dashing about, trolling for Alaska's three electoral votes, darting from state to state and speech to speech. He had lost five pounds and looked haggard when he appeared in the first televised debate, seen by more than sixty-five million people. That night Kennedy, looking fit and relaxed, quickly established by his performance that the challenger belonged in the ring. White sympathetically noted in his book "the electronic cruelty of the camera to [Nixon's] countenance. . . . On television, the deep eye wells and the heavy brows cast shadow on the face and it glowered on the screen darkly." This was the year, White added, when television won the nation away from sound to images. What the two candidates said in their four debates mattered little: "rarely has there been a political campaign that discussed issues less or clarified them less." (There would be other televised campaigns that clarified issues even less, but these were still in the future.)

In the final week of the campaign Nixon surged back and nearly overtook Kennedy. This led critics to charge later that the press, by overstressing Kennedy's enthusiastic crowds, had cost Nixon the election. Teddy White instead credited the Republican's final surge to the belated use, in the campaign's last days, of the Republican's leading vote-getter, President Eisenhower. Ike had all along been eager to do more in the campaign; he fumed at Kennedy's promise to get the country "moving forward" again after Eisenhower's do-nothing presidency; he was outraged at Kennedy's talk of a "missile gap"—which, after the election, proved not to exist. On the hustings, drawing big crowds, Eisenhower's avuncular authority made Kennedy look young and unready. Yet Nixon, determined to win on his own in order to get out from Eisenhower's shadow, delayed too long in calling for his help.

It is certainly true that most reporters liked Kennedy and disliked Nixon—"To be transferred from the Nixon campaign tour to the Kennedy campaign tour," White wrote, "was as if one were transformed in role from leper and outcast to friend and battle companion." This affected the tenor of much of the reporting by the fifty or sixty national correspondents who covered the campaign, White acknowledged, yet even a liberal candidate soon learns that when he gets into some difficulty, reporters may have sympathy for the man but their interest in pursuing the story is greater. What made the Nixon camp different was its bitter belief that the press was the enemy and could safely be ignored. The Nixon strategy was to use television to go over the heads of reporters; on the campaign trail itself the press was walled off and frozen out. There were trips when not a single newsman was aboard the Nixon plane. As White noted, "Kennedy would as soon have dismissed his co-pilot as have dismissed the rotating trio of pool reporters who rode his personal plane everywhere." In a later interview with a newspaperman, Teddy talked more candidly than he had in his book, because in the book his remarks might have sounded too biased: "You're on a campaign plane with ten or twelve guys, and Kennedy walks back and says, 'Hey, Teddy, come on up and have a nightcap with me.' And, even though you've spent eighteen hours with him that day, you're eager to talk about the day's events. But when Nixon walked through the plane, every reporter was looking fixedly out the window. Eighteen hours with Nixon was enough."

Presumably, what reporters were trying to avoid was a matey chitchat with Nixon, not a serious interview. As Teddy White observed in his book in a frustrated footnote, it was impossible for him, as for most reporters, "despite repeated and personal effort, to meet or talk with Mr. Nixon privately or discuss his campaign with him." Therefore, "however long [a reporter] may travel with a man," he is apt to gather wrong impressions about someone "with whom he was forbidden personal contact." Teddy, in fact, was sometimes not even on the regular press plane that accompanied Nixon but was confined to the "zoo plane," which was for photographers, with all their equipment, and strays like himself who had no newspaper or magazine credentials.

This makes all the more remarkable the objectivity White achieved in his reporting of the Nixon campaign, and his constant attempt to understand the lone, insecure, self-isolated candidate. In his reporting, White was helped by a little-known and unusual arrangement. He had come to know Richard Clurman, chief of correspondents for *Time* magazine, and with characteristic gall he asked Clurman if he could read the files of *Time*'s political reporters, which would give him advance tips on what both political camps were up to, and what people in both parties were saying, on and off the record. Clurman obliged. Had Clurman asked Harry Luce whether he should turn over such files to Teddy? (Luce's answer might well have been no.) He had not; he was simply accommodating a friend whom he considered, as a former *Time* correspondent, a member of the club. In this way White was helped in his coverage of West Virginia by reading the files of *Time*'s White House correspondent (and later columnist) Hugh Sidey. In those days, Sidey told me, he held Teddy in "special awe"; he remembered him in a trench coat, "the kind you hang grenades from. He worked hard, ate the bad meals."

Among the correspondents, White had one special distinction, Sidey said. "Kennedy was so upbeat, wry, gracious. We were all such hotheads and made no bones of our opposition to

Nixon's staff, his record, his personality. But I never heard Teddy even in private knock Nixon. He thought he was very bright. Teddy was never a man to burn his bridges."

Sure enough, in years to come, Nixon would himself become the central figure in another volume of Teddy's *Making of the President* series.

A third of a century later Teddy's book on the 1960 campaign remains a page-turner, full of fascinating details and shrewd judgments. It won the Pulitzer Prize. It created a new genre of political journalism; four years later there would be a dozen or more imitators, but Teddy's sequel in 1964 would outsell them all. Politicians as well as the public admired *The Making of the President 1960*. General Charles de Gaulle read it, hoping to understand what he regarded as the excessive democracy of the Americans. Once, Richard Clurman made the mistake of taking Teddy along with him to Number 10 Downing Street to interview Harold Wilson, the British prime minister. Wilson spent the entire time interviewing Teddy about American politics. Canada's prime minister, Lester "Mike" Pearson, used Teddy's book as a manual in running his own campaign.

The Making of the President differs from the many "quickie" books by journalists that are just as quickly forgotten. Teddy followed the scholarly standards he had learned from John Fairbank at Harvard. Arthur Schlesinger later wrote that only another journalist would appreciate Teddy's performance, his need to "be everywhere, talk to everybody, sit up all night writing out his notes, take a plane at dawn to cover another candidate halfway across the continent and then, when it is all over . . . sit down at his typewriter and labor for months to distill the angry chaos into a coherent narration." Only a historian, Schlesinger added, could appreciate Teddy's skill in "selecting the critical points out of filing cases full of material, in checking and cross-checking to get the best possible account of an episode that every participant remembers differently, in cutting and concentrating and throwing away, in transforming experience into history. . . . The historians of the future will stand permanently in his debt."

Chapter 17

THE GOOD—OR BAD—OLD DAYS

Though Teddy and Harry renewed their friendship and resumed a fragile working relationship, their differences over China were always a barrier between them.

Shortly after Teddy had finished *The Making of the President 1960* and was casting about for something else to do, he and Carl Mydans, the *Life* photographer, talked about going back to China to do a report for *Life.* The Communists, in their eleven years in power, had cruelly crushed opposition and might now feel secure enough to allow the two men in.

Teddy went to see his friend Edward K. Thompson, the managing editor of *Life,* who liked the idea but said there had "always been a problem with Harry." Teddy assured him that Luce had never held their dispute against him, or "it's been so long he's forgotten about it." Nonetheless, Thompson sent him off to see Luce. Thompson remembered well what then took place, because both Teddy and Harry afterward described the conversation in the same words. Teddy, seeing Luce grope around for an answer to his proposal, said, "But Harry, I want you to know that I have changed my mind about China."

Harry replied, "*You,* Teddy, may have changed *your* mind, but *I* haven't. NO!"

■　■　■

When Teddy at the age of sixty-three wrote in his autobiography, "I still insist, and know, that I was right and he was wrong in telling the story of China," he was right in talking about the period when he was on the scene, reporting the collapse of Chiang Kai-shek's regime. Luce was right in insisting that if the Communists came to power things would get worse.

Teddy had stated his case against Chiang in *Thunder Out of China,* the book that caused the break between him and Harry. But when it came time to reissue that book, in 1961, the year in which Teddy wanted to return to China with Mydans, Teddy conceded Harry's point in a new introduction: "Nor could one foresee how the rigid dogmatic fancies of this Yenan leadership, so curiously charming in the hills, could become such a terrifying policy and practice fifteen years later. . . . For what [the Communists] achieved in their lust to apply a logic of government to the anarchy of China was to make all China a prison."

How deeply Luce himself felt on the subject of China can be seen in the bizarre, testy, defiant speech he made to the editorial staff of *Time* gathered for dinner after Eisenhower's election. In his rambling remarks he said:

> Now we are *for* objectivity. This may surprise some of you. . . . There is objective truth in the universe. . . . There is scientific truth and there is moral truth. . . . Majorities do not make truth. Intellectual facts do not make truth. What is the objectivity we are against? The alleged journalistic objectivity . . . a claim that the writer presents facts without applying any value judgment to them. That is modern usage and that is strictly a phony. It is that I had to renounce and denounce.
>
> So when we say the hell with objectivity, this is what we are talking about. . . . Now this does not mean that value judgments are bad. . . . Quite the contrary. It means that 75 percent of the business of recognizing, selecting and organizing facts is having a correct value judgment. And that is just as true for the Associated Press or the United Press as it

is for *Time,* whether or not they have the intelligence to recognize it. . . .

The slaughter of millions of Chinese by the Mao regime was due in part to American ignorance and confusion concerning the issue. American journalism was very much implicated in that mistake. I think we might all of us take a vow tonight that, God help us, we will not be again an accessory before the fact to the murder of mankind.

Many of the people in the room disagreed with Harry's single-mindedness about China and felt ashamed of the magazine's prejudiced coverage of the Eisenhower campaign. But they resented these excesses most of all because they discredited that part of Luce's editorial credo that they did agree with. They liked editorializing in what they wrote, and therefore they had to put up with the boss when he overdid it. From day one, thirty years earlier, *Time* had been an opinionated magazine, crackling with prejudices, designed to irritate and amuse as well as to instruct, and providing dozens of small pleasures to those who crafted its irreverent judgments.

Such outspoken rejection of editorial evenhandedness, gleefully practiced by those who worked at *Time,* riled conventional newspaper editors, as it was meant to. Luce said on one occasion: "The press today is to a large extent the press-which-gives-the-public-what-it-wants. If newspapers are not doing their job for the Republic it is because they are concentrating too much on pleasing the people. Here is the sacred paradox of democracy. The people are to be served, not necessarily to be pleased."

Deeply ingrained in Luce was the belief that responsible journalism owed readers not just information but guidance. *Time* had no editorial page and, as Tom Matthews put it, "always felt hoarse and strangled without it." In compressing the week's news, *Time* combined facts and judgments, flooding its news stories with opinions in a way that shocked the respectable journalistic establishment of the day. As Luce once wrote,

"*Time* will not allow the stuffed dummy of impartiality to stand in the way of telling the truth as we see it."

The judgmental journalism that Luce exercised in the news columns is now commonplace in newspapers and magazines that once denounced the practice. Sometimes these subjective responses are labeled as commentary or analysis, but at other times news and opinion are simply combined in the same story. This amounts to a radical shift away from the earlier belief in an antiseptic delivery of the news, untainted by the reporter's own opinions and biases.

It was Joe McCarthy who cured newspapers of this noble illusion. Once newspapers examined their own role in inflating McCarthy into a national scourge, they discovered that he had shrewdly taken advantage of two of their most vulnerable practices. One was their delight in printing sensational accusations by anyone considered newsworthy. The second weakness was the press's haste to print accusations without first giving the accused a chance to reply. Today the press makes a conscious effort to reach the accused for comment. Fair journalism also requires that readers be given some clue as to the reputation and motives of the person who makes an accusation—a practice that would once have been considered unacceptable editorializing in the news columns.

Even if he couldn't get assigned to China, Teddy White was still eager to work for the Luce magazines, particularly on political stories that would be useful when he wrote his next *Making of the President* book. One day he turned up in the office of Ralph Graves, the text editor of *Life,* with a story suggestion about two extremely wealthy men competing to be governor of New York State. On the Republican ticket was Nelson Rockefeller, always grinning, waving, and saying "Hi-ya" to the masses, though incapable of remembering the names of anyone he had just met. Running against him as a Democrat, but no match for

Rocky in pandering to the populace, was the lugubrious liberal Averell Harriman (known around *Life* as "Honest Ave, the hairsplitter"). Teddy knew them both well.

Graves liked the proposal but was quickly cautioned by Teddy: "I think it might be a good idea to check with Luce." When Graves did so, he told me, "Luce's eyebrows jumped up, and stayed up for as long as I can ever remember, then he said 'Good!'"

Teddy's friend Ed Thompson, the managing editor, wanted to welcome him back to *Life* with a big splash. Since both of the candidates were impressive collectors of art, Thompson proposed to illustrate Teddy's article by setting Rockefeller's masterpieces against Harriman's. Luce liked both the layouts and Teddy's piece. But he made a private request to Thompson, who was one of Luce's favorite editors: "Please don't get into the habit of running pieces by Teddy too often. I don't want the word to get around that I have completely made up with him." Thompson scrupulously followed Luce's instructions until he felt it safe to put Teddy back on the staff, as *Life*'s leading political writer, in 1962.

On the day President Kennedy was shot, *Life*'s presses were about to start printing seven million copies of the issue dated November 23, 1963, when Teddy, having rushed back from lunch on hearing the news from Dallas, burst into the managing editor's office crying, "This is my story!"

Who else had a better claim? Of all the contemporary figures he had written about, Teddy had admitted only three heroes to his pantheon—General Stilwell, Chou En-lai, and Kennedy. Stilwell was dead; Chou had betrayed Teddy's illusions about him; only Kennedy was left among his heroes.

"Kennedy played White like a flute," Ben Bradlee once told me. "Of course he played all of us that way." In the days when Bradlee was *Newsweek*'s Washington bureau chief and Senator

John F. Kennedy was his Georgetown neighbor, the Kennedy and Bradlee children were often together, and the parents didn't bother to maintain the proper distance between journalist and source. Conceding this professional lapse in his relationship with Kennedy, Bradlee added, "But we also played *him*." The "we" included Teddy White.

Told to get to Dallas that Friday afternoon as quickly as he could, Teddy passed the hat around among his colleagues at *Life*. After collecting about three hundred dollars in expense money from them, he was off to the airport. En route he learned over the cab's radio that Kennedy had died and that his body was being flown to Andrews Air Force Base outside Washington. Teddy switched to the Washington shuttle, and when he arrived in the capital shoved a pile of money into a cabbie's hands, hired him for the evening, and directed him to Andrews, which they reached just as the blue-and-white *Air Force One* glided to a landing. The rear door was opened and the coffin lowered to the ground. Teddy noted that "Jacqueline Kennedy, her raspberry-colored suit still smeared and stiff with blood, appeared, helped by Robert Kennedy into the gray Navy ambulance that carried the coffin."

After watching Lyndon Johnson, the new president, descend from *Air Force One,* to be flown by helicopter to the White House, Teddy instructed his cabdriver to head for the hospital where Kennedy's coffin had been taken; there he saw "Mrs. Kennedy for a moment, still bloodstained, and so numb of expression that I could not bring myself to speak to her."

A week later, Teddy got an urgent call from Jackie Kennedy. That memorably funereal Thanksgiving weekend had been emotionally wrenching for the entire nation: the nation's radio stations played hours of somber music and television endlessly replayed scenes of sorrow—the slow funeral march through crowded Washington streets, Kennedy's body lying in state, the burial at Arlington cemetery. Now, from her seclusion in the Kennedy compound at Hyannis Port on Cape Cod, Mrs.

Kennedy called to say she had something she "wanted *Life* magazine to say to the country" and asked Teddy to write it. She would have a Secret Service car pick up Teddy in New York City.

Teddy called his editor, Ed Thompson, asking him to hold the presses at *Life* until Teddy learned what Jackie Kennedy had to say. Thompson agreed to do so, though waiting would cost the magazine thirty thousand dollars an hour. Teddy ran into his first difficulty when he called Secret Service and was curtly informed that as the president's widow, Jackie Kennedy could no longer order up Secret Service cars and drivers. Teddy thought of flying to the Cape, only to be told that bad weather had grounded all planes. (He checked with his brother Robert, the head of the National Weather Service in Washington, who said a northeaster or a full-scale hurricane was building up near the Cape, and no flights would be possible.) At last, in a hired limo with chauffeur, Teddy set off for Hyannis Port in a heavy rainstorm.

He was mindful of how much this trip was delaying the magazine, so when he arrived at the Kennedy compound he began in brisk, businesslike fashion to interview the president's widow. Then he sensed that it wasn't that kind of occasion at all: he had been summoned "as a friend who also happened to be a journalist." He slowed himself down to let her talk at her own pace and in her own way. He had a tape recorder with him but decided against using it. He began taking notes instead, beginning with her appearance: "dressed in black trim slacks, beige pullover sweater . . . eyes wider than pools . . . calm voice." Some of what she said, he decided, "was too personal for mention in any book but one of her own," and this he left out. She spoke in her whispery voice for two hours, keyed up, alternating in narrative between memory and feelings, but always without tears, even when reliving those awful moments in Dallas just one week earlier. First, she said, there had been a noise that sounded like a backfire. "He looked puzzled, then he slumped forward. He was holding out his hand. . . . I could see a piece of his skull coming off. It was flesh-colored, not white. . . . Then he slumped in my lap, his blood and his brains were in my lap. . . . All the ride to the hospital I kept bending over him, saying Jack, Jack, can you hear me, I love you, Jack. I kept holding the top of his head down, trying to keep the brains in . . . but I knew he was dead."

She had summoned Teddy to Hyannis Port, she said, because she didn't want history to forget her husband. She continued: "For a while I thought history was something that bitter old men wrote. But Jack loved history so. . . . I want to say this one thing, it's been almost an obsession with me, all I keep thinking of is this line from a musical comedy. . . . At night before we'd go to sleep . . . we had an old Victrola. Jack liked to play some records. His back hurt, the floor was so cold. I'd get out of bed at night and play it for him . . . the song he loved most came at the very end of the record, the last side of *Camelot,* sad *Camelot:* 'Don't let it be forgot, that once there was a spot, for one brief shining moment that was known as Camelot.' " She added: "There'll never be another Camelot again."

His interview completed, Teddy went off to a servant's room to write his story on a borrowed typewriter. Matching her own taut and tense but tearless recital, and despite his own inner turmoil after a physically and emotionally exhausting week, he wrote with the speed of a professional, finishing his report in forty-five minutes. He showed it to Jackie Kennedy for her approval; then, from a wall phone in the Kennedy kitchen, he telephoned New York to dictate his story to two of his editors, Dave Maness and Ralph Graves.

By then it was two in the morning. I remember Maness's concern at that late hour that some of the article seemed too overwrought. He read back to Teddy one passage about Camelot that sounded mawkish. Teddy responded, "Yes, isn't that beautiful?" In this way, with great quickness of mind, he alerted us that Mrs. Kennedy—who had just joined him in the kitchen—was right beside him at the phone. In New York, editorial fastidiousness gave way to the feeling that a genuine emotional experience should be allowed full expression.

In the end, as Jackie Kennedy intended, history had not been left entirely to bitter old men to write. "Camelot," whether used romantically or in irony, became the word by which Kennedy's brief, shining moment would thereafter be remembered.

In the spring of 1964, six months after Kennedy's assassination, Harry Luce stepped down as editor in chief of his magazines. At the age of sixty-six, he had lost some of his fervor to change the world and was more willing to accept it. Harry and Clare were spending more time in Phoenix, where they found the climate more agreeable than in New York. But whenever he did visit New York and lunch with his editors, it was he who, as always, dominated the conversation, by an easy informal understanding with his successor, Hedley Donovan. Shorn of his favorite title, editor in chief, Luce was now called editorial chairman, but the magazines were still his, and he was still referred to, in a kind of mock tribute, as The Proprietor. At these editorial lunches he was as curious as ever about events but now more willing to yield in argument, recognizing that those around the table followed the news more closely than he did.

Teddy wrote to him: "There are certain things that I absolutely refuse to believe: like Harry Luce retiring. Imagine! Do you realize what this does to all my generation? We've been able to think of ourselves as boys all these years because you were there in the background to take care of us if things went wrong. . . . As a reporter I feel orphaned by the retirement of the greatest of American editors."

Just how different the new era would be became evident at a grand dinner for the staffs of the Luce magazines at the New York Hilton to mark the transfer of power. Both Luce and Donovan exchanged bouquets of admiration in their speeches, but Donovan had something more on his mind. As managing editor of the ever-so-earnest *Fortune* magazine, he had never approved of the bias, the impish smart-aleckiness, and the readiness to wound that had marked *Time* magazine. He told his audience that the Luce magazines could be proud of some of the enemies they had made, but some others were "acquired rather casually." As for politics, he said, the vote of the Luce magazines should be independent, "not in the sense of some snooty or finicky disdain for political parties. And certainly not independent in the sense of any wishy-washy confusion as to what we believe. But in the sense that we are no way beholden to any party."

Though Luce had not read Donovan's speech in advance, he could not have been surprised by it: one of Hedley's conditions in taking the job of editor in chief was that the magazines would be politically independent. That year *Life* for the first time editorially endorsed a Democratic presidential candidate, Lyndon Johnson, even though Clare Boothe Luce was campaigning vigorously for the Republican Barry Goldwater.

Under Donovan, there were still clashes of opinion on the magazines, but fewer causes for heartburn among the editors. Like the rest of American journalism, the Luce magazines were becoming fairer, freer of partisanship, and devoid of passion. In time they would become parts of a vast conglomerate whose primary goal was profit, and whose primary interest was entertainment. A similar change would come over the great television networks once their bold, innovating, domineering founders had left the scene.

If the recent era in which Harry Luce and Teddy White flourished now seems long ago and far away, it is because television changed journalism as radically as the invention of gunpowder once changed warfare. In 1972, five years after Luce's death, *Life,* losing money despite millions of subscribers, suspended publication as a weekly. Television had first stolen its advertisers, then many of its readers: the best of still photographs, arriving in the mail days after the event, could not compete with pictures that were transmitted by satellite as the news happened and were complete with motion and sound. Newspapers were similarly devastated: in the first thirty-five years after television's arrival, the number of American households taking newspapers declined 40 percent.

The wicked old press lord was gone. Most of the nation's newspapers had become chain-owned monopolies run by pragmatic executives who thought a too-vigorous expression of a newspaper's opinion was self-indulgence and bad for business. Opinion is now molded by a new elite of celebrity journalists, highly visible and highly paid and mostly centered in Washington. They can be seen on Sunday television shows, lecturing—or bullying—public officials who by the nature of their jobs have to be more circumspect than their taunting cross-examiners. In their ambition to guide and shape public opinion the celebrity journalists can be every bit as arrogant, with their encroaching personalities, as the old press lords—and are much more visible than faceless owners like Hearst, Pulitzer, and Luce were.

Members of this new breed are a strange hybrid: half journalist, half entertainer. Their chief competition in the clamor for public attention is not other journalists but other entertainers, including television preachers who wrap their political messages in simplistic theology, and brassy talk-show hosts on call-in radio who substitute stridency for thought. Authority has been democratized. Everyone feels entitled, if not to fifteen moments of fame, at least to two minutes of attention.

But any longing for a more orderly past, when the news was clearer and the commentary more profound, is false history. What remains attractive about that earlier day—a time with its own tribulations and discontents—is a vital sense of possibility. There existed the conviction that the United States, if it was not, as Harry Luce believed, operating under a special dispensation from Providence, was still the best of all worlds and about to become better. There was a confidence that consensus could be reached on any issue among people of goodwill. All this was in the very air that Harry Luce and Teddy White breathed.

As Teddy White neared his fiftieth birthday, his wife decided to give a dinner party for him. Mostly the guests would be people of consequence. In making up the list, Nancy and Blair Clark of CBS, a friend of Teddy's since Harvard, ran into a problem: Teddy had too many friends. They resolved it by limiting invitations to friends who had known Teddy before the year 1946, but they agreed to make exceptions of two of his later friends, inviting Jackie Kennedy and Adlai Stevenson (though as things turned out, neither could come).

The list included some distinguished public servants whom Teddy had come to know during his European exile (such as Paul Hoffman), but many were Teddy's friends from the China days. Would there be awkward encounters among them, even though fifteen years had passed since the Communists conquered China? Harry and Clare Luce would be there. So would Teddy's favorite Harvard professor, John K. Fairbank, with his wife, Wilma; Fairbank suspected that Luce regarded him as an agent in the devil's workshop. John Paton Davies, Teddy's State Department companion on his trip to Communist Yenan, was one of the diplomats Luce blamed for the loss of China. In turn Fairbank and Davies held Luce largely to blame for the failure of American policy in China. But such animosities, if they still existed, were submerged that night in the common wish to celebrate Teddy.

The guest list of old China hands also included *Life* photographer Carl Mydans and his reporter wife, Shelley, a popular couple on no one's enemy list. John Hersey was there also, the only one whose presence Luce seemed to be worried about. An unfavorable review of Hersey's latest novel had just appeared in

Time, and in some agitation Harry told Mike Bessie, Teddy's editor, that he wanted Hersey to know that Luce had had no advance knowledge of the review. (Bessie saw the two talk together but never learned whether Luce had been able to placate Hersey.)

In fact, most people who were at that dinner in a little Manhattan restaurant on East Fifty-eighth Street could remember little years later, except that everyone, and especially Teddy, had a good time. Partly, Nancy said, memories might be hazy because there had been so much booze. Even so meticulous a man as Arthur Schlesinger, who can usually document any occasion by quoting from his journal, could remember little of what was said that evening, as he was not keeping a diary at that time. He did recall Clare's predicting that, come the revolution, she and Teddy would be on the same side of the barricades. But Schlesinger's strongest impression of the evening, listening to the speeches by Harry and Clare, was that each was trying to outdo the other as the one who treasured Teddy more.

CURLING UP WITH THE POWERFUL

Perhaps the high point of Teddy White's journalistic career was when, as he put it, he stood "on the bridge" of the ship of state alongside its skipper, President Kennedy. The very phrase suggests Kennedy's gift for making whoever might be of help to him—including sympathetic journalists—feel included in a great enterprise.

At the time Teddy White enjoyed a formidable reputation as the man who had invented a new kind of political journalism—a handbook for journalists and politicians alike, which changed forever the way political campaigns would be waged and how they would be reported. He signed a contract to produce five more *Making of the President* books, one every four years—"so long as I can still totter around after the goddam caravan in 1980." With each new volume his name would be better established, but this increased stature would also make him a target of criticism. The process, familiar throughout American life, is sped by envy: once someone becomes a celebrity, he is less esteemed in his own field, where he is now tested by more exacting standards.

White's decline from his high peak of influence began rather abruptly. His second book, *The Making of the President 1964,* had no candidate as appealing as Jack Kennedy, nor did it have an electoral race as dramatically close as that of 1960 had been.

And in writing about Lyndon Johnson's landslide, he managed to antagonize the central figure in his tale. "That Teddy White made a hero out of Kennedy and a bum out of me," the new president complained.

"I was barred from the White House, my press pass lifted, until just before the end," Teddy complained in return.

"I of course voted for Lyndon Johnson," Teddy wrote later. "However much I loathed his style, there seemed to be a coarse greatness in his purpose." Teddy in those days could hardly have favored Johnson's opponent, Barry Goldwater, whose conservatism disturbed Teddy and whose flippancy about nuclear bombs ("Let's lob one into the men's room of the Kremlin") alarmed him. Yet once again, in *The Making of the President 1964,* White succeeded admirably in concealing his own views as he described how a motley army of unknowns in each camp devised campaign strategy, raised vast sums of money, blackened the opponent's reputation, manipulated the press, and either won or lost. Now, spotlighted by Teddy, these unsung technicians soon became highly paid specialists in their dark arts, and celebrities themselves.

Even though he had a solid book contract, Teddy helped to finance much of his reporting by doing preliminary articles for *Life,* articles that, as Luce wrote Teddy, were "just about the best reading in the field of contemporary history that I have read since I read you the last time. In fact, why don't I just firm it up and say *the* best?"

The book sold well; Teddy now had imitators but no real competitors. Even right-wing reviewers like William F. Buckley, Jr., in a front-page article in the New York *Herald Tribune,* praised White as "the best political reporter in the language," though in his familiar condescending manner Buckley also called White "an Eagle Scout liberal" who "knows literally, but absolutely, *nothing* about economics in the best Democratic tradition." Only years later would Buckley more generously acknowledge that White had risked derision in that landslide year of 1964 by daring "to say that Goldwater had galvanized dissatisfaction in America that would not be put down by the facile rhetoric and quick-fix social legislation" of the Democrats.

By that time, Buckley had come to know Teddy, who called on him for an interview when Buckley, in a gesture of frivolity and gall, ran for mayor of New York City: "He began to ask questions and to take those copious notes of his, neat save for the cigaret ashes that spilt on them. I was feeling saucy and answered two or three of his questions with a levity not entirely appropriate. He would suppress a smile, even as his eyes would twinkle. Finally, he put down his pencil and said: 'Look, Mr. Buckley. I am doing business now. We will make friends later.' "

Shortly after *The Making of the President 1964* was published Teddy took off to Europe with his family for what "was to be 18 months of indulgence, exploring past and future as fancy took me," recognizing that "my taste for politics had slackened." But it was only election campaigns, and not politics itself, that he was tired of. Nor was he capable of relaxing for long. In Europe, he got to thinking about power, its acquisition and its use, and became interested in Julius Caesar, who amassed great power and then abused it. As he once told Donald Straus, who had been in Harvard classes with him, "I have an erotic bang out of power. I'm in love with power." In Rome he immersed himself in the study of Caesar's life and times, then got himself invited to the Rockefeller Foundation's beautiful estate on Lake Como, Villa Serbelloni, where he wrote his first and only play, *Caesar at the Rubicon*. The play covers the six weeks when Caesar, ambitious to rule Rome, sat beside the river Rubicon, waiting, maneuvering, and intriguing to see whether, after nine years of successfully waging war in Gaul, he would be welcomed by the Roman Senate, or, if not, whether he should seize Rome and set himself up as a dictator, bringing to an end five centuries of democratic government.

The play had a two-week tryout in Princeton, where Don

Straus saw it with the Whites and felt that "it wasn't a bad play," though it never reached Broadway. Later it was published in book form as *Caesar at the Rubicon: A Play About Politics*; it reads well, perhaps better than it may have played.

By then, his long holiday over, it was time for Teddy once more to crisscross the United States, interviewing politicians and gathering material for his next book, *The Making of the President 1968*. Whenever his travels took him near Phoenix, where the Luces had a winter retreat, he would write Harry to ask whether he could "drink a cup of friendship" with them, and he could count on an instant invitation if they were in residence.

In the sunny twilight of Luce's retirement, Teddy was a welcome burst of effervescence, cockiness, and gossip. The Luces lived in a house whose patio bordered the Arizona Biltmore golf course. There, following his doctor's orders, Luce played nine holes a day, riding in a golf cart driven by Andy, his caddy. Before lunch each day, Harry and Clare also swam in their heated pool, slowly sidestroking back and forth, talking to each other. They played bridge, or relaxed over a new enthusiasm of theirs, television—the medium that would shortly destroy *Life* magazine.

When Harry and Teddy got together, they would quickly lock horns in amiable combat over issues. It was almost like old times. At their last meeting, Luce at one point remarked, "It's all right to interrupt, Teddy, but not too much!"

To the end of his life Luce enjoyed philosophical disputation. One of the frequent visitors to Phoenix was Father John Courtney Murray, a friend for twenty years. It was Murray, a brilliant Jesuit theologian, who articulated the philosophy that made possible the election of a Roman Catholic as president. Traditionally, the Church of Rome shared power with autocratic governments the world over, forbidding dissent; Murray and his American colleagues worked out the rationale whereby the Catholic Church, in nations where it was a minority, could participate democratically in the life of a pluralistic society. Murray and Luce loved arguing.

"I don't think I ever met a man with a more objective mind," Murray said of Luce. "He always tried to see all sides of any question. His arguments were intelligently conceived and reasonably affirmed. He never belabored the obvious. That's why he was never dull."

Father Murray added: "He's the only man I know who can *will* a golf ball two hundred yards."

But the physical vigor that sustained Luce for so long gradually began to give way. He had concealed from his colleagues in New York an earlier heart attack, explaining a prolonged stay in Phoenix by saying he had pneumonia. In retirement he kept his body active by golf, and his mind sharp by occasional speeches ("They force me to rethink an issue").

One Sunday morning in February 1967 Harry canceled a golf date, feeling fatigued and ill. The next day his doctor, noting his high fever, ordered him taken to a hospital in an ambulance, though Luce insisted that he was really all right. He was restless in the hospital, frequently getting out of bed, over his nurse's objections. At three in the morning, after he had gotten up to go to the bathroom, the nurse heard him cry "Jesus!" and then a loud thump. He was dead of a coronary occlusion.

His funeral was held at the Madison Avenue Presbyterian Church in New York City, where he had worshiped for many years. As a procession of limousines drove up, photographers jostled to take pictures of the notables—governors, senators, business leaders, publishers, educators, writers—among the eight hundred who attended. Perhaps many who came expected to hear a conventional, respectful recital of a distinguished figure's achievements. Instead they heard a moving and personal account of Luce's lifetime commitment to serving his God, delivered by Harry's friend and pastor, the Scots-born David H. C. Read, a man of plainspoken eloquence who had spent many hours with Luce jointly exploring the mysteries of belief and doubt. Of Luce he said:

> On quick analysis, perhaps a complicated man—an idealist who made his judgments with utter realism; a man with his roots in the world unseen who joyfully plunged into the arena of the world we know, accepting its challenges and delighting in its gifts. . . . To talk with him was a signal to shift the mind into high gear, for his was never in neutral.
>
> [Beneath the complexity was the simplicity of] a man of faith. That faith was not a vague quality of humanistic hope. It was not the surface adornment of an otherwise self-sufficient personality. It was a quite specific faith in the sovereign God and Creator through Jesus Christ His Son. . . . This simple belief that behind the chaos of men and nations there is a divine purpose accounts for his fascination with news of all kinds, and his conviction that both the nation and the world have a destiny to pursue.
>
> [Also from] what you might call a mellow Calvinism came his sense of sin and grace. This may seem far from the sophisticated approach of the magazines that are his brainchildren, but . . . a healthy understanding of human sinfulness kept his idealism within the bounds of common sense, and a reliance on the mercy of God ruled out cynicism and despair.
>
> Henry Luce, with all his energy and drive, with all his brilliance and wit, with all his agility of mind, with all his power and influence, was at heart a pilgrim. He was not ashamed, in a sophisticated environment and a nihilistic age, to see life as a pilgrimage—a pilgrimage with a purpose and a goal.

And so Dr. Read ended with Bunyan's hymn:

> *Who would true valor see,*
> *Let him come hither;*
> *One here will constant be,*
> *Come wind, come weather;*

> *There's no discouragement*
> *Shall make him once relent*
> *His first avowed intent*
> *To be a pilgrim.*

We who worked on Luce's magazines had of course always known the centrality and depth of Luce's faith. But I can't recall that in the secular atmosphere of his magazines he ever based any argument, in discussions with his editors, on religious authority. To me, that day, Dr. Read joined together the two sides of Luce's character in a way I had never fully understood before.

After the church service, Clare Boothe Luce invited some of Luce's closest colleagues to the Luce apartment. Jim Bell, who had covered the Hiss-Chambers trials for the magazines, shared a taxi ride with Teddy White. He remembered that Teddy spent the entire trip berating John Hersey—who was not at the funeral—for not having made up with Luce.

When Teddy returned from Europe in 1967, he was disturbed as much by the divisive atmosphere he found in the country as he was by the actions the government was taking, both of which he blamed on Lyndon Baines Johnson, "the worst president, with the exception of Warren G. Harding, of the 20th Century." First there was Vietnam, a peculiarly ugly and unwinnable war that was dividing the nation. Teddy's China experience had turned him against the use of American troops on the Asian mainland; his McCarthy-era memories made him reluctant to tangle with the generals, where his patriotism might again be called into question. He made several brief trips to Vietnam, covering the political rather than the military scene, but found that as a well-known correspondent he was kept "cocooned from reality" by officialdom. He wrote little about Vietnam and felt guilty about it afterward.

Teddy also blamed Lyndon Johnson for "probably the most thoughtless of the many acts of the Great Society," the Immigration Act of 1965. This, White felt, "was to change the texture of America, thoughtlessly and forever," when it shifted away from traditional European immigrant quotas toward Asian and Hispanic quotas. The arrival of hundreds of thousands of Latin Americans, legally or illegally, across the nation's porous southern frontier troubled him. In the determination of many Hispanics to retain their own language and customs Teddy saw a threat to the unity of the nation. Of course, in the big cities of the East and Midwest there had always been enclaves where European immigrants, particularly the older among them, had clustered, clinging to the language and customs of their homeland while their children became "Americanized." But to Teddy, the Hispanics in their vast numbers and their political influence, and in their pressure to have their children taught in Spanish in the public schools, were a challenge to the American vision of itself as a melting pot. His friend Richard Clurman thinks that White, who loved America, was offended by those who did not, including separatists among blacks, and those browns who refused to assimilate. He was put off by black demands for "entitlements" and special privileges. From his ghetto upbringing Teddy had retained a firm belief that this was the land of opportunity only for those who worked at it.

Teddy had never been a racist; he had earlier called the treatment of black people "the greatest imperfection in American life" and had chronicled and celebrated the courage of northern freedom riders who risked their lives to give southern Negroes the vote; and as a foreign correspondent in China he had deplored the way American GIs contemptuously dismissed Chinese soldiers as "slopeheads." Yet his attitudes were changing, a part of a growing conservatism in him.

"Teddy hated black militants," his son, David, told me. David remembers coming down from Harvard to join his father; they were to have lunch at a dockside restaurant and then take the ferry together to their summer home on Fire Island. David arrived wearing a red armband in support of a student strike at Harvard and a button reading "Free Bobby Seale," the Black Panthers' leader. Teddy ordered David to take off the red band and the button before entering the restaurant, or he wouldn't buy him lunch. They argued, but neither gave way, and the two equally stubborn men took the ferry to Fire Island without lunch.

In the second volume of Teddy's memoir, which he started and then abandoned, he acknowledged something he never elsewhere admitted in print, that "somewhere between 1965 and 1968, my devotion to the party of my youth, the Democrats, began to fade. . . . The Great Society and the Vietnam War, combined, were the forcing bed of a change within myself." The changes taking place in America, said his son, David, produced "a rigid reflex in him that forced him to the right." Many of his friends, distressed by this drift, mistakenly attributed his change to opportunism, to his desire always to be close to those in power, as the country itself turned more conservative.

The year 1968 confirmed Teddy's forebodings about the state of the nation. It was the year the Reverend Martin Luther King, Jr., and Bobby Kennedy were murdered. It was the year of unrest in the ghettos and angry confrontations on college campuses. It was the year L.B.J. decided not to stand for reelection, then held his designated successor, Vice President Hubert Humphrey, on a tight leash for so long—Humphrey felt unable to express his own misgivings about Vietnam until too late in the campaign—that this may have cost Humphrey the election. Humphrey was an old friend of Teddy's. He might not have been the right choice for president, but Teddy, like most of the press, and indeed like most of Humphrey's political colleagues, regarded Humphrey as a man who brought honor to the craft of politics. The majority of the press certainly had little use for Richard Nixon, who won the election, but Teddy, as usual, reported him with sympathy: "Richard Nixon was . . . not a very trusting person. Life had made him that way. There hung over him the wary loneliness of a man always excluded from the company of those he admired."

Nixon's campaign promise that he had a "plan" to end the Vietnam War proved hollow. But Nixon's daring opening to China gave a delighted Teddy a chance to return to the country he most longed to see again. He reentered China carrying the credentials of the Luce magazines, but with no Harry Luce around now to challenge his judgments.

Among the reporters bound for China, Teddy was the acknowledged expert, a role he savored. On the flight to Beijing, Teddy sat next to William F. Buckley, Jr.; they good-naturedly needled each other across the Pacific, but then Buckley, in a column, mischievously described Teddy as "ecstatic at the prospects of visiting his old haunts and of justifying his early optimism about the vector of Chinese Communism." In another column, Buckley sourly criticized journalists who had "fallen all over themselves praising a despotic regime" because they were eager to be invited back.

At a diplomatic reception the American press contingent was lined up to be greeted by Teddy's old hero Chou En-lai. John Chancellor felt a twinge of embarrassment for Teddy when Chou passed Teddy without a flicker of recognition, then warmly greeted another old China hand, Phil Potter of the Baltimore *Sun*. On another occasion, Buckley, Chancellor, Teddy, and James Michener were out for a walk when Teddy decided to buy something from a vendor. The vendor couldn't understand Teddy; it took Michener, who also spoke Chinese, to complete the transaction. In retelling the story Buckley made the episode seem not a confusion about dialects but a question of Teddy's claim to speak Chinese.

Teddy himself described a happier memory: of the grand dinner in the Great Hall of the People, when Teddy boldly pressed his way to the head table, where the leaders sat. He was challenged by both American and Chinese security people.

Chou En-lai and Patricia Nixon, seated next to each other, saw his predicament. "Perhaps they were bored with their conversation, for I do not think [they] had much in common to discuss. Simultaneously both waved to their agents to let me through, and both, as I came forward, tried to explain why they had beckoned to me. Chou En-lai, his English by now rusted away, could only say that I was 'old friend, old friend,' pointing at me. And she, believing I had approached to talk with her, was saying the same thing."

A week later, at a photo opportunity in the beautiful city of Hangchow, where Nixon and Chou En-lai, with "affected nonchalance," strolled over the moon bridges together, Nixon spotted Teddy among the press observers and pointed him out to Chou, who remarked, "But that is Teddy White. He has not come back to China since the liberation." Teddy writes: "I was angry with the entire manipulative voyage; I had tried without success for twenty years to reach Chou En-lai and ask him if I might have a visa to revisit China, so I shot back: 'It's not my fault I haven't been able to come back.' . . . My command of Chinese had by then rusted away, so I relied on the official interpreter, who said that Chou En-lai had responded, 'Maybe it's both our faults.' . . . It sounded like the Chou En-lai I had once known."

The Making of the President 1972 was an ill-fated book that would have a succession of unfortunate personal consequences for Teddy, including the collapse of his marriage to Nancy.

Mike Bessie, Teddy's editor, said that during each two-year period when Teddy was writing a new volume, Nancy did not have a place in her home she could call her own. Teddy's working materials were scattered over the living room, the dining room, the bedrooms. This time, Nancy insisted, things had to be different. She found a garden apartment for rent in the neighborhood and suggested that Teddy write his book there; she added that if he insisted on writing it at home, she would divorce him. Teddy, not wanting to change his settled habits, refused the offered apartment. That, Nancy said, was "the final straw" in a marriage that was already strained; she began a divorce proceeding.

When Clare Boothe Luce learned of it, she invited Nancy to stay with her during the trauma of the divorce. Clare knew what it was like. After all, her most successful play (and movie) was *The Women,* a wickedly catty comedy about women living uneasily together in Nevada while establishing residency for a Reno divorce.

For all of his renown, Teddy White was now a lonely man. He moped about his empty town house, and to his friend Bernie Frizzell, an American journalist in Paris, who proposed to visit him, he wrote: "You're welcome to stay. I must say you may find me a very silent and morose companion as my mood is not of the best. . . . I still miss Nancy."

A few months later, when Leonard Lyons, a gossip columnist, reported that Teddy was retiring, Teddy replied: "Please don't embalm me before I'm ready. It's true the divorce last year threw me a bit . . . and I was exuding gloom, like gefilte fish exudes jelly, all through the spring."

One day a letter came to Teddy from Hawaii, where Clare Boothe Luce now lived: "Now get yourself a nice *traditional* wife—pretty, plump and pliant, whose only goal in life will be to make Teddy happy. Pretty hard character to find in these days of the Liberated Woman. Aloha, Clare."

Teddy was indeed discovering that a good woman is hard to find. As he wrote Bernie Frizzell: "Between sex and love I would settle now for companionship. I'm an old sexist, male chauvinist and I find most women of my middle-class ambiance either much too hard, much too tough, much too much on the make—or else, very girlish, very unstable, very unformed and stupid, and unable to carry on a companionship of equals."

Though he might talk, he-man style, of "chasing babes," he

was in fact somewhat puritanical in matters sexual. In time Teddy would marry a woman with as much independence of mind as he, Beatrice Kevitt Hofstadter, a professional historian and widow of the distinguished professor of American history Richard Hofstadter. In his earlier days Teddy had sometimes grandly referred to himself as the historian; now in his writing he felt more comfortable describing himself modestly as the chronicler or the storyteller.

At the peak of his career, Teddy was a target for every journalistic competitor. The kind of election reporting he had single-handedly pioneered had developed into a cottage industry. Among the two hundred or so reporters on the campaign trail in 1972, eighteen were writing books. Teddy was also under pressure from the editors of the Associated Press, who told their staff, "When Teddy White's book comes out there shouldn't be one single story in that book we haven't reported ourselves," and from Abe Rosenthal, the managing editor of *The New York Times,* who warned his reporters and editors, "We aren't going to wait until a year after the election to read a story in Teddy White's book that we should have reported ourselves."

The arrival of herd journalism in campaign coverage meant that there was even a reporter along writing a book about the reporters themselves. In *The Boys on the Bus,* Timothy Crouse, who himself admired Teddy, wrote:

> Many of the new generation of campaign reporters looked down on White as a pathetic, written-out hack. They saw him as a political groupie who wrote flattering, mawkish descriptions of major politicians in order to keep them primed for later books. His 1968 book, with its penitently overkind description of Richard Nixon, had taken a beating from reviewers. . . . By 1972, the traveling press openly resented Teddy. They felt he was a snob, that he

placed himself above the rank and file of the press. White would suddenly appear in some press-room, embracing old friends on the campaign staff, and would immediately be ushered off to the candidate's suite or the forward compartment of the plane for an exclusive interview. And the reporters would grumble about Teddy White getting the royal treatment.

Against this stands the testimony of David Broder of *The Washington Post,* the best political reporter of the next generation, who wrote: "To colleagues on the press bus, he was the boon companion, the most appreciative audience for our tales, the kindest critic of our work, the man whose unending curiosity and ebullience lifted our spirits when we were tired or jaded or hung-over. So great was his enthusiasm for the story he would not let us become cynics."

Perhaps these different responses had something to do with which of his colleagues Teddy considered his professional equals.

White's privileged access was particularly galling aboard the Nixon plane, where not only the candidate but all his top aides, a grim and uncommunicative bunch, hated and disdained the press. Teddy and Nixon hit it off. They shared the same foreboding about the country's future, a fear that, like ancient Rome, the United States might lose its world leadership not by defeat but by an inner moral crumbling. It was White's conviction that history would cast "Richard Nixon as one of the major presidents of the 20th Century, in a rank just after Roosevelt, on a level with Truman, Wilson, Eisenhower, Kennedy." In his enthusiasm for reporting the sweep of Nixon's victory over George McGovern, White all but ignored the scandal over Watergate that in the last weeks before the election was building up around Nixon. Mike Bessie was fearful that Teddy's panegyric would look foolish if Nixon was about to be impeached just when the book was due to come out. He gave Teddy a few extra pages and a tight deadline to work in some catch-up references to Watergate. Over at *The Washington Post* one day, Ben Bradlee got a phone call from Teddy, who "in that funny little voice of his said 'Who are these guys Woodward and Bernstein? And make it quick because it's costing me a buck and a quarter a minute.' "

As usual, *The Making of the President 1972* became a bestseller, despite a number of skeptical reviews. The criticism that angered Teddy most came from a friend, the columnist Anthony Lewis, who wrote on the op-ed page of *The New York Times*:

> Theodore H. White is so awesomely diligent a reporter, so accomplished a political animal and so engaging a person that criticizing him seems almost a sacrilege . . . but it is time for someone to say that White has written a bad book.
>   . . . Alas, one detects in Teddy White some of that unfortunate pleasure in curling up with the powerful. . . . White lets us know that he spoke with Mr. Nixon on the telephone 15 minutes after the astronauts landed on the moon. The President's "astonishing mind ranged over football metaphors, the spirit of exploration, plans to initiate space missions. His mind had all the facts in hand, had presorted them into patterns." It really is embarrassing to read such stuff from Theodore White.

Furious, Teddy asked for equal space on the op-ed page to answer Lewis. Told that the *Times* would allow him only a 450-word reply in the letters-to-the-editor column, Teddy decided to write Lewis directly:

> I found your column to be vicious, personal and destructive. What makes me so sad is what has happened to someone I once admired. I have become increasingly appalled. . . . The case of Tony Lewis is the case of a reporter wearing the robes of a High Priest.
>   You start out by saying that this is a bad book. Possibly

true. What I've been trying to do over these years is to describe man as individual under the pressure of forces. I am eaten by uncertainties always, and grow more uncertain as I grow older. . . . You *know* what is good and bad. In the very deepest sense I find you blood brother to Richard Nixon. . . . Your world is a mirror image of his—a world of good and bad.

[You have become rigid in] the civil war that now rages among liberals in this country, the effort of each group to strip the label of liberal from the other, as if it were a floor pass awarded by the Sanhedrin of Good Men or a badge issued by the police. . . . You have developed an intolerance for different opinions that baffles me.

Those I love most in the world—my friends, my children, the people I work with—pleaded with me to write the kind of book you denounce me for not having written. I could not, because I do not see it that way—and not for the pleasure of curling up with the great (have you ever tried to curl up with Richard Nixon? He's uncurlable).

Two years later, trying to atone for his misbegotten book, Teddy wrote another one, called *Breach of Faith,* which in its soft indictment might as well have been called *Poor Richard's Almanac.* In it Teddy reproached Nixon for having shaken the public's trust in its government, but he did so grudgingly: "If one hates Nixon enough, it is easy to describe the implacable vindictiveness and tenacity of the man as more important than his tremendous courage; the recurrent gusts of panic or fury as more important than the long thoughtfulness . . . the cheapness and nastiness of his tactics as more important than the long-range planning of his exceptional mind. I am not," he insisted, "competing in the piety and outrage sweepstakes."

How lightly Teddy felt about Nixon's involvement in the Watergate scandal can be judged by an interview he gave years later to *People* magazine: "If I had to do it again, I'd retitle it *Guilty of a Small Crime,* for Nixon's crime was not commensurate with, say, that of Lyndon Johnson plunging half a million boys into Vietnam."

Alongside Teddy White's misjudgments, and all that can be said professionally against him—that he hustled, flattered, pandered—it must be recognized that at key moments in his life he stood his ground, rightly or wrongly, for what he believed. His defiance of Harry Luce over Chiang Kai-shek once cost him a job he prized greatly; his stubborn support of Nixon, and his blindness to Nixon's misdeeds, separated him from family and friends and eventually damaged his political reputation.

On a tour to promote his new book, Teddy often captivated reporters who interviewed him with his quick gift of gab and his knowing tales of famous people. But his observant interviewers would also describe Teddy "starting his third pack of Marlboros" or "pouring himself another Scotch and water" or "taking a long sip of his bourbon." (Teddy told a *Wall Street Journal* reporter: "I write with coffee and rewrite with bourbon.") A reporter for the *Chicago Tribune,* looking at Teddy with an unkinder eye than Teddy directed toward those he interviewed, said that Teddy "looks like Grumpy of the Seven Dwarfs, heavy of jowl, thin of hair, his ears protruding . . . reptilian eyes blinking out behind horn-rimmed glasses."

He had reached the stage of recognition where he invited parody, and he had to endure this one by Nora Ephron:

> White flicked a cigarette ash from his forty-sixth Marlboro of the day and took the last sheet of one-hundred-percent rag Strathmore parchment typing paper from his twenty-two-year-old IBM Executive typewriter. It was the 19,246,753rd piece of typing paper he had typed in his sixty years. He was tired. He was old and tired. He was also short. But mainly he was tired. He was tired of writing the same book over and over again. He was tired of being

taken in, taken in by John F. Kennedy, Lyndon Johnson, General Westmoreland, Richard Nixon . . . tired of being made to look like an ass, tired of having to apologize in each successive book for the mistakes he had made in the one before.

"Teddy didn't know how to handle success," his daughter, Heyden, said.

His friend Richard Clurman said that Teddy was "the worst handler of his celebrity of anyone I ever knew." At a dinner Teddy would be seated between two women who would ask him about politics. Teddy would answer, "I don't want to talk bullshit like that."

Often, Teddy's boorish behavior can be explained by his drinking, but depression and frustration added to his troubles. Perhaps, as athletes lose a step, performers lose their looks, and singers lose their top notes, he felt his creative juices drying up. Insecure, he knew his lesser work was being overpraised, while younger rivals, feeling he was overrated, could hardly wait to topple him.

"I'm getting tired of the President series," he wrote Frizzell. In 1976, when it came time to do the next-to-last volume of the series, Teddy went out on a few preliminary campaign forays and filled two notebooks with his tiny handwriting, but he had lost all sense of freshness and discovery and concluded: "I could sit at home [watching TV] and learn as much or more about the frame of the campaign as I could on the road." Of course this wasn't true. His sharp powers of observation and his knowledge of the people involved, more than his writing talents, gave his books strength. But in his negative mood, his writing troubled him too: "What you are trying to do is the hootchy-kootchy to get them into the tent. It's demeaning and degrading; in a way it makes you feel slimy."

In fact, Teddy at his best wrote taut, vivid, and powerful

narrative, but his attempts to impart drama to his writing frequently led to purple passages, reaching for metaphors, and jumping to conclusions. Fortunately, in Teddy's overwritten prose a plainer truth could usually be discerned. Editors found it easier to remove excesses from his copy than to infuse life into other writers' prose that had none.

In the Jimmy Carter election year, Teddy found himself "in a clouded time, not knowing whether it is twilight or dawn"; he "no longer knew how to string the stories together in any way that connected with history." He abandoned the book. (The final volume in the series was written in 1980, by which time his publisher decided that *The Making of the President* was no longer a selling title; it was called, with characteristic Teddy grandiosity, *America in Search of Itself.*)

Yet at a moment when Teddy White seemed to have exhausted his talent, he set out to write his memoir, which ranks among the best books he ever wrote. Plainly Teddy had a compulsion to write; it was as if he were following a Cartesian necessity: I write, therefore I am. From the memorable description of growing up in a Jewish ghetto in Boston to his days of achievement and controversy in Asia, in Europe, and in American politics, Teddy examined with frankness and honesty, and sometimes pain, his own role as a witness in a world of unsettling changes. Near the end of his memoir he tells of visiting his hometown of Boston during the Massachusetts primary of 1976 and, on impulse, deciding to visit the home he grew up in on Erie Street in Dorchester. He was irritated when the cabdriver asked ten dollars over the meter but soon understood why the cabbie wanted hazardous pay.

> . . . [White] had seen this kind of desolation in other American cities—the blank places, the burned-out hulks, the boarded windows, the caries of the inner urban community. But this had been home. Frightened at being fearful of the streets where he had once courted girls and played hit-

the-ball, he nonetheless went on [past] the little Hebrew school on Bradshaw street, where he had first learned and then taught the language of the Bible. [It had] been vandalized . . . razed to the ground.

The cab turned onto Erie Street.

> . . . Empty lots and tumble-down near-ruins flanked the silent street where gardens once grew and mothers strolled with babies. The driver had speeded up on this desolate street and had overshot the mark, when White realized he had passed his own house. He asked the driver to back up. And there it was—a derelict of a house, with a tin number plate saying "74" on the doorpost . . . standing by itself, the neighboring houses on either side and behind long since torn down. . . . The old steps to the porch were rotting and twisted; the house itself was askew; on the upstairs floor where his grandmother had reigned as tyrant, the windows were either smashed, open to the wind or boarded up. Four bells with names attached indicated that four families now lived on the bottom floor, which had once housed David White and his family. . . .
> White was peering over the wire-mesh fence of what had been the garden of his birthplace when several black children materialized, yelling, "Hey, man, what y' doing?" Then followed a dignified but scowling black man, who challenged, "What you doing here, man?" . . . White told him about the cherry tree, the day lilies, the garden, the tulips, as they all had been. Gradually the man's suspicion faded. . . . The black man offered the information that there was still a pear tree in back and the old grapevine had still been there when they'd moved in several years before.

White, telling the story with sadness but without rancor, was so shaken by his visit to Massachusetts and to his birthplace that this experience "more than anything else had derailed the grand scheme" to complete his *Making of the President* series. He could no longer so firmly hold to the belief that had sustained him, that in America, the land of opportunity, the political process, for all its weaknesses, was serving the common good, which in the end would prevail. Having lost that swaggering conviction, he did not feel capable of writing a confident political history of his times. He could only offer instead what proved to be better, his own history as witness to it.

In the last years of his life, Teddy White found himself drawn back to the first years of his career. In 1982, a third of a century after the tumultuous events in China, many of the American survivors of that era gathered at Arizona State University, in the presence of East-West scholars of a later generation, to assess the wreckage. Some were State Department experts, their careers blackened in the McCarthy recriminations; others were journalists who had covered China during that era.

Teddy had been invited to attend but begged off because his mother, bedridden and blind at ninety-three—and testy because she could no longer read the books she loved—was seriously ill. He sent a rueful, almost apologetic, message to the conference: "We were all very young men, ignorant men, unskilled men. China was a mystery to all of us, as it remains to this day a mystery to the most learned scholars. We never knew who was doing what to whom or why. We could not penetrate Chinese politics. We lived on the slope of a volcano; we could see its steaming, record an eruption now and then, knew the landscape was heaving, and all of us sensed that this volcano would blow its top."

Most of the conferees, less shaken by doubt, felt satisfied that they had correctly foretold the collapse of Chiang's regime. But among the diplomats, in particular, there were differences about whether the Communists, when they came to power, should have been welcomed by the United States as an improvement or simply accepted as a new dictatorship, also unattractive, that the United States would have to reckon with. At that late date no one argued, as Teddy and Annalee Jacoby once did, that there had been a magic moment at the end of World War II when, with a friendly gesture from the United States, the Chinese Communists might have been detached from the Russians and become our allies. That this happy solution did not occur Teddy and Annalee Jacoby had blamed on the dark power exercised at the time by Harry Luce.

If at the Arizona conference, Luce-bashing resembled an Olympic competition, it was John Hersey who won the gold. In a luncheon speech Hersey described how Luce had set out to adopt Teddy White, "to take possession of him. As he had done, in a different but no less paternal way, over the years with me." Hersey then told how four years later, he and Teddy "had, not without pain, torn ourselves away" from Luce. Hersey sent White a draft of his Arizona speech, producing an emotional reconciliation between the two friends, who had long since drifted apart. Teddy wrote Hersey: "You caught him as well as anyone can possibly catch another man. . . . I have no differences with you on Luce's drives: money and Christianity. And I'm glad you got his Christian character. This he believed in above all. . . . He was not simply a pilgrim to the shrine; he was a Crusader. He would bash in anyone's skull whom he considered an infidel (as he thought of you and me). He might well have been among the warriors who stormed Jerusalem in 1099."

White was pleased to learn that Hersey, the mishkid, was at work on a book about the Christian missionaries in China: "I, myself, get fonder and fonder of Christ as I get older. That's because I am quintessentially Jewish, and so was Christ. I *want* to believe. But the Jewishness in me has come out as a cold and cynical observation of the gap between the word and the message and the deed and the horrors that come from the message."

Teddy, who had always envied Hersey for sharing Luce's Christian religion, was wrong about faith's being at the root of the difference between himself and Hersey. Hersey, who called himself moderately liberal politically, had drawn away from

Teddy on political grounds, convinced that Teddy had "developed a reverence for wealth and power" that had corrupted him. "My own view of the rift," Hersey wrote to me shortly before his death in 1993, "was that it was not a matter of religious beliefs—I was a longstanding agnostic by that time . . . but of politics. I thought Teddy had gone around the bend; his love affair with Nixon stands for me as the saddest and strangest lapse in Teddy's judgment."

Nonetheless, Hersey gently replied to Teddy:

> I, too, cherish our old friendship, Teddy. We have a lot to remember. I don't know about you; I kind of enjoy our differences, whatever they may be. . . . I don't believe they have to do with believing or not believing (I don't, by the way, believe in Christ in any churchy sense, I don't in fact believe in an institutional God—though I do delight in the gift of life and in the incredible diversity of things in this amazing universe); I don't think they have to do with being Jewish or gentile, or with anything political. They have to do with differences in temperament—those quirks that make us interesting people, if we are. That's why I can get some pleasure from them; you're so full of life when we argue, you're so *you*! The pain is that our worlds have drifted apart and we seem to be at a greater distance from each other than we really are.

One day in May 1986, as Teddy sat facing his typewriter, he suffered a massive stroke, and he died two days later at the age of seventy-one. Several months earlier he had asked Richard Clurman to make funeral arrangements for him. He wanted a service at a prominent synagogue on New York's Fifth Avenue but insisted that the rabbi should make no remarks in English, simply reciting the Kaddish in Hebrew. Unlike Luce's funeral, where the emphasis appropriate to a man of Luce's deep faith was on a pilgrim's confronting eternity, Teddy's service, though held under the roof of a temple, made only a minimal gesture to formal religion. As at Luce's service, there were limousines waiting outside, and inside the temple were many distinguished names and familiar faces. But, in the kind of ceremony that has become increasingly fashionable in the secular second half of the twentieth century, there were few references to pain and death, and scant attention to faith and belief.

Senator Pat Moynihan, who, like Teddy, had been criticized by liberal friends for detecting some redeeming qualities in Richard Nixon, spoke of what he called the central theme of Teddy's work, quoting from *Caesar at the Rubicon:* " '. . . the terrible conflict between the idea of liberty and the idea of order. Rarely does any civilization harness the two; but when that happens, the results can be spectacular and magnificent, as they were in Republican Rome, in ancient Athens, in England at its apogee, in the United States for how long we do not know.' "

That uncertainty about his beloved country had darkened Teddy's last years. He had earlier described an idea "which had become obsessive with me after twenty years of American politics—of how the cities as they are cannot be saved, any more than the Vietnam war could be won." And thus, in Teddy's view, the American civilization he cherished would endure, said Senator Moynihan, dramatically repeating Teddy's phrase, "for how long we do not know."

Mostly, however, speakers, celebrating Teddy's achievements, kept their remarks light, talking about Teddy's human qualities, his enthusiasm, his eccentricities. John King Fairbank, the Harvard tutor who had introduced Teddy first to China, then to journalism, said, "I taught him for two years and learned from him for forty." Teddy's daughter, Heyden, spoke too: "My father's love for us . . . enfolded us, taught us, kept us safe, and made us strong." Plainly the intent of the occasion was to console the living with amusing and affectionate remembrances of a friend who had once been among them but had now departed. Which was just the way Teddy White, who acknowledged himself "soft on the human race," had wanted it.

ACKNOWLEDGMENTS

I t was Nancy, Teddy White's first wife—aware that I had known both Teddy and Harry Luce—who proposed that I write a book about the unusual friendship of the two men, a friendship that survived so many personal and professional strains. When I decided to do so, she cooperated freely in interviews, never once asking what my own attitude was toward either Harry or Teddy, and never asking to see what I had written: behavior I found admirable. Her daughter, Heyden White Rostow (Teddy's literary executor), gave me access to Teddy's papers at Harvard, with no strings attached. She and her brother, David, both of them journalists, were spontaneously forthright in interviews with me, to ensure that I understood their father's character.

Harry Luce's son Henry Luce III, who had been a colleague of mine at *Time* when he was a writer and correspondent, let me roam freely through Luce's papers. Happily, Alan Brinkley, who was chosen as Luce's biographer, believes that research materials should be open to anyone who wishes to use them. I am grateful to them both. My friend Jason McManus, who inherited Luce's proud title of editor in chief, gave me permission to use the Time Inc. archives, where Elaine Felsher as archivist was cheerfully helpful.

Harry's sister, Beth (Mrs. Maurice T. Moore), had vivacious

memories of the spartan days she and Harry shared while growing up in a missionary family in China. Carl and Shelley Mydans, old China hands and longtime friends of Teddy's, not only
shared their memories of him with me but read the three China
chapters to guide me through the complexities of Chinese politics half a century ago. Similarly, John Paton Davies of the State
Department, with whom Teddy flew to Yenan, read the Yenan
chapter and made useful suggestions. Edward K. Thompson,
the managing editor of *Life* in its great years—and the man I
later succeeded as the editor of *Life*—volunteered crucial anecdotes of his life with Teddy and Harry, even though my book
would compete with the memoirs he was writing. I spent a
pleasant afternoon with John Hersey on Martha's Vineyard,
reminiscing about the old days; he later wrote me a letter about
his differences with Teddy, which is quoted in the final chapter.
Whittaker Chambers's son and daughter, John and Ella, zeal-
ously protective of his reputation, generously allowed me to
quote from his letters to Luce and from staff memos that he
wrote.

Only after I had finished the manuscript of this book did I
come into possession of a surprising letter that Chambers had
written. Though as fellow senior editors at *Time,* Whit and I
were colleagues, we had little in common, and I assumed that he
considered me, like most of the *Time* staff, as leagued against
him. In 1956, eight years after Chambers had quit *Time,* he answered a letter from his friend Ralph DeToledano. "What dis-
turbs me most," Chambers said, "is that Griffith has gone to
Nwswk." DeToledano had got his facts wrong; I hadn't. Yet
Chambers was moved to comment: "Tom Griffith was one of
Time's really good editors. I incline to think that, all his limitations allowed for, he was almost the only one. I mean an editor
who edits well, not by being able to give reasons always for
what he does, but by editing well even when he doesn't know
why he did it. Art and instinct . . . But Griff and I were never

friends. Griff is far to the left of me.* . . . I do not think Griff is a hatchet man. I think he means to act honorably, and usually succeeds."

Reading this letter for the first time, nearly forty years after it was written, I was pleased that it was so free of his frenetic suspicions of an earlier day, his vituperative dismissal of his colleagues, in *Witness* and in memos to Luce, as fools or knaves if they were not members of his tiny cell of loyalists. His agonizing experiences in the Hiss case had obviously mellowed some of his judgments and begun a change of attitude in him that I describe in later chapters of this book. But I have not altered what I wrote about him during his days at *Time,* which accurately reflects the atmosphere of the period, and how I then felt.

In three years of interviewing, I found that those who knew Teddy or Harry, or in many cases knew both of them, had such vivid impressions of them that they—with one exception— eagerly offered their reminiscences. Among people I am indebted to are Teddy's brother Robert and sister, Gladys, Teddy's widow, Beatrice Hofstadter White, Wilma Fairbank, John Kenneth Galbraith, Arthur Schlesinger, Annalee Jacoby (now Mrs. Clifton Fadiman), Dmitri Kessel, William F. Buckley, Jr., Allen Grover, Simon Michael Bessie, Richard M. Clurman, Frank White, Joseph Kastner, Ben Bradlee, Blair Clark, John Chancellor, Hugh Sidey, David Maness, Robert Ajemian, Marvin Kalb, Ralph Graves, Don Cook, Osborn Elliott, David Halberstam, Louis Harris, Philip Kunhardt, Tillman and Peggy Durdin, Robert "Pepper" Martin, Donald Straus, Al Ravenholt, Jacques Barzun, Stephen R. MacKinnon, and Robert Herzstein. Only Art Buchwald, a friend of Teddy's in their Paris days, declined to be interviewed, pleading that he was saving his impressions to write about them himself.

---

*That is, I supported Franklin D. Roosevelt's New Deal, which means that politically I belonged to the mainstream majority of that day.

Though I was free to write of Harry and Teddy without any imposed constraints, I cannot escape (and do not want to) the accumulated feelings, prejudices, and influences of forty-five years spent in Luce's organization. This book is dedicated to eight of my colleagues in the days immediately after World War II, when peace seemed finally at hand, only to be abruptly replaced by the Cold War, a time so full of misunderstandings, anxieties, frustrations, and occasional triumphs that all of us were marked, and sometimes scarred, by them. In the days when I edited the National Affairs section of *Time,* we did battle in what was known around the office as the "bloody angle." The only difficulty in singling out these colleagues is that I must then slight the impact upon me of so many others—writers, researchers, editors, production workers, artists—who were friends and associates during my years on *Time, Life,* and *Fortune.* It can be said of Harry Luce that he put together a lively crew of dedicated, knowledgeable, and talented craftsmen.

In Luce's last years, after he had made Hedley Donovan the editor in chief and took for himself the title of editorial chairman, I became deputy to them both, with the clumsy title of senior staff editor of all our publications. My office sat between theirs. On days when Luce was in town I would be summoned to his office around ten-thirty in the morning—we were late starters at Time Inc. Both of us, having digested the morning papers by then, would chat about the day's news, or Luce would recount what some senator, diplomat, or businessman had said to him at dinner the night before. Now that he was no longer so bent on changing the world, and was content merely to understand it and to savor its follies, I found these exchanges enjoyable; we could differ without having to argue. Impressions like these, I realize, have affected subconsciously the tone of this book; perhaps they have also helped me to understand the complexity of the relationship between Harry and Teddy.

Most of all, my gratitude goes to four people intimately involved in this book. My wife, Caroline, not only fed, encouraged, and sustained me throughout but, with her own years of experience in journalism, helped me in the research and, with discriminating good judgment and the empathy that comes from more than a half century of marriage, was a tactful, sometimes rigorous, but always understanding critic of my ideas and my prose. Robert Manning and I have been friends for nearly forty years, during which time I was his editor at *Time* and he my editor at *The Atlantic.* A perceptive man of high spirits and caustic Irish wit, he read the manuscript chapter by chapter as it was written and, knowing most of the people involved, gave me wise counsel. My literary agent, Robert Lescher, who has stood loyally by me for years, found the right editor and publisher for this book. Robert D. Loomis justified his well-established reputation as a sympathetic, enthusiastic, and demanding editor. He kept me from wandering down fascinating but ultimately irrelevant byways, keeping me to my central theme, the relationship between two remarkable men.

SELECT BIBLIOGRAPHY

Chambers, Whittaker. *Witness.* New York: Random House, 1952.
———. *Odyssey of a Friend: Whittaker Chambers' Letters to William F. Buckley, Jr.* New York: Putnam's, 1969.
Crouse, Timothy. *The Boys on the Bus.* New York: Random House, 1973.
Fairbank, John King. *Chinabound.* New York: Harper & Row, 1982.
Halberstam, David. *The Powers That Be.* New York: Knopf, 1979.
Hersey, John. *Life Sketches.* New York: Knopf, 1989.
Herzstein, Robert E. *Henry R. Luce.* New York: Scribner's, 1994.
Judis, John R. *William F. Buckley, Jr., Patron Saint of the Conservatives.* New York: Simon & Schuster, 1988.
Kobler, John. *Luce, His Time, Life and Fortune.* New York: Doubleday, 1948.
Luce, Henry. *The Ideas of Henry Luce.* Edited by John Knox Jessup. New York: Atheneum, 1973.
MacKinnon, Stephen R., and Oris Friesen. *China Reporting.* Berkeley: University of California Press, 1987.
Martin, Ralph G. *Henry and Clare.* New York: Putnam's, 1991.
Matthews, T. S. *Name and Address.* New York: Simon & Schuster, 1960.
———. *Angels Unaware.* New York: Ticknor & Fields, 1985.
Neils, Patricia. *China Images.* Savage, Md.: Rowman & Littlefield, 1990.

Stilwell, Joseph W. *The Stilwell Papers.* Edited by Theodore H. White. New York: William Sloane, 1948.

Swanberg, W. A. *Luce and His Empire.* New York: Scribner's, 1972.

Weinstein, Allen. *Perjury: The Hiss-Chambers Case.* New York: Knopf, 1978.

White, Theodore H. *The Making of the President 1960.* New York: Atheneum, 1961.

————. *The Making of the President 1972.* New York: Atheneum, 1973.

————. *In Search of History.* New York: Harper & Row, 1978.

White, Theodore H., and Annalee Jacoby. *Thunder Out of China.* New York: William Sloane, 1946.

The World of Time Inc. Vols. 1 and 2 edited by Robert T. Elson. Vol. 3 edited by Curtis Prendergast. New York: Atheneum, 1973. A company history that takes seriously its responsibility to be candid.

COLLECTIONS

The papers of THEODORE H. WHITE are in the Houghton Library at Harvard. Because much remains to be done in cataloguing them, I am grateful to Caroline Preston, curator, for guiding me through the maze.

Most of the papers of HENRY R. LUCE relating to journalism are to be found in the archives of the Time Magazine Company in New York. (Other papers of his, and of Clare Boothe Luce, are in the Library of Congress in Washington, D.C.)

The W. A. SWANBERG papers are at Columbia University. His biography *Luce and His Empire* won him a Pulitzer Prize, though it is marred by prejudice and political naïveté. He was an earnest and thorough researcher, however, and his papers at Columbia are a rich treasury.

The DAVID HALBERSTAM papers are at Boston University. His interviews with people at Time Inc. for *The Powers That Be* show him to be as indefatigible and searching a questioner as was his friend Teddy White.

INDEX

ABOUT THE AUTHOR

THOMAS GRIFFITH was born in Tacoma, Washington. After graduation from the University of Washington, he became a police reporter on the *Seattle Times* and then assistant city editor before winning a Nieman Fellowship at Harvard. He then joined *Time* magazine, serving first as a writer and then as an editor. Over the years he edited every section of the magazine—including foreign news, which he edited for seven years—and rose to assistant managing editor. He became deputy to Henry R. Luce and Hedley Donovan, Luce's successor as editor in chief of the Luce publications, and then became the editor of *Life* in its final years as a big weekly magazine. When *Life* suspended publication in 1972, he turned to writing articles for *Fortune* magazine and essays for *Time* and became *Time*'s first and only media columnist. He also wrote a bimonthly column, "Party of One," for *The Atlantic*. He is the author of two previous books, *The Waist-High Culture* and *How True: A Skeptic's Guide to Believing the News*. He and his wife live in Manhattan and East Hampton.

ABOUT THE TYPE

This book was set in Sabon, a typeface designed by the well-known German typographer Jan Tschichold (1902–74). Sabon's design is based on the original letterforms of Claude Garamond and was created specifically to be used for three sources: foundry type for hand composition, Linotype, and Monotype. Tschichold named his typeface for the famous Frankfurt typefounder Jacques Sabon, who died in 1580.